DEEP
ROOTS

PRINCETON STUDIES IN
Political Behavior

Tali Mendelberg, Series Editor

DEEP ROOTS

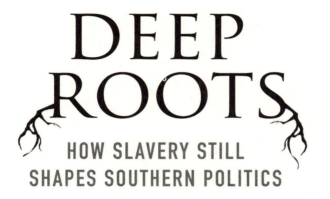

HOW SLAVERY STILL
SHAPES SOUTHERN POLITICS

AVIDIT ACHARYA
MATTHEW BLACKWELL
MAYA SEN

PRINCETON UNIVERSITY PRESS
PRINCETON AND OXFORD

ISBN 978-0-691-17674-1

Library of Congress Control Number: 2017963019

British Library Cataloging-in-Publication Data is available

This book has been composed in Sabon Next LT Pro, Trade Gothic LT Std and Trajan Pro

Printed on acid-free paper. ∞

Typeset by Nova Techset Pvt Ltd, Bangalore, India
Printed in the United States of America

3   5   7   9   10   8   6   4   2

This book is dedicated to
Usha Acharya,
Jayaraj Acharya,
and Hugo Blackwell-Sen

CONTENTS

TABLES

FIGURES

ACKNOWLEDGMENTS

This book unfolded as a series of informal lunchtime conversations while all three of us were assistant professors at the University of Rochester's Political Science Department. Over time, our informal conversations turned to several core themes—themes that we believed characterized some of the most important questions in American politics. Why is the South so reliably conservative? Why have white Southerners been so conservative, particularly on issues related to race and redistribution? Does this make the United States more conservative than other Western democracies? As we continued to debate these ideas, we kept coming back to historical forces. And, motivated by many papers in political economy, we began to explore the connection between contemporary Southern politics and the South's slave past, gradually bringing in data and developing our argument about the historical persistence of political attitudes.

Several years later, this intellectual journey has culminated in this book. Along the way, we have written several papers and engaged scholarship from across different fields, including political science, history, economics, African American studies, women's studies, sociology, and statistics (to name a few). We have talked with scholars from across substantive and methodological areas. All three of us have moved away from wintry Rochester to three very different departments (two in Cambridge and one in Palo Alto), have grown our families, and rediscovered other research areas. However, our interests keep bringing us back to the idea that contemporary politics is, in part, a function of historical forces and traditions.

Our intellectual trajectory was aided and encouraged by the help of many scholars. We are indebted to many conference, seminar, and workshop participants who listened to early versions of this project and who provided valuable feedback. The questions, criticisms, and comments we received at these presentations helped immeasurably in making this researcher stronger, more nuanced, and more comprehensive. We are especially grateful to conference or seminar participants at the University of California-Berkeley, Columbia, the Harvard Department of Government, the Harvard Kennedy School, the Harvard Law School, the London School of Economics, Princeton, Stanford, the Maxwell School at Syracuse University, CIDE (Mexico City), the University of Kentucky, the University of Notre Dame, the University of Pennsylvania, the University of Pittsburg, the University of California-Riverside, the University of Chicago, the University of Chicago Law School, the University of Washington, the University of Warwick, Washington University-St. Louis, the University of Wisconsin, the University of Virginia, Yale University, and the University of California-San Diego. This list also includes participants at several national academic conferences, including the 2013 Conference on Empirical Legal Studies, the 2014 American Political Science Association Meeting, the 2015 Midwest Political Science Association Meeting, the 2015 European Political Association Meeting, and the 2014 Society for Political Methodology Summer Meeting.

We are also fortunate to have many supportive, thoughtful, and, importantly, critical colleagues with whom we have had ongoing conversations (online or in person) about this project. This list is long and includes scholars from across disciplines, methodological and substantive specialities, and departments, especially those at the Stanford Department of Political Science, the Harvard Department of Government, and the Harvard Kennedy School. We are especially grateful to Jim Alt, Steve Ansolabehere, Larry Bartels, Matt Baum, Adam Berinsky, Lisa Blaydes, Ray Block, Larry Bobo, Adam Bonica, Corey Brettschneider, Christia Spears Brown, David Campbell, John Carey, Dan Carpenter, Amy Catalinac, Charlotte Cavaille, Adam Chilton, Andrew Coe, Cathy Cohen, Dara Kay Cohen, David Darmofal, Lauren Davenport, Andrew Eggers, Stanley Engerman, Ryan Enos, Bernard Fraga, Luis Fraga, Archon Fung, Sean Gailmard, Claudine Gay, Scott Gehlbach, John Gerring, Martin Gilens, Steve Hahn, Morgan Hazelton, Mike Henderson, Michael Herron, Jennifer Hochschild, Vanessa Holden, Dan Hopkins, Will Howell, William Hubbard, Jeff Jenkins, Nathan Kalmoe, Josh Kertzer, Gary King, Morgan Kousser, Chryl Laird, David Laitin, Jennifer Larson, Ben Lauderdale, Alexander Lee, Corrine McConnaughy, Ryan Moore, Suresh Naidu, Nathan Nunn, Brendan Nyhan, Eric Oliver, Orlando Patterson, Mark Peffley, Dianne Pinderhughes, Ellie Powell, Kevin Quinn, Karthick Ramakrishnan, Marc Ratkovic, Andrew Reeves, John Roemer, Thomas Romer, Cyrus Samii, Alex Sarabia, David Sears, Gary Segura, Ken Shepsle, Ken Shotts, Paul Sniderman, Arthur Spirling, Dustin Tingley, Stewart Tolnay, Stephen Voss, Leonard Wantchekon, Matthew Winters, Christina Wolbrecht, and Jon Woon.

We are especially thankful to participants in our book conference: Justin Grimmer, Marc Meredith, Robert Mickey, Eric Schickler, Michael Tesler, and Vesla Weaver. The thoughtful comments, critiques, and suggestions of these scholars helped us immensely in terms of clarifying our thoughts and moving the book project forward. We are extremely grateful for their time and for their investment in this project. In addition, the comments of several anonymous referees helped us sharpen our arguments and shore up empirical analyses. Although we do not know who they are, we are enormously indebted to their feedback and engagement.

We should also add that this book would not have been possible without the welcoming environment toward political economy and rigorous empirical inquiry that is the trademark of the University of Rochester Department of Political Science, where the three of us embarked on this project. For that reason, we are especially indebted to our Rochester colleagues, including Adam Cohon, Stanley Engerman, Gerald Gamm, Robin Harding, Gretchen Helmke, Hein Goemans, Stuart Jordan, Bethany Lacina, Dick Niemi, Michael Peress, Bing Powell, Lynda Powell, Larry Rothenberg, Curt Signorino, and others. Susan Hagen of the University of Rochester media office pressed us on how to make this work resonate with a public audience.

Heather O'Connell and Adam Slez have been particularly helpful to us. Their work, which maps 1860 county borders onto modern-day county borders, started us on many of the analyses that we present in this book. We're grateful to them for sharing their data with us. The Cooperative Congressional Election Survey (CCES), supported jointly by Harvard University and MIT and under the guidance of Steve Ansolabehere, provided additional sources of data. Steve, Eitan Hersh, and Ariel White were extremely helpful to us in working with Catalist LLC data, which provide some of the evidence in chapter 8. Jim Alt helpfully passed along historical voting rights data. Inès Crosas, Lauren Greenawalt, Melissa Kappotis, Michael Morse, Alexandra Pagano, Amanda Pearson, and Scott Trufan have provided valuable research assistance over the years. We are also thankful for financial support from Harvard's Weatherhead Center for International Affairs, which supported our book conference, and from Harvard's Institute for Quantitative Social Sciences. We are grateful to our editors at Princeton University Press, Eric Crahan and Tali Mendelberg. Both have provided us with ongoing feedback and support, and we are indebted to them for their engagement with this project.

We are also grateful to our friends for their ongoing support. Among the folks who have provided support, encouragement, and good cheer are Achal Acharya, Andrew Arbaugh, Tim Brandt, Andy Crepeau, Brian Costello, Aarjan Dixit, Erin Dress, Katie Elliott, Jill Downer, Dana Howard, Katherine Hughes, Alice Jayne, Sarah Kenney, Adam Levine, Ben McKean, and Janson Wu.

Lastly, we extend our deep gratitude to our families, without whom this book would not have been possible. Avi thanks Katie Ramsey for her comments, unwavering support, and confidence in this project, and Devin for the comments he is likely to have only after it's too late. Matt thanks his parents for their lifetime of support and Hugo and Mac for bringing joy and brightness to what can be a long and arduous process. Maya thanks the entire family, including her parents, Pradeep, Yasi, Shayan, and, most of all, Hugo.

A.A.
Stanford, Calif.

M.B.
Cambridge, Mass.

M.S.
Cambridge, Mass.

DEEP
ROOTS

CHAPTER ONE

INTRODUCTION

*"98% probably of white people in
Mississippi were segregationists.
My family was, my father was, I
was, everybody was. Everybody
that I knew was for segregation."*

Greenwood, Mississippi, resident

Greenwood, Mississippi (2010 pop. 15,205), is, by all accounts, a typical town in the Mississippi Delta. It isn't big, but it is bigger than many others in the area. The town's gridded streets line up in a roughly north-south direction, and its two rivers—the Tallahatchie and the Yazoo, parts of the web of smaller rivers forming the Mississippi flood plains—roughly encircle it. North of the Yazoo, historic mansions line Greenwood's "Grand Boulevard," and cotton and corn fields dot the roads leading away from the city. South of the Yazoo, in the historic city center, long-standing restaurants and shops—some of which have been in existence for decades—continue to serve Delta specialties like broiled shrimp and crabmeat. But perhaps Greenwood's greatest claim to fame, at least today, is serving as the birthplace and former home to a number of great blues artists, including Robert Johnson.

Looking around the town—and elsewhere in the broader Mississippi Delta region—it is easy to see remnants of older, different times. The Mississippi Delta is an alluvial plain, and its system of rivers have provided rich, fertile soil for agricultural use for two centuries. To cultivate these lands in the early 1800s, white entrepreneurs forced the transportation of enslaved African Americans westward into this region. The area is part of the broader hook-shaped region of the South known as the Black Belt, due to the rich color of the soil. Together, the fertile land, the "inexpensive" enslaved labor force, and the area's navigable rivers made cities like Greenwood the engines behind "King Cotton," with Mississippi

The quote in the epigraph comes from the film *Booker's Place: A Mississippi Story*, directed by Raymond De Felitta. Courtesy of Raymond De Felitta.

providing roughly 480 million pounds of ginned cotton in 1859—nearly a quarter of all cotton production in the United States that year.[1] In turn, this production helped to propel the nation through the Industrial Revolution in the late nineteenth century. This past is evident today in Greenwood's Grand Boulevard district, with its mansions and wide, tree-lined streets. A sign on the outskirts of town still proudly welcomes visitors to "Greenwood, Cotton Capital of the World."

But, as in many cities across the Mississippi, these economically rich times did not last. Starting in the 1940s, the mechanization of cotton production dramatically reduced the need for agricultural labor; in tandem with the Great Depression and the migration of African Americans out of the rural South, cities like Greenwood fell into cycles of recession, further exacerbated by racial tensions through the 1950s and 1960s. Between 1940 and the present day, close to half of the population of the Mississippi Delta left for opportunities elsewhere, and, today, downtown Greenwood is peppered with boarded-up buildings and vacant lots. In the traditionally African American neighborhood of Baptist Town, just outside the city center, many abandoned shotgun-style houses line the streets, calling to mind a past when mostly black agricultural workers lived there.

Forces such as these have hit African American communities in Black Belt cities like Greenwood particularly hard. In Greenwood, which was sixty-seven percent black in 2010, the unemployment rate for African Americans is nearly twice that of the state average, which in turn is higher than the national average. Incomes for African Americans in Greenwood are also lower than state and national averages, with half of Greenwood families headed by African Americans living in poverty. The median income of the city has been around half of the national median income for most of the last decade. Residential and institutional segregation is also persistent. For example, following the legally mandated desegregation of public schools in the 1960s, many Black Belt towns such as Greenwood established private "segregation academies" for white students, leaving desegregated public schools mostly African American and starved of resources. Today, Greenwood High School is ninety-seven percent African American, while the nearby Pillow Academy—founded in 1966 to provide segregated schooling for Greenwood's white children—is ninety percent white.[2]

These racial divides are echoed in the political environment of the Delta. At a city level, the politics of cities like Greenwood have followed the trajectory of African American politics more generally (although, as we will discuss throughout this book, this has not always been the case). Since African American voters today tend to overwhelmingly side with the Democratic Party, this means that Greenwood—like other majority-black cities throughout the Black Belt—has sided with Democratic candidates.

The same does not hold, however, for Greenwood's *white* residents. For example, in 2008 and 2012, Democratic presidential candidate Barack Obama won *nearly no support from the area's white voters*.[3] Indeed, at the county level, nearly all of the votes of Leflore County's white residents went to Obama's two Republican opponents, John McCain (2008) and Mitt Romney (2012). This pattern—black voters supporting Democratic candidates, but white voters overwhelmingly supporting more conservative candidates—is one we see again and again throughout the South's Black Belt.

Greenwood's historical and political trajectory contrasts with another Southern city, Asheville, North Carolina (2010 pop. 83,393). Whereas Greenwood's fertile land was its primary natural resource, Asheville's location in western North Carolina was by far less friendly to large-scale agriculture, setting its course on a different path. Indeed, Greenwood was settled primarily as a base for the production and shipment of cotton, but Asheville and Buncombe County, a region in the Blue Ridge and Smoky Mountains, was settled with the intent of establishing a trading outpost. For that reason, the city remained small for most of the eighteenth and nineteenth centuries, and it was only upon the arrival of the turnpike and the railroad later in the nineteenth century that the area started to blossom. For the early parts of the twentieth century, its crisp climate and mountain location made it a desirable vacation destination for Southerners from hotter lowland areas, and, over time, its boardinghouses started housing travelers from around the country.

Asheville today stands in contrast to the cities of the Black Belt in its demographic and economic profile. Of city residents, 43.3 percent have bachelor's degrees or higher, a figure that far outpaces both the North Carolina average (27.3 percent) and the national average (30.4 percent). In addition, a thriving tourist industry brings visitors to Buncombe County's famous Blue Ridge mountains and to cultural attractions like the Biltmore Estate. The city is also home to a variety of other industries, including health care, grocery and retail, and higher education, with the University of North Carolina at Asheville generating a well-educated workforce. In terms of the city's minority populations, only around fifteen percent of Asheville residents (and six percent of Buncombe County residents) are black, but inequality between people of different races is more muted than elsewhere in the South (though still present). The median 2010 black household income in Asheville was thirty thousand dollars per year; the same measure in Greenwood was around half that: seventeen thousand dollars. Both were lower than the corresponding white household income, but the black-white gap in Asheville was, and continues to be, narrower.

Importantly, Asheville also differs from Greenwood in its politics. In 2008, for example, Democrat Barack Obama won over most of Buncombe County's *white* voters. In fact, he won the county with fifty-seven percent of the vote, but blacks make up only six percent of the population. Assuming that Obama won every single black vote, he still won over half of the white vote—a very high figure in the U.S. South. Of course, many of these votes surely came from the retirees and the university students who call Asheville home. But, even accounting for this mobile population, many whites whose families have lived in the Asheville area for generations supported a fairly liberal, black candidate. This is a voting pattern that is corroborated by Asheville's long-standing reputation as a relatively progressive Southern city, where, for instance, Lyndon Johnson won sixty-two percent of the vote in Buncombe County against Barry Goldwater in 1964. In comparison, Johnson only received 6.4 percent of the (overwhelmingly white) vote in Leflore County, Mississippi.

These two cities—Greenwood and Asheville—are illustrations of the broader puzzle that we explore in this book. The South has strong intraregional differences in political attitudes, a fact long noted by political scientists such as V. O. Key, who wrote about this in his seminal work, *Southern Politics in State and Nation*. Places like Asheville, Atlanta, Nashville, and Charlotte are relatively liberal in their politics. Even whites in rural areas away from the old plantation counties, like northeastern Alabama, vote for Democratic candidates with some frequency. But in Black Belt cities such as Birmingham, Greenwood, and Jackson, white voters are among the most ideologically and politically conservative in the entire country, despite these cities having large numbers of African Americans who lean in a Democratic direction. These differences in turn are reflected in national policy. As scholars such as Key have noted, the Southern Black Belt is one of the most conservative parts of the country on issues of redistribution, civil rights, and law enforcement, and politicians from these areas have been at the forefront of fighting for conservative causes at the national level and have been so for generations. Thus, a key question for understanding American public opinion specifically— and American politics more broadly—is what explains these important patterns. Why are whites in Greenwood so conservative and why are whites in Asheville comparably more liberal? Why did these differences develop? And why do these differences persist? In a time of increased polarization and divided polities, these are remarkably relevant questions.

This contemporary puzzle forms the basis for this book. However, even though this puzzle focuses on regional differences in *present-day* political beliefs, we believe that the most compelling explanation for such present-day differences lies in the *history* of these places. Specifically, we argue in this book that *political attitudes persist over time, making history a key mechanism in determining contemporary political attitudes*. Looking at regional differences across the U.S. South, we focus this argument on the "peculiar institution" that drove the South's economy and politics for nearly 250 years: chattel slavery. We argue that Southern slavery has had a lasting local effect on Southern political attitudes and therefore on regional and national politics. Whites who live in parts of the South that were heavily reliant on slavery and the inexpensive labor that the institution provided—such as Greenwood (sixty-eight percent enslaved in 1860) and other places in the Southern Black Belt—are more conservative today, more cool toward African Americans, and less amenable to policies that many believe could promote black progress. By contrast, whites who live in places without an economic and political tradition rooted in the prevalence of slavery—places like Asheville (fifteen percent enslaved in 1860, for example)—are, by comparison, more progressive politically and on racial issues. These regional patterns have persisted historically, with attitudes being passed down over time and through generations. As we discuss below, this persistence has been reinforced both by formal institutions, such as Jim Crow laws (a process known as *institutional path dependence*), and also by informal institutions, such as family socialization and community norms (a process we call *behavioral path dependence*). Present-day regional differences, then, are the direct, downstream consequences of the slaveholding history of these areas, rather than being simply attributable exclusively to contemporary demographics or contemporary political debates.

To go back to our original question, what explains regional political differences in cities like Greenwood versus places like Asheville? Why are whites so much more conservative in the Black Belt versus other parts of the South? What we argue in this book, and what we show using empirical evidence, is that the differences in the politics of cities like these can be traced in part to one important fact: places like Greenwood were places where the local economy was rooted in slavery prior to the Civil War, but places like Asheville were not. The history of these areas, in tandem with attitudes being passed down over time via behavioral path dependence, helps drives these political differences.

1.1 HOW CAN HISTORY SHAPE POLITICAL ATTITUDES?

Many people may think that the claim that the past still somehow shapes our political attitudes is outlandish. We tend to think of our political beliefs as well reasoned and carefully considered, or, at worst, determined by what's happening around us right now. In terms of slavery and Southern white attitudes, it seems implausible that something that happened so long ago, and which has since been abolished, could possibly affect people's attitudes today. It seems remote to think that all of the things that happened between 1860 and today haven't served to diminish those sorts of influences.

This is a reasonable viewpoint—one shared by many political observers and scholars of public opinion. Slavery ended over 150 years ago, at a time when the U.S. population numbered around thirty-one million, about ten percent of what it is today. In the 1850s, roads in the United States were mostly unpaved, horses and wagons were the modal form of transportation, and railroads were just beginning to replace steamboats as the standard way to transport goods across the country. Alexander Graham Bell wouldn't make his first telephone call for another twenty-five years, and the Wright brothers wouldn't take their first flight for fifty more. Women couldn't vote, there were only thirty-three states in the United States, and Buffalo was America's tenth largest city. This younger United States had also yet to face the wave of internal and international migration that would characterize the twentieth century. Much has changed in American society and culture in the 150 years since slavery was abolished.

From the vantage point of politics and of race relations, these changes appear especially salient. The institution of slavery was itself permanently abolished, initially by the Emancipation Proclamation (1863) and more forcibly by the defeat of the South in the U.S. Civil War (1861–65). The subsequent involvement of the federal government during Reconstruction (1865–77) brought additional progress, including the enactment of the Thirteenth, Fourteenth, and Fifteenth Amendments to the U.S. Constitution, which together formally abolished slavery, established for all residents the right to equal protection of the laws, and guaranteed newly freed African Americans the right to vote. Although historians have questioned the extent to which these amendments were enforced (as we will discuss later in this book), slavery as a formal institution had collapsed by the 1860s, marking a significant transition point in the American racial order. Many have argued that the inclusion of African Americans into public life moved, at best, in fits and starts, but it would be misleading to say that these massive political and economic forces didn't substantially shift and shape political and social attitudes through history.[4]

Additional movements toward equality have been made in the twentieth century, further distancing the United States from its slave past. To name some milestones, the 1920s and 1930s saw the remarkable rise of African American visionaries in disparate fields, including literature (Langston Hughes, Zora Neale Hurston), the arts (Marian Anderson, Josephine Baker), and athletics (Jesse Owens, Joe Louis, Jackie Robinson). Within politics as well, the voice of black political and intellectual leaders such as W.E.B. Du Bois, Marcus Garvey, and Booker T. Washington guided the nation toward a fairer treatment of African Americans. By the 1960s, these efforts had culminated not just in the formal constitutional disavowal of state-mandated segregation (with the Supreme Court ruling in 1954 of *Brown v. Board of Education*), but also with the massive grassroots civil rights movement. From a legal perspective, landmark pieces of legislation brought new protections for minority rights; these included not just the far-reaching Civil Rights Act of 1964 and the Voting Rights Act of 1965, but also the Fair Housing Act (1968), the Equal Opportunity and Employment Commission, and the promotion of minority hiring by state and federal governments via the use of affirmative action. In terms of criminal justice, many jurisdictions have stronger sentences for hate crimes or other kinds of crimes targeted toward minority groups. And the political inclusion of African Americans has extended not just to the 2008 election of Barack Obama, the nation's first black president, but also the appointments of two Supreme Court Justices (Thurgood Marshall and Clarence Thomas), two Secretaries of State (Condoleeza Rice and Colin Powell), two Attorneys General (Eric Holder and Loretta Lynch), and numerous other high-level federal and state officials. Scholars have also demonstrated progress toward equality in white attitudes on race during this time especially in the period following the civil rights movement and especially on questions of institutionalized discrimination.[5]

The South has been no exception to this progress. A visitor from the 1860s would hardly recognize the city of Atlanta today. In the 1860s, Atlanta was a small city (pop. 9,554, about the size of Greenwood), mostly reliant on local railroads for business and trade. Today, Atlanta is a reflection of the "New South," home to a large and growing black middle and upper class—one that contributes significantly to the local economy and provides substantial cultural contributions to the city. In more recent years, Atlanta and other cities like it have lured many middle- and upper-class African Americans away from cities in the North and back to the South. For many African Americans, this "New South" is a far more welcoming environment than many parts of the racially segregated North.

HISTORICAL PERSISTENCE IN POLITICAL ATTITUDES

On the other hand, we also know that institutions and norms (and also political attitudes, as we will discuss) change remarkably slowly over time. Slavery was abolished only around 150 years ago—which represents the lifetime of two seventy-five-year-olds put together. As reminders of how close this past is to us, the last person believed to be born into slavery died only in the 1970s, while the last recognized living child of former slaves died in 2011.[6] Thousands of people alive during the early part of the twenty-first century were born during the times of sharecropping in the 1920s and 1930s. For many Americans living in the U.S. South, and also for many Americans whose grandparents and parents have migrated to other parts of the country, these connections represent a close temporal and generational contact with slavery and its aftermath. The past that we consider here simply was not very long ago, and certainly not when compared to broader events in human history.

This historical persistence also permeates the culture of cities and regions. For example, while many things in Greenwood, Mississippi, have changed, many other things have not. In the city center, the famous local restaurant Lusco's has been a town mainstay, run by the same family since 1921. (Until desegregation in the 1970s, the restaurant was "for whites only"; other restaurants in town responded to desegregation by turning into private "supper clubs.") In terms of an even older past, just outside of the city, a visitor can still see long-staple cotton farms or stop by some of the abandoned shotgun style homes that housed thousands of African-American agricultural workers earlier in the twentieth century. Within the city, traditionally working-class and sharecropping neighborhoods remain African American neighborhoods; neighborhoods north of the city continue to be white neighborhoods. Greenwood today in many ways resembles Greenwood from the 1950s and 1960s; the town so captures the feelings of the pre-civil rights movement Deep South that it was a substitute for Jackson, Mississippi, in *The Help*, a 2011 motion picture about African-American women in domestic employment.

These facts point us to the possibility of a historical persistence in terms of not just ambient culture, but also political attitudes, a key component of what we argue in this book. Going back further in time, for example, many of the defining cultural institutions in Greenwood can be traced to the area's deep ties to chattel slavery. At its peak shortly before the Civil War, the Southern United States had an enslaved population of four million people. This constituted nearly one-fourth of the entire population of the U.S. South. In looking at the country as a whole, one in eight Americans were enslaved. In terms of whites' interactions with the institution, this translated into more than one in four Southern families holding enslaved people as property, and, in places like Greenwood and elsewhere in the Black Belt, where up to ninety percent of people in some counties were enslaved, this number rose to almost one-half of white families. Just like other places in the Mississippi Delta, the area had a significant prevalence of slavery, with sixty-eight percent of Leflore County's population enslaved in the 1860s. Of course, the impact of slavery was not limited to the South. Many Northern cities reaped the economic fruits of enslaved labor, including in the building of roads, buildings, parks, and universities. Later on, industrial centers across the North benefited from the cheaper production of cotton, a labor-intensive and lucrative crop, and other extracted resources. But it was in the Black Belt of the American South that the institution of slavery was the most firmly and intimately embedded and where it had its furthest reach.

The impact of slavery on the Southern economy and on Southern politics hardly ended once the Civil War was over in 1865. As historians have argued, slavery created an entire way of life that was utterly and completely dependent on the provision of cheap labor, and this varied region by region, depending on slavery's prevalence. When the institution was forcibly removed by war, Southern whites who were heavily reliant on the institution of slavery looked for other ways by which to maintain and protect the social and economic order. Depending on how reliant an area was on black labor, this meant turning to both formal institutions and informal customs to reign in newly emancipated black workers and potential black voters. After all, if black workers left, there would be no one to cultivate lands, maintain infrastructure, build roads and railways, operate newly profitable mining and timber production, and provide domestic labor. And if blacks could freely vote, then the entire political system of the South—and one upon which the Black Belt was particularly reliant—would be thrown into tumult. Thus, the brief optimism of racial progressives during the period of Reconstruction succumbed to the Southern Redemption following the Compromise of 1877 and the significant withdrawal of federal involvement from Southern politics. Southern white elites consolidated and regrouped politically, forging new alliances with whites who had previously supported federal intervention. One player left out of this new power dynamic was the black freedman, who had limited independent political or economic power.

In the absence of federal government intervention, Southern politicians, a group dominated by Black Belt interests, moved the region toward a system that largely restricted participation in social, economic, and political life to whites. These efforts stopped legally short of violating the Reconstruction Amendments to the U.S. Constitution—at least as interpreted by Southern judges and by the U.S. Supreme Court.[7] Over the course of the thirty years following Reconstruction, a variety of anti-black state laws made it difficult, if not impossible, for African Americans to pull themselves out of poverty and economic dependency. These laws made it difficult for blacks to vote, hold jobs (especially as skilled laborers), travel freely, or gain access to education.[8] Vagrancy laws made it illegal to be unemployed and tended to target blacks; anti-enticement laws made it illegal for whites to try to recruit black workers from other white men's lands. Together, these laws and practices formed a network that strongly limited the ability of freed former slaves to become economically independent and to exercise their political rights. In this way, Southern politicians filled the vacuum left by emancipation with a system of segregation and subjugation known as Jim Crow.

The institutions that came out of Reconstruction are just part of the story, however. For Southern whites—particularly those living in

Black Belt areas where slavery had been the dominant system of labor—cultural institutions and informal norms reinforced differing political attitudes. Segregation, racial policing, social punishments for interracial fraternizing and interracial relationships, and—above all—racial violence worked together to reinforce the idea that blacks were somehow inferior, less deserving, and more worthy of this kind of subjugation. These non-institutional behaviors and attitudes were a necessary companion to the laws that implemented these ideas: if whites truly believed that blacks were inferior, then it would be easier to inflict economic hardship, racial violence, and the denial of political rights—and all of these things were necessary for whites to maintain their political and economic positions. This operated in tandem with informal and socially rooted organizations like the Ku Klux Klan and other social networks. The goal was the same as with the formal institutions: to keep blacks in a subjugated position, economically and politically. This arrangement also appealed to poorer whites in these areas, who derived a significant psychological benefit from white supremacy. The net effect of this reaction was that whites "dug in," creating an environment that reinforced culturally, socially, and politically the idea that blacks were racially inferior.

As we shall see below, these reactions were particularly strong among those who had the most to lose—that is, those whites living in the Black Belt. Greenwood, for example, was the location of the 1954 kidnapping and lynching of fourteen-year-old Emmet Till, an African-American teenager who was allegedly caught whistling at a white woman; Till's body was found in the Tallahatchie River with a cotton-gin fan tied around his frame. (The white men who confessed to killing Till were acquitted by an all-white jury in nearby Tallahatchie County, Mississippi.) Although instances such as these are no longer prevalent, they have not been completely extirpated. In 2015, for example, a white supremacist shot and killed nine black churchgoers in Charleston, South Carolina. The shooter, from nearby Richland County, South Carolina (sixty percent enslaved in 1860), had written earlier that he "chose Charleston because it is the most historic city in my state, and at one time had the highest ratio of blacks to Whites [*sic*] in the country."[9]

1.2 BEHAVIORAL PATH DEPENDENCE

The story of this book speaks to larger questions about the political culture of a place. Scholars from many fields—including political science, sociology, and history (among others)—have noted a striking resilience of regional differences in political attitudes and political outcomes across nations, states, and localities. Alexis de Tocqueville famously traced the contours of the political culture of the early United States, contrasting it with its European predecessors.[10] Many have noted the longstanding political differences between the South and the rest of the United States, starting in the earliest days of the colonies and continuing through today. But this variation poses its own puzzle: How do these political cultures develop and persist across time? While there are a variety of ways the past can influence the present, in this book we focus on channels of persistence that operate via a mechanism we call *behavioral path dependence*.

Just like path dependence in institutions, which have been widely studied,[11] we argue that ideas, norms, and behaviors can be passed down as well, and they interact with institutions, reinforcing each other over time. This type of path dependence posits that behaviors, not just institutions, become self-reinforcing; once we start down a path of development in political culture, it becomes harder and harder to extract ourselves from that path. Similar to religion and language, attitudes—including political and racial attitudes—are passed down from generation to generation, fostered and encouraged by families and social structures, such as schools and churches.[12]

While conceptually distinct from institutional path dependence (mainly in the outcomes that it seeks to explain), behavioral path dependence does not exclude institutional channels of reinforcement over time. Rather, it incorporates institutions and behavior by emphasizing the interplay between them and the reinforcement mechanisms that strengthen each one. In the Black Belt South, for instance, local governments, to the extent they could, participated and sanctioned the enforcement of anti-black laws: the localized Black Codes gave way to state-sanctioned Jim Crow laws, put into place by numerous state constitutions that were enacted at the turn of the twentieth century. In turn, as many have argued, Jim Crow laws have given way to increased incarceration rates, increased racial violence, and laws that are otherwise unfavorable to African Americans. As these institutions gained hold in the South, reversing them and fully integrating blacks into society became increasingly difficult and the institutions became more important to Southern whites. Of course, any path can be disrupted, and many of these institutions were eventually (and effectively) undermined by the civil rights movement, the Civil Rights Act of 1964, and the Voting Rights Act of 1965. These laws were, as we discuss below, quite effective in addressing racial inequalities, particularly with regard to economic indicators and education; however, such interventions have been less effective in addressing regional persistence in political attitudes and political culture.

At its core, behavioral path dependence suggests that the political attitudes of a place or a region—such as the Black Belt—can persist across generations, nurtured by institutions, laws, families, and communities.

This idea of path dependence in politics more broadly suggests that significant historical forces, and the attendant political economic and political incentives that they produce, can create patterns that pass down through generations over time—and these patterns can outlast the original institutions and incentives. For example, looking at Greenwood, a possible explanation is that its history of slavery and its subsequent reliance on black labor has contributed to the development of more conservative political and racial attitudes among whites. We will show in this book that these attitudes have persisted over the course of the twentieth century. Thus, whites living in Greenwood and in other parts of the Southern Black Belt are more conservative today than are whites living elsewhere, even though those institutions that initially spurred on these attitudes— slavery, sharecropping, *de jure* disenfranchisement—are no longer in existence.

BEHAVIORAL PATH DEPENDENCE COMPARED TO OTHER APPROACHES

Looking across the U.S. South, path dependence in political attitudes suggests that some part of the variation in political, and specifically racial, attitudes that we see today in the U.S. South is fundamentally related to events that happened in the distant past. This is a break from what research in political science and public opinion might tell us.

Of course, the questions of how Americans formulate their political beliefs are not new. However, most of these predictions and analyses hinge on *contemporary* factors. As we discuss throughout this book, a number of studies have examined race relations—and specifically whites' attitudes on race-related issues or toward minority groups—by looking at present-day demographic characteristics, such as the share of the population that is black, how frequently blacks and whites interact, and contemporary patterns of segregation. Other inquiries focus on electoral politics. During each election cycle, teams of journalists, pundits, and scholars set out to understand why certain places politically swing the way they do and what this means for national and state electoral maps. For example, what is an area's level of unemployment? What is its average income? What is the racial, gender, and age composition of a particular city? Who won in the last election and by how much? Still other inquiries use survey data to make predictions about political outcomes. For example, we know that wealthier people tend to be more conservative, so what is a person's income? Employment or marital status? Race or gender? These sorts of present-day economic indicators and individual characteristics can tell us a lot about partisan leanings and political and racial attitudes.

Other scholars and political analysts focus on a slightly different question, which is what contemporary factors serve to change people's minds. Campaigns have spent millions of dollars and marshaled countless volunteer hours trying to mobilize voters, predict their behavior, and assess which kinds of appeals work and which don't. Other studies have used randomized controlled trials to assess the most effective sorts of mailers, telephone solicitations, and in-person contact. The result of all of this? In terms of increasing voter turnout—perhaps the simplest change—the most powerful known interventions have managed to increase turnout by around nine percentage points. In terms of changing people's minds—a more complicated task—some powerful interventions have found impacts, but whether the impacts are long lasting remains to be seen. Indeed, the bulk of this research, which focuses on contemporary factors and contemporary interventions, implies that large changes in the political attitudes and behaviors of Americans are rare, costly, and short-lived.[13]

These studies are important. However, they miss an important aspect of political reality—the hugely powerful legacies of past institutions. For that reason, we are not surprised by either the lack of findings or, if there are findings, results that are substantively small or fade quickly. Mailers, phone calls, or volunteer canvassers would not significantly alter the effects of a century and a half of history in places like Greenwood, Mississippi, or Asheville, North Carolina. And they certainly would not attenuate history's role in shaping attitudes on long-standing questions involving race relations, affirmative action, or voting rights. We think, as we will illustrate later in this book, that important interventions throughout the twentieth century—including the mass mobilization of tens of thousands of African Americans during the course of the civil rights movement—have had powerful effects on attenuating institutional outcomes and the expression of racial hostility over time. We also think that contemporary demographics are one possible legacy of these historical forces. However, at the root of our argument is the idea that behavioral path dependence means that patterns of attitudes change quite slowly. Counties like Leflore County, Mississippi, are places with 150 years of white dominance over a subjugated African American population—a relationship that had its roots in the political economy of antebellum slavery and its aftermath. These forces have spurred on certain kinds of political attitudes. In other words, contemporary factors can only take us so far in explaining the gulf in political attitudes that exists between the Southern Black Belts and other parts of the South and, by extension, other parts of the country.

1.3 THE ARGUMENT OF THIS BOOK

In this book, we argue that the unique political, economic, and social history of the South has created a set of divergent political cultures that persist in some form through to the present due to the path dependence of political attitudes. There are three crucial components to our argument. *First*, in looking at the U.S. South, we document that Southern whites who live in areas where slaveholding was more prevalent are today more conservative, more cool to African Americans, and more likely to oppose race-related policies that many feel could potentially help blacks. That is, we demonstrate a direct connection between a long-abolished economic institution and contemporary political attitudes. That this connection has lasted over 150 years presents a puzzle for when and how the attitudes within the South diverged along these lines and why they have persisted until today.

This leads to the *second* component of our argument, which is that these attitudes grew out of the historical incentives to subjugate African Americans—incentives that strengthened through the antebellum period and morphed in the postbellum period into significant institutional and social customs designed to keep blacks in socially, politically, and economically marginalized positions. As W.E.B. Du Bois noted, "Emancipation left the planters poor, with no method of earning a living, except by exploiting black labor on their only remaining capital—their land."[14] Slavery, emancipation, and their aftermath left a lasting mark on the South, but one that we argue was not uniform across the former slave states. In Black Belt locations such as Greenwood, the white business and political elite were greatly affected by the abolition of slavery and took great pains to ensure that their economic enterprise could continue and their political power could be maintained. The era of Jim Crow that followed was state sanctioned but also depended on local enforcement to achieve its ends. We believe these historical forces, both their relative presence and absence, shape the racial order of the South, as well as the way that Southerners thought—and continue to think—about race, politics, and policy. Differences in these historical forces led to a widening gap between the Black Belt and the rest of the South in the late nineteenth and early twentieth centuries.

The *third* component of our argument is that these divergent historical attitudes have been passed down over generations to create, in part, the contemporary political cultures we detect today. In other words, Americans' political attitudes are in part a direct consequence of generations of ideas that have been collectively passed down over time, via institutions such as schools and churches and also directly from parents and grandparents—that is, via behavioral path dependence. As we shall see, however, some outcomes have attenuated over time with interventions such as the Civil Rights Act and the Voting Rights Act, but the gulf in political attitudes among whites living in the South continues to exist today.

Our hope is, therefore, that we push our collective understanding of what shapes and forms contemporary political opinion and contemporary political behavior further, beyond contemporary factors. In doing so, we hope to show that our political attitudes today are intimately inter-twined with, and shaped by, those political attitudes of our parents and grandparents, nurtured by historical institutions and by intergenerational socialization. That is, deep political predispositions and social attitudes are in part the product of historical forces that subsequently create and drive the intergenerational transmission of attitudes, norms, and preferences. For that reason, we think that looking at the history of places like Greenwood, Mississippi, is very important in trying to understand why whites in these sorts of Black Belt cities are not only more conservative than whites living elsewhere in the South, but they are also some of the most conservative people in the entire country.

Ultimately, our argument in this book concerns the core idea that the formation of public opinion more broadly can have historical roots. In turn, attitudes can persist over time and across multiple generations via behavioral path dependence. History shapes contemporary political culture.

1.4 HOW THIS BOOK IS ORGANIZED

A brief roadmap will orient the reader to our book's organization. We start in chapter 2 by presenting an overview of the key theoretical concept underlying our analysis, namely that of behavioral path dependence. This chapter aims to situate this theory within the broader literatures of historical institutionalism, American political development, political behavior, and studies of Southern politics originating in Key's seminal book *Southern Politics*. We lay the groundwork for the rest of the book by examining how nonpolitical customs and norms could be transmitted over time and by considering other examples of this kind of transmission outside of American politics, including some important recent studies in comparative politics and in political economy. Although previous studies have alluded to the fact that attitudes can persist over time, ours is the first to fully develop this concept within the context of behavioral path dependence and political attitudes.

The rest of the book is then organized into three parts. Part I develops the main analysis documenting path dependence of political attitudes among white Southerners. Specifically, we examine the contemporary effects of American slavery, showing the predictive power of slavery on contemporary Southern white political attitudes. This forms the core part of the empirical puzzle that we explore in later sections of the book. Part II then brings the narrative back in time to the antebellum, Civil War, Reconstruction, and post-Reconstruction periods. Here, we argue that the relationship we see between slavery and present-day political attitudes might have its roots in the economic and political incentives growing out of slavery and, importantly, its collapse. Part III then takes up how path-dependent forces shaped the trajectory of political attitudes at the local level, across generations. In this part we highlight what we call the "mechanisms of reproduction," which drive behavioral path dependence. These include both intergenerational socialization and mechanisms of institutional reinforcement. Finally, we also explore how the legacy of slavery is not uniform across outcomes—some effects of slavery persist, while others have been significantly attenuated by the federal interventions of the twentieth century.

PART I: THE CONTEMPORARY EFFECTS OF SLAVERY

Part I establishes our main evidence for behavioral path dependence in political and racial attitudes in the American South, relying on several data-driven analyses to show that the South's slave past predicts regional behavioral outcomes today.[15] The goal of Part I is to show, using data and examples, that *historical patterns predict contemporary attitudes.*

Chapter 3 presents the core empirical evidence for the possibility of path dependence in political attitudes. We show that Southern counties that had higher shares of slave populations in the time period before the Civil War are today areas where whites are (1) more likely to be conservative in terms of their partisan self-identification and (2) more likely to oppose policies that many believe could benefit African Americans, such as affirmative action. These are also areas of the U.S. South where various measures show that (3) whites have the coolest views toward blacks as a group. Figure 1.1 previews the data and findings from this chapter and shows measures of white political preferences disaggregated by region of the country: non-South (which includes the Midwest, Northeast, and West Coast), formerly low-slave Southern counties, and formerly high-slave Southern counties.[16] The figure shows that, across all measures, non-Southerners are more liberal—they are more likely to identify as Democrats, to support affirmative action, and to say that slavery has hurt the ability of blacks to work their way out of the lower class. Within the South, formerly low-slave areas are more likely to express these views as well. *It is within formerly high-slave areas that whites are the most likely to oppose the Democratic party, oppose affirmative action, and express sentiments that could be construed as racially resentful.* We present these and other results in chapter 3. And, as we show, although these results may be surprising, they hold up even in the face of a battery of statistical tests.

Chapter 4 addresses questions that many skeptical readers will have, which is whether these results aren't simply being driven by contemporary factors such as present-day demographics. First, we address the important counter-arguments that these findings are simply being driven

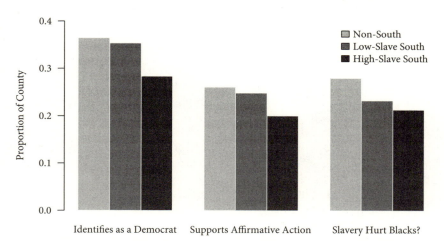

Figure 1.1. White attitudes on race-related issues. Low-slave refers to counties in the U.S. South that had fewer than 25% of the county population enslaved; high-slave refers to counties that had more than 25% of the population enslaved.

by contemporary black concentrations or population mobility over time. We are motivated in these questions by the seminal work of V. O. Key, who noted that one of slavery's legacies was in the high shares of African Americans living in this part of the country today. A voluminous literature following Key has made the point that white populations, being threatened by large numbers of African Americans, develop more conservative views and stronger antiminority attitudes—a mechanism that the literature refers to as "racial threat." As we show in chapter 4, however, this explanation does not fully explain the distinctiveness of the Black Belt. Once we account for the prevalence of slavery in the Southern Black Belt, the effects of contemporary black populations on white political and racial attitudes disappear. This is an important point, and, because it contradicts a significant literature in American politics, we discuss it at length. We also consider whether our findings are being driven by substantial population sorting over time, leading to demographic changes in the Black Belt. Although the evidence on this point is thinner, we nonetheless find that this explanation does not appear to be fully driving our results. Instead, we argue that the forces at play do not originate in contemporary demographics, but, rather, in the historical economic incentives for oppression and antiblack policies, which, via behavioral path dependence, continue to shape attitudes today.

PART II: THE ORIGINS OF THE U.S. RACIAL ORDER
IN ECONOMIC AND POLITICAL INCENTIVES

Part II addresses the questions left open by the empirical findings in part I. If our findings that whites who live in former parts of the slaveholding South are more racially conservative aren't explained by demographic factors, then what explains this pattern? We argue in this part of the book that the answer lies in the complicated historical institution of slavery itself: that is, the economic and political system of slavery and its collapse led whites living in areas most dependent on slavery to be more conservative, and more cool or hostile toward African Americans.

How is it that slavery has led to whites who were reliant on it to become more racially conservative? And when did these differences come to light? Chapter 5 examines the historical progression of political differences between the slaveholding Black Belt and other parts of the South. Slavery affected much of antebellum politics, leading to some cleavages between the Black Belt and nonslaveholding areas in the antebellum period, but these differences were mostly rooted in economics, rather than the question of slavery. In elections that focused on Southern rights and the future of slavery, low-slave areas were just as likely to support the institution as high-slave areas. Similarly, on race and the treatment of enslaved people, we are unable to distinguish meaningful differences between high- and low-slave areas. If anything, it appears that whites living in low-slave areas saw slaveholding as a means of economic upward mobility. It is not until the Civil War and its aftermath that we can detect meaningful partisan differences between former slaveholding and nonslaveholding areas. Slavery had a massive impact on Southern society and politics in the antebellum period, but the political geography we find today only begins to develop in the years leading up to the Civil War and immediately after, suggesting the important role that the threat of the collapse of slavery played in exacerbating and fomenting regional differences in politics and over the treatment of African Americans.

This addresses *when* the political geography of slavery solidified into the patterns we see today. But *how* did these differences come about? Chapter 6 tackles these questions conceptually by looking more closely at the end of slavery through the periods of Reconstruction and, later, Redemption. We argue that emancipation was a critical juncture in the development of Southern politics and for race relations in particular. Emancipation, and all that came with it, altered the incentives faced by Southern white elites, especially those living in former high-slave areas to promote the (1) economic and (2) political suppression of blacks. Indeed, Southern whites—and particularly Southern Black Belt elites—had created a business economy that was reliant on labor-intensive agriculture (such as cotton farming) and extraction. The success of these industries was predicated on the generous provision of inexpensive and renewable labor. For these elites, the end of slavery meant the end of this steady supply of workers, threatening their income sources and economic status. As negotiation replaced coercion in the owner-laborer relationship, owners sought to find new ways to reestablish their control over their mostly black labor force.

With the passage of the Reconstruction Amendments, newly freed blacks could and did vote, creating a panic among whites who lived in areas where blacks outnumbered them. Rather than accede to a free black vote, whites in these areas often turned to voter suppression and ballot stuffing, using the numbers of blacks living in these areas as a way to accumulate greater political power. These economic and political incentives led Southern whites to engage in widespread racial suppression and intimidation, not just via legal means (e.g., Black Codes) but also via extensive localized racial violence and intimidation. In chapter 6, we show that there were more lynchings, more instances of convict leasing, and more votes to disenfranchise blacks in high-slave areas. These interventions worked in tandem with a more conservative racial culture, one that emphasized social segregation in homes, schools, churches, and businesses. This broader racial order, steeped in white supremacy, offered poor whites in the Black Belt a concrete advantage over the local black population and led to their strong support for the system.

PART III: THE MECHANISMS OF PATH DEPENDENCE

Part III turns the question toward examining the forces that have led to path dependence in political attitudes. How can we explain the fact that economic and political incentives dating back 150 years continue to affect political attitudes in the present-day period? Part III attempts to draw the line between point A (slavery) and point B (today) by looking at the mechanisms that drive behavioral path dependence, as well as important interventions that occurred both before and after the civil rights movement.

Chapter 7 traces the path of persistence by discussing two primary mechanisms by which behavioral path dependence takes place: (1) intergenerational socialization, and (2) institutional reinforcement. As evidence for intergenerational socialization, the chapter demonstrates that the racial attitudes of children in the post-1965 era are positively correlated with the racial attitudes of their parents, and that the effect of slavery is weaker in the subsample of whites who currently live in the South but did not grow up there. As evidence for institutional and environmental reinforcement, it shows that parts of the South that mechanized their agriculture earlier (therefore more quickly reducing their reliance on cheap labor to fuel the cotton economy) are areas where slavery's effects on whites' political attitudes today are weakest. It also shows that slavery's effects are amplified in places that saw greater violence (as measured by lynchings) and moderated in areas where black concentrations are higher and in areas where school desegregation took place, both suggesting that social interactions between white and black residents could serve to either reinforce or attenuate the effect of slavery.

These findings set the stage for chapter 8, which tackles the regional differences within the South during and after the civil rights movement, including the important interventions of the Civil Rights Act of 1964 and the Voting Rights Act of 1965. These interventions, as the chapter documents, were massively impactful and suggest an optimistic view about what our findings mean for American politics today: that these changes can come from within the United States and affect both behavioral and institutional outcomes. The civil rights movement helped change the way that millions of people think about race and race relations, while the Civil Rights Act of 1964 helped secure the protection of laws for millions of African Americans, and the Voting Rights Act of 1965 made it possible for millions of blacks to exercise their rights under the Fifteenth Amendment for the first time. In spite of the persistent legacy of slavery that we find in attitudes, it appears as though these interventions attenuated the effects of slavery in other areas, particularly in differences in local white and black populations in terms of education, income, and voting. This raises the fundamental conceptual question of why some legacies of slavery persist, but others do not. We argue that the concentrated efforts of federal interventions and black protest groups in high-slave areas led to an accelerated pace of change in these areas that reduced the mid-twentieth-century gaps between high- and low-slave areas.

We conclude in chapter 9 by considering these questions in the broader context of national politics. We argue here that America's slave history has affected our politics on a broader level, making the United States in part more conservative on racial issues, including redistribution, welfare, and law and order. We also consider what our findings mean for the future of policy interventions. Our conclusion is not without optimism: our history has shown that there are effective modes of intervention, particularly when it comes to economic inequality and educational disparities. Effective interventions might have an important role to play in the attenuation of path-dependent attitudes. However, our results also suggest the importance of vigilance: in the absence of interventions—both institutional and cultural—there is a possibility of retrenchment.

Our ultimate conclusion, however, is straightforward: history plays a deep and important role in how we understand contemporary political attitudes and, by extension, contemporary politics.

1.5 OUR METHODOLOGICAL APPROACH

This book relies on data analysis and quantitative methods. We use data from a variety of public opinion surveys, including the Cooperative Congressional Election Survey (CCES) and the American National Election Studies (ANES). We also use other kinds of economic indicators and demographic statistics, including from the U.S. Census, the United Nations, and other outlets. Because we attempt to analyze large quantities of data, we often turn to regression analyses and other kinds of statistical modeling, including matching, instrumental variables analyses, and other kinds of correlations and corrections. Sometimes, we look at very long-term patterns, such as basic relationships between things that happened in 1860 and the political culture of today; other times, we look within decades to tell a story about a particular time period. We also note that significant advances in data collection and survey techniques mean that these sorts of approaches were far from feasible even as little as twenty years ago. For example, some of the surveys we leverage here—including the Cooperative Congressional Election Survey—survey tens of thousands of people via online sampling, a strategy that results in far greater geographic coverage and thus enables our inquiry. Inevitably, there are times when no quantitative data of sufficient quality exist to generate a quantitative answer to a particular question. In these cases, we draw upon a broad set of work in political science, history, economics, and sociology.

Throughout, we have attempted to translate our quantitative analyses into straightforward substantive interpretations. It is our view that quantitative analyses add little unless they can be interpreted in meaningful, substantive ways. We therefore opt in favor of graphical representations and other, more intuitive ways of presenting this kind of information, leaving the more technical material to our other published work.

In terms of historical exposition, we attempt to keep our discussion brief and focused on the goals of our book. Volumes could be and have been written about the history of these time periods and contexts; indeed, we draw on this work to help us connect the dots along the behavioral paths that we study. But our contribution to the story of the South is a theoretical and empirical analysis of how political culture comes to be in a particular place. In the spirit of other political scientists who have studied path dependence, this story is dynamic and so will require historical context, but we attempt to keep the focus on the general processes at work.

We hope that by understanding these processes, we can begin to predict how behavioral path dependence will operate beyond the American South. In short, history informs our story, but it is not the story itself.

The story of this book is largely a story of place. Our key theoretical concept, behavioral path dependence, describes how social and political behaviors are passed down from one generation to the next through parent-child socialization and socialization within communities, schools, churches, and other kinds of local networks.[17] As well, these behaviors are reinforced and moderated by local institutions and shocks.

This suggests that the right unit of analysis in detecting behavioral path dependence is the local *community*. If behavioral path dependence operates locally at the level of the community, it is natural to take small communities as the unit of analysis in seeking quantitative evidence for behavioral path dependence. Where a person lives is often a good predictor of his or her heritage even though we know that people move over the course of their lives. For instance, those who currently live in an area that was once home to a large number of cotton plantations are more likely to have familial or communal ancestors that participated in slavery in some capacity than are those who currently reside in areas with very little slavery before the Civil War. Prior studies of behavioral path dependence, which we discuss in detail in the next chapter, have also followed the practice of using the local community as the unit of analysis.

In our study, we therefore use the county as our main unit of analysis. This follows a long line of research in Southern politics, dating back at least to V. O. Key, who showed an impressive variation in attitudes and voting patterns across counties within each of the Southern states. Local communities are often smaller than counties and occasionally cross over county boundaries, but, for our purposes of measurement, counties provide a reasonable approximation to estimate how political attitudes may vary with the influence of slavery. We supplement our county-level analyses with analyses at the individual and family levels.

1.6 CONCLUSION

We conclude this introduction by highlighting what we believe to be the core contributions of this book. The first is that we show that *political attitudes are in part path dependent*, making history an important component to the study of politics. Here, we show that America's history with slavery, emancipation, and Reconstruction has fundamentally influenced white Southerners' political attitudes. This history, as we show, has made whites who hail from areas where slavery was more prevalent more conservative—particularly on racial issues—than they otherwise would have been. History matters and shapes our politics, beliefs, and attitudes. And it does so via the important channels of institutional path dependence and behavior path dependence.

Second, we show that *Americans' attitudes on race can, in part, trace their origins to the economic and political incentives borne out of the mass enslavement of African Americans*, and that this varies regionally depending on the historical prevalence of slavery. We use data and other quantitative techniques to show that Southern whites—particularly those in the Southern Black Belt—had huge incentives to use informal institutions and localized customs to try as much as possible to recreate the system of institutionalized subjugation that slavery had once provided. We show that, once slavery ended, other institutions—some formal and some informal—arose to take its place. However, although we use the example of slavery and black-white relationships here, we believe that economic and political incentives matter significantly in structuring race relations, not just in the United States, but across other societies as well.

Third, we show that *not all legacies of slavery are the same*. As our analyses illustrate, important legislation like the Civil Rights Act of 1964 and the Voting Rights Act of 1965, along with the societal change instigated and moved forward by the civil rights movement and subsequent leadership from African Americans and other groups, have been successful in reducing systematic inequalities between black and white Southerners. Furthermore, these interventions have significantly attenuated differences between high-slave and low-slave parts of the South. However, these institutional and cultural interventions have done little to attenuate the differences in political attitudes across these same parts of the South. Even as all Americans, including Southerners, have moved away from overt racism, the present-day relationship between racial and political conservatism and slavery remains similar to that seen in the middle of the twentieth century.

CHAPTER TWO

A THEORY OF BEHAVIORAL PATH DEPENDENCE

> I met a little blue-eyed girl—
> She said she was five years old;
> "Your locket is very pretty, dear;
> And pray what may it hold?"
> And then—my heart grew chill and sick—
> The gay child did not flinch—
> "I found it—the tooth of a colored man—
> My father helped to lynch."
>
> *Poem by Bertha Johnston*

Slavery arrived in Texas later than it did in other parts of the South, but, even so, it quickly became important to the Texas economy and to the state's development. The city of Waco, Texas, illustrates this importance. Like many other Texas cities, Waco was small in the 1840s and 1850s—mostly inhabited by plantation farmers who grew cotton along the Brazos River. By 1860, however, the town was rapidly growing. According to the 1860 U.S. Census, Waco's McLennan County had around 4,000 free citizens, 270 of whom owned 2,300 slaves. This reliance on slavery and on labor-intensive agriculture led many citizens to support secessionist causes and to send many men and resources to the Confederate Army. Today, some 150 years later, Waco continues to adhere to these conservative, agricultural roots. McLennan County leans in a solidly Republican direction, having voted for the Republican candidate in every presidential election since 1980.[1]

Waco's conservative nature is long-standing, and, in the early twentieth century, the city was particularly conservative on racial issues. One of the most infamous and gruesome lynchings took place in Waco—the lynching of Jesse Washington in 1916. Washington was an area farmhand who had been accused of the rape and murder of a white woman. Within days of being accused, Washington had been arrested, questioned, and put on trial. Jurors deliberated for four minutes before finding Washington guilty; as

Johnston, Bertha. "I Met a Little Blue-Eyed Girl." *The Crisis*, July 1912.

he was being led away through Waco's main square, however, an unruly mob intervened. What happened next was repugnant by any standard. As two thousand people looked on, Washington was tortured, his toes and genitals mutilated, and he was kept alive while being burned repeatedly. He took hours to die. Among the spectators were hundreds of white children, some of whom participated in the torture while others kept parts of Washington's corpse as souvenirs. When asked why he brought his son, a white father—carrying the child on his shoulders—explained using a racial epithet: "[M]y son can't learn too young the proper way to treat [black people]."[2]

Washington's lynching in Waco was hardly an isolated instance of these sorts of public rituals. Throughout the early twentieth century, generations of Southerners—including children—participated not just in racial violence but also in other kinds of racial abuse, including beatings, exploitation, and, of course, segregation. These injustices operated within a larger fabric of norms that sociologists have called "racial etiquette," which buttressed the Southern racial hierarchy by structuring interactions between blacks and whites.[3] These traditions illustrate the heart of this chapter. How did norms like these promote racist attitudes within Southern society? Do they help explain the differences that we see today between the old slaveholding South and those parts of the South that were less reliant on slavery? Do they provide a connection between slavery and the present?

Motivated by examples like Jesse Washington's lynching, we argue that the answer is provided by a concept that we call *behavioral path dependence*. We define behavioral path dependence as path dependence in behavioral outcomes, including in attitudes, norms, and beliefs. Substantively, behavioral path dependence means that once the culture of a community has moved along a path, it becomes firmly rooted and difficult to reverse or change. The theory helps to explain not only many of the patterns we see across the contemporary South but also a broad range of findings from economics, sociology, and political science that we discuss in this chapter.

For behavioral path dependence to explain contemporary differences in political (or racial) attitudes, it must address two interrelated issues. First, how did the political culture come about in the first place? That is, how did behavioral paths diverge? Second, why was the chosen path not completely reversed or altered by future events or interventions? On the first issue, the literature on path dependence refers to such divergences as *critical junctures*—a concept developed by Ruth Berins Collier and David Collier in the context of labor movements in Latin America.[4] Like them, we posit that there are times in history when the choices leaders make are dramatically influenced or altered by significant events. These choices then close off paths down the road, making it difficult for society to revert back to a path that wasn't chosen. In the American South, one such critical juncture was the time around and immediately after the abolition of slavery, when Black Belt elites faced strong economic and political incentives to reinforce a racial hierarchy that would allow them to maintain their economic and political power. The formerly high-slave areas of the South started down a particular path that was distinct from the ones followed by other parts of the South or the North, and, once chosen, it became difficult to deviate from this path.

Second, we must consider why the path that was chosen has not been completely reversed or altered by future events or interventions, particularly if (as is the case with slavery) the incentives and institutions set at the time of the critical juncture either fade or disappear altogether. Why do differences in behavioral outcomes linger for decades if not centuries? For behavioral path dependence to operate, attitudes and behaviors must be subject to what are called *mechanisms of reproduction*. Using the case of the American South, we isolate two such mechanisms. The first, as the example of white children's participation at Jesse Washington's lynching shows, is intergenerational socialization. Children tend to follow in the footsteps of their parents and grandparents, learning from them not just language and religion but also racial and political attitudes. The second is institutional reinforcement. Just as norms can be inherited through families, institutions can reinforce societal norms and behavior, which in turn maintain these institutions in a self-reinforcing equilibrium. On the flipside, when the supporting institutions disappear, the equilibrium is disrupted and the behaviors and attitudes that these institutions supported decay naturally over time. The speed of decay, we argue, is also affected by other interventions.

We organize this chapter as follows. First, we provide a conceptual overview of "behavioral path dependence," outlining more precisely how it both builds on and differs from existing concepts. Throughout, we illustrate this concept via our example of regional variation in political attitudes in the American South, although we leave many of the finer details and empirical investigations to subsequent chapters. Next, we discuss behavioral path dependence in previous work in political science and economics in order to assess its usefulness as a generalizable concept. We then turn to the mechanics of how behavioral path dependence might operate with regard to slavery and emancipation, and we explore the origins of behavioral path dependence. For this, we build on the concept of a critical juncture, linking it to the important period between slavery's abolition and the end of Reconstruction. Finally, we discuss mechanisms of reproduction, specifically how attitudes and behaviors are passed down within communities over generations. We focus on two mechanisms: (1) intergenerational socialization and (2) institutional reinforcement. We conclude by discussing the idea of behavioral decay, and how certain institutional interventions can hasten this decay.

2.1 THE CONCEPT OF PATH DEPENDENCE IN INSTITUTIONS AND BEHAVIORS

Political scientists, sociologists, and other social scientists have long used the concept of path dependence to explain persistence in the social world over time. At its broadest, path dependence means "that what happened at an earlier point in time will affect the sequence of events occurring at a later point in time," or that the past influences how things are structured or operate today.[5] Political scientist Margaret Levi proposes a narrower definition:

> Path dependence has to mean, if it is to mean anything, that once a country or region has started down a track, the costs of reversal are very high. There will be other choice points, but the entrenchments of certain institutional arrangements obstruct an easy reversal of the initial choice. Perhaps the better metaphor is a tree rather than a path. From the same trunk, there are many different branches and smaller branches. Although it is possible to turn around and clamber from one to the other—and essential if the chosen branch dies—the branch on which a climber begins is the one she tends to follow.[6]

Levi's definition suggests that path-dependent processes are difficult to alter or reverse and may become more entrenched as time goes on and the tree grows. Changing course may be hampered by various feedback effects, or what Paul Pierson refers to as "increasing returns processes." That is, part of what makes a path-dependent process difficult to reverse is the fact that "the relative benefits of the current activity compared with other possible options increase over time."[7] For example, once a bureaucratic agency is created, it becomes difficult to abolish since its staff have a vested interest in keeping it open. The central implication of these reversion costs is that there can be great deal of historical consistency—more specifically, persistence—in political outcomes.

While path dependence is a widely used concept in the social sciences, it is typically associated with the analysis of institutions—things like laws, government entities, and bureaucracies—rather than attitudes, public opinion, or individual-level beliefs.[8] This is in large part because the concept's main area of application has been in the field of historical sociology, which takes the *structure* of relations between individuals (rather than the *attitudes and beliefs* of individuals) as its fundamental unit of analysis. Despite this, path dependence has much to contribute to the study of political behavior and public opinion. In fact, political behaviors of today may have deeply entrenched roots in past events and behaviors. This is our main argument.

We develop this connection by introducing the concept of *behavioral path dependence*, which we take simply to be *path dependence in behavioral outcomes*, including in attitudes, behaviors, norms, and beliefs. Substantively, the concept refers to the fact that once the social and political psychology of a community has proceeded down a certain path, the behaviors and culture of that community can become entrenched and difficult to reverse. Looking at the American South, once antiblack attitudes developed in places like Greenwood, Mississippi, or Waco, Texas, they were passed down to children, grandchildren, and great-grandchildren. Deviating from this path became very difficult over time, even when the original forces that gave rise to the attitudes either receded or attenuated—as the example of slavery and emancipation show.

A key implication of behavioral path dependence, then, is the persistence of behavioral outcomes over time and across generations. Looking at the politics of the South, behavioral path dependence helps us address several important questions. Why have the effects of slavery (and its demise) lasted so long? Why and how did these attitudes emerge as distinctly important? And how did these attitudes become ingrained over time? In addition, we can link behavioral path dependence to specific regions, which helps to explain why we see variation in whites' political attitudes *today* across the South.

We note some commonalities between what we argue here and the broader concept of path dependence. First, behaviors may be self-reinforcing in the long-run, but this is not necessary for behavioral path dependence to operate. For example, within the Black Belt, whites continued to benefit from the racial hierarchy they established with slavery—particularly in reinforcing ways through the early twentieth century. But even though whites benefited from racial norms for much of Southern history, federal legislative efforts in the twentieth century have substantially curtailed certain social "benefits." Specifically, whites no longer have legally privileged positions in schools, at the voting booth, and in employment. Nonetheless, as we discuss in chapter 3, we can still detect evidence of path dependence when we see regional variation in contemporary political attitudes across the South. Second, as with institutional path dependence, there are other "choice points" (to use the language of Levi) at which the paths could deviate, but entrenched ways of thinking make it hard to pivot. Thus, interventions designed to change certain outcomes might fail to influence the underlying behavior or attitudes.

What do we mean by path dependence in "institutions" versus "behavior"? To explain this distinction, we consider Douglass North's definition of an "institution" as the "humanly devised constraints" on political, economic, and social behavior.[9] Thus, laws, codes, and rules fit in the category of "institutions." While institutions shape and constrain human choices, research on political behavior has often drawn on social psychology research to argue that there are "behavioral forces" that work alongside these constraints. For example, intrinsic preferences, beliefs, ideologies, and attitudes of individuals all constitute behavior. Thus, we define "behavior" as a broad category of forces that can be either intrinsic to the individual or shaped by culture.

Although separating behavioral forces from institutional constraints is conceptually useful, they can also operate in tandem or reinforce one another. In the American South in the early twentieth century, formal institutions created Black Codes to codify antiblack sentiment, and, in turn, these rules created norms for how whites and blacks could behave in social or private settings. For example, segregated public transportation was often the first introduction for both white and black children to the world of Jim Crow, providing a government-backed lesson in the relative status of whites versus blacks.[10] Over time, whites internalized the justifications for the laws they created, and, through lived experience with these institutions, antiblack sentiment was further reinforced. We document this symbiosis in significantly more detail below, particularly when we discuss the post-Reconstruction and early twentieth-century periods. For now, we note that, at a conceptual level, institutional mechanisms (i.e., rules, laws, and local ordinances) can, over time, influence behavioral path dependence by reinforcing particular attitudes, values, customs, or beliefs.

Importantly, behavioral forces sometimes conflict with institutions. For example, after serving alongside blacks during World War II and fighting a common enemy, many white veterans found their preexisting racial views changed. The institutions of the military sharply conflicted with the attitudes held by whites in the Jim Crow South. Serving in the war marked a turning point for some white soldiers, who pushed for social change after returning home. But, for others, it was easier to revert back to the familiar racial hierarchy of their Southern home. For example, the historian Jason Sokol describes how two soldiers—one white and one black—took the train back home to the South after being discharged: "As the train rumbled across the country, the two dined together and passed the time telling stories. [The black solder] felt they had transcended 'this race nonsense' and 'became tight.' As the train passed into Texas and Louisiana, [he] realized his mistake. The white soldier assumed a posture of superiority and informed [him] that the war was over, they were back in the South," reverting back to using racial epithets and reminding the black man that he wasn't "an American soldier anymore."[11] This example suggests that conceptually separating behavioral forces from institutional constraints is useful. Most returning white veterans ultimately readjusted to life in the South, but not all. And whether a white veteran eased back into the Southern racial hierarchy depended on the strength of behavioral forces relative to the institutional constraints.

OTHER EXAMPLES OF BEHAVIORAL PATH DEPENDENCE

Although the literature does not use the term "behavioral path dependence" as we define it in this book, our concept of behavioral path dependence has substantial support from previous work.[12] Indeed, behavioral path dependence applies to many political and social phenomena. It helps us understand not only divergence in political and racial attitudes across the American South but also long-term patterns in political opinion, attitudes, and other behaviors.

For example, political scientists such as V. O. Key recognized the persistence of political attitudes over generations. In one paper, Key, writing with Frank Munger, observed that partisan shares in Indiana's counties remained stable despite dramatic changes in the local political economy over a period of eight decades.[13] Specifically, Key and Munger noted that farmers who had moved to Indiana self-segregated across county boundaries according to where they came from: some migrated from the South, others from the Northeast. Since there was very little political exchange across these migrant communities, each retained the politics they brought with them, which over time resulted in observable regional partisan patterns. Commenting on the stability and durability of public opinion, Key and Munger wrote that:

> the long persistence of county patterns of party affiliation despite changes in "interest" and the disappearance of issues that created the pattern, and the existence of contrasting patterns in essentially similar counties, point toward a "political" grouping at least to some extent independent of other social groupings. It may also be that the continuity of the life of the party group is not a smooth and uninterrupted flow, as might be inferred from electoral analysis alone … yet the net effect over long periods is the maintenance of similar party divisions.

Thus, patterns of political attitudes can outlive the forces that produced them.[14] Even major events such as migration do not completely unravel the political attitudes held by a community.

Subsequent research, largely in comparative politics and economics, uses behavioral path dependence to study the evolution of human behavior, particularly political attitudes. One notable early example is work by Mattei Dogan, who suggests that contemporary radicalism in the Toulouse region of France might be traced to heresies committed by the Cathars who lived in this area in the twelfth century. In response to these heresies, Pope Innocent III initiated a punitive campaign known as the Albigensian Crusades between 1209 and 1229, which reinforced the spirit of Catharism that in turn persists to this day. According to Dogan, even in the 1960s—some eight centuries later—"[r]emnants of the Cathar spirit still persist. Anticlerical Radicalism found its favorite homeland in [the] area" once occupied by the Cathars and their supporters.[15]

Other studies have also found lasting effects on political attitudes, including long-lasting effects on regional variation in voting—one of the outcomes we examine in later chapters. For example, a notable study by Nico Voigtländer and Hans-Joachim Voth examines German towns between World War I and World War II, and shows that the Nazi Party's vote share is higher in towns that had Jewish pogroms during the Black Death of the fourteenth century—a persistence in culture of nearly half a millennium.[16] A more recent study by Volha Charnysh shows that an anti-Jewish pogrom in 1941 predicts town-level opposition to European Union accession in 2003, as right-wing populists used anti-Semitic rhetoric to spread opposition to EU membership.[17] Another study, by Jason Wittenberg, examines voting patterns in the 1948 and 1990 elections in Hungary—years before and after the communist period—and shows that places where the right did well in 1990 coincided with those where it did well in 1948.[18] Also looking at Eastern Europe, work by Leonid Peisakhin shows that communities that came under Romanov rule after the partition of Poland in 1772 exhibit behavioral patterns today that are very distinct from adjacent and otherwise similar communities that fell under Habsburg rule.[19] Finally, ongoing work by economists Nicola Fontana, Tommaso Nannicini, and Guido Tabellini finds that the communist vote share in Italy has been persistently higher in the country's northern areas where the Nazi occupation and Italian civil war lasted longer.[20]

Other studies that have looked exclusively at cultural attitudes (rather than voting or political partisanship) also suggest that behavioral path dependence plays a role in shaping these sorts of ostensibly nonpolitical attitudes. For example, a well-known study by Nathan Nunn and Leonard Wantchekon shows that African communities that were targeted more heavily by the Atlantic slave trade several hundred years ago exhibit less trust in others (including in government) than those that were not as heavily targeted.[21] In another study, Luigi Guiso, Paola Sapienza, and Luigi Zingales examine the origins of differences in civic traditions between Northern and Southern Italy, showing that cities that experienced self-government in the Middle Ages have higher levels of civic capital today than those that did not.[22]

What do these studies tell us? First, this body of research suggests that behavioral path dependence is a broadly generalizable phenomenon, one that is not just limited to our example of the American South in the wake of slavery's collapse. To the contrary, behavioral path dependence helps to explain regional differences in political outcomes and cultural attitudes in contexts as diverse as southeastern France, parts of Africa, or western Ukraine. Second, these papers suggest that the persistence of attitudes and political viewpoints can last a long time—possibly even centuries. For example, the study on the slave trade's effects on Africans' modern-day attitudes finds that effects persist as long as three hundred years, while the study linking anti-Jewish pogroms on Nazi voting in Germany finds effects persisting for half a millennium; meanwhile, the analysis of the French Cathars conjectures an effect lasting eight hundred years.

However, the literature, though fascinating, does not settle cohesively around any unifying concept thus far; each work explains what appears to be an idiosyncratic phenomenon. But, taken together, this literature does suggest there is a generalizable explanation for how historical forces as disparate as the African slave trade, Jewish pogroms, and American slavery predict contemporary political attitudes. These patterns, we believe, can be addressed by the concept of behavioral path dependence.

2.2 CRITICAL JUNCTURES AND THE MAKING OF DIVERGENT PATHS

How does the process of behavioral path dependence begin? Looking at the American South, a key question is how and when the political and partisan paths of high-slave and low-slave areas diverged. This is an important question not just for scholars; understanding the nature of the divergence could help us assess when and how other such events might engender change, and will possibly help us evaluate what interventions, if any, could help attenuate differences.

Looking at regional variation in political attitudes across the American South, behavioral path dependence provides several points of origin. One possibility is that whites who settled in different parts of the South have always been different, dating from the colonial period until today. (Some historians embrace this view of cultural persistence.[23]) This line of reasoning implies that centuries-old cultural values and beliefs that predate slavery also drive political and racial attitudes today. Furthermore, this would suggest that slavery is not a causal factor in driving attitudes. In fact, it is the antebellum cultural folkways that drove both the adoption of slavery and current political attitudes.

Another possibility, which is what we argue in this book, is that slavery itself was a key factor in triggering the slaveholding South to diverge from areas that were less reliant on slavery. Although the institution developed over the course of more than one hundred years, it collapsed relatively quickly—within ten years over the course of the Civil War and its immediate aftermath. The economic and political incentives before and after the war fell quickly out of alignment, leading Black Belt counties to move promptly to contract the rights of newly freed blacks. And yet this would not be the first time that elites whose power was undermined by the forced removal of an institution upon which they relied heavily would do their best to reverse these changes. When Napoleon's armies forcibly removed seignorial institutions in Western Germany, local elites tried to set up informal institutions to replace the ones that were abolished.[24]

To help evaluate these possibilities, we consider the possible origins of behavioral path dependence more broadly. For this, we rely on the notion of a critical juncture, a concept from the literature on path-dependent processes. The idea put forward by this work is that there is a "critical juncture," a time period when a path-dependent process begins to unfold. The events that take place at this critical juncture put society on a particular long-term development trajectory.[25] Paul Pierson and Theda Skocpol explain this concept succinctly:

> Outcomes at a critical juncture trigger feedback mechanisms that reinforce the recurrence of a particular pattern into the future.... [Path dependence] highlights the role of what Arthur Stinchcombe (1968) has termed historical causation in which dynamics triggered by an event or process at one point in time reproduce themselves, even in the absence of the recurrence of the original event or process.[26]

How can we recognize critical junctures? Typically (though not always), the critical juncture is a *shock* that shapes incentives and leads actors to make choices that alter the path that society has been taking, triggering a new feedback mechanism that starts a new path. In other words, a critical juncture is a point at which there are several possible paths, and only one is chosen. Later on, the paths not taken are no longer options.

Looking at the existing literature documenting examples of behavioral path dependence, all studies show some such critical juncture. For example, in Voigtländer and Voth's analysis of the persistence of anti-Semitism in Germany mentioned above, the relevant shock is the massive reduction in the European population caused by the Black Death, an event that triggered the panicked environment in which the pogroms took place. In Peisakhin's analysis of Polish attitudes also mentioned above, the relevant shock is the first partition of Poland, and in Fontana, Nannicini, and Tabellini's analysis of Italy, it is the Italian civil war and Nazi occupation of northern Italy between 1943 and 1945. In other works on path dependence, such critical junctures correspond to the Glorious Revolution in England, the decolonization of Africa, and the defeat of the Germans in Cameroon during World War I.[27]

Looking at the American South, this concept of critical junctures naturally points us to the Civil War and, especially, the abolition of slavery in 1863. This shock was followed by the defeat of the South in the Civil War (1865) and dramatic changes to the Southern political economy during the brief period of Reconstruction (1865–77) and later Redemption (circa 1877–97). Two major changes took place relatively abruptly during these periods that had profound effects on the Southern political economy. First, Southern blacks were freed and now earned higher wages than before, which threatened the economic viability of the Southern plantation economy. Second, blacks gained the right to vote, which dramatically increased the size and nature of the electorate, creating the potential for both a change in representation and a shift in policies enacted by local and national governments. In fact, a large number of African Americans were elected to political offices in this period.[28] The potential for such dramatic political change threatened the interests of the existing white elite, who sought to reverse these changes by disenfranchising blacks with poll taxes, literacy tests, and whites-only primaries. In chapter 6 we provide more details on the events that followed this critical juncture in Southern history.

More conceptually, the events surrounding the Civil War and emancipation of slaves map onto the critical junctures framework. First, this was a time when society (not just politicians but also individuals) had to make choices about the kind of system that would replace slavery. Second, making these choices at this point closed off options later on. Specifically, once the American South moved along the path of Black Codes, residential and school segregation, and, eventually, Jim Crow, it was difficult—if not impossible—to revert back to the status quo at the time of emancipation. Indeed, by the early twentieth century, millions of Southerners—both black and white—were born into Jim Crow and its socially sanctioned system of discrimination, one that differed from slavery but was nonetheless impactful in structuring white-black interactions. Last, these choices have the possibility of creating a feedback loop. Once Black Codes were in place, and once blacks assumed a subjugated role within an ostensibly free society, a feedback loop began.[29] Whites across the class spectrum benefited from the system and, until the political and economic incentives shifted, had no impetus to change it. The economic elite of the Black Belt gained more control over the labor force, and poor whites were able to maintain the psychic benefit of not being at the bottom of the social hierarchy along with freed blacks. All of these factors point to this critical time period as being a critical juncture.

We have implicitly referred to the first few decades after the abolition of slavery as the critical juncture, although it hardly seems like a "moment" in history, especially as thousands of pages have been written on the events unfolding in this time period. Indeed, while some readers may not think that it is appropriate to refer to what occurs over the course of decades as being "abrupt," this timeframe is relatively brief in the life of a nation. As we develop in further detail in the chapters that follow, it is hard to overestimate the importance of slave institutions in the South and how their collapse reverberated through the South's political economy. Indeed, although slave numbers began increasing dramatically starting in the late eighteenth century, slave labor had been central to the South since African slaves arrived at the port of Jamestown, Virginia, in 1619. This society, one that was built upon slave labor, existed for nearly 250 years before losing its power and economic prestige within a fairly short amount of time. Viewed through this macroscopic lens, we consider the demise of slavery in the South as a key critical juncture that set the South on a distinct path.

2.3 PERSISTENCE AND THE MECHANISMS OF REPRODUCTION

As we described above, behavioral path dependence involves persistence in behavioral outcomes (such as political attitudes, ethical values, customs, and beliefs) well after the conclusion of the events of the critical juncture. But what maintains the persistence? How is it that behavioral path dependence can cause persistence over decades, possibly even centuries?

We consider two forces behind this persistence, which are sometimes called the "mechanisms of reproduction" in the path dependence literature.[30] These are: (1) intergenerational socialization and (2) institutional reinforcement. These broad categories are not mutually exclusive and both could operate in tandem. In addition, while both apply to our example of the American South, other contexts might see behavioral path dependence happening primarily via one channel versus the other. For example, in their analysis of the effect of the Atlantic slave trade on contemporary Africans' attitudes on trust, Nunn and Wantchekon examine both institutional and what they call internal channels of persistence, and conclude that "both channels are important, but ... the internal channel is at least twice as large as the external channel."[31]

INTERGENERATIONAL SOCIALIZATION

One of the most important channels by which behavioral path dependence operates is via socialization between older and younger generations—for example, between grandparents, parents, uncles, and aunts and their grandchildren, children, nieces, or nephews. From an early age, children are exposed to the political, racial, and religious attitudes of their parents and older relatives, and, from this early socialization, they develop attitudes that are often similar to those of their parents, relatives, and members of their local communities. This emulation extends not just to likes and dislikes (e.g., hobbies or sports) but also to norms that are more consequential, including language, religion, and politics. In fact, a number of studies have shown that partisanship is stable over time and across generations. For example, work by Don Green, Bradley Palmquist, and Eric Schickler presents evidence that partisanship is stable over the life cycle: political socialization takes place early in the life of an individual, and remains fairly stable throughout the individual's lifetime.[32] In addition to this, a wide body of literature shows that the most important determinant of an individual's partisanship and party affiliation is the ideology of his or her parents. In particular, M. Kent Jennings, Laura Stoker, and Jake Bowers look at cross-generational political attitudes and find that "[p]artisan attitudes and attitudes with a strong affective or moral component (e.g., racial and school prayer attitudes) are most likely to be passed on from parent to child, as are religious orientations."[33]

The idea that intergenerational socialization is a powerful force has been influential in the fields of public opinion and voter behavior, but also in fields cognate to political science, including economics and cultural anthropology. For example, anthropologist Robert Boyd, biologist Peter Richerson, and economists Alberto Bisin and Thierry Verdier argue that cultural change takes place relatively slowly and is constrained by the influence that parents have on their kids. In particular, Bisin and Verdier develop a model of parent-child socialization in which parents attempt to endow their children with their own values and preferences.[34] Several other studies have documented instances of intergenerational socialization. This includes findings that boys in Bangladesh who witness marital violence at home are more likely to be perpetrators of marital violence themselves and that American sons are significantly more likely to serve in the military if their fathers served.[35]

Several papers explicitly reference the parental transmission of attitudes as a key explanation for behavioral path dependence. For example, Alberto Alesina, Paola Giuliano, and Nathan Nunn show that agricultural societies that adopted the plough over four thousand years ago are less favorable to women today than those that adopted other tools for agriculture, such as the hoe or the digging stick. Moreover, they show that first-generation American women whose parents immigrated from plough-heritage societies have a lower female labor-market participation rate than those that did not. Since an individual's community and institutional environment changes significantly after moving to a different country, the authors interpreted this finding as evidence that parental socialization matters.[36] Parental socialization is also a key explanation for the behavioral path dependence in Voigtländer and Voth's analysis of persistent anti-Semitism in Europe and Nunn and Wantchekon's study of the origins of Africans' mistrust.

The South is no exception to this pattern of parental socialization, and several works—mostly in sociology and anthropology—show how racial attitudes were passed down from one generation to the next.[37] For example, squarely in line with what we would expect from intergenerational socialization, historian Jennifer Ritterhouse argues that children in the American South were taught to observe *racial etiquette* or *racial learning*.[38] That is, young white children who might not have understood the complicated political and economic history of slavery and Reconstruction would still know to address black people using racial slurs, while black children would know to address white people (including white children) with respectful titles. Racial violence, to which white children were often witnesses, provided further "lessons." For example, Ritterhouse analyzes photographs of lynchings and finds that white children are present in around a third of historical photographs.[39]

INSTITUTIONAL REINFORCEMENT

As we noted above, behavioral path dependence is conceptually distinct from institutional path dependence in the sense that it speaks to behavioral outcomes (such as differences in attitudes, behaviors, norms, and beliefs) while institutional path dependence speaks to differences in institutional outcomes (such as differences in how bureaucracies develop). However, the two often operate together. Behavioral path dependence specifically allows for the possibility that both institutions and culture work in tandem, reinforcing one another and creating feedback effects that propagate both attitudes and institutions. Nevertheless, can behavioral path dependence be explained by a purely structural theory of path dependence that allows processes of feedback and increasing returns to affect behavior as well as institutions? For example, did slavery affect contemporary attitudes through its enduring effect on institutions? Are the effects of slavery felt today primarily because the South created policies such as Jim Crow, segregation, and disenfranchisement? Our answer to these questions is that culture and institutions work in tandem and persist over time because they *reinforce each other*.

Prior work on behavioral path dependence is divided on the role of institutions versus culture in explaining persistence. For example, Wittenberg emphasizes the importance of church institutions in explaining the persistence of right-wing values in Hungary, while Nunn and

Wantchekon's study on Africans' mistrust of strangers and Alesina, Giuliano, and Nunn's study on plough- versus hoe-based agriculture focus more on cultural mechanisms such as socialization within the family to explain their persistence results. Guiso, Sapienza, and Zingales's analysis of modern-day Italy goes so far as to say that even institutional persistence is explained mainly by behavioral path dependence, rather than the other way around.[40] Nevertheless, despite differences in emphasis, almost all of these works recognize that institutions and culture reinforce each other, that the effects of each are often difficult to parse, and that both influence key outcomes.

In the U.S. South, the demise of slavery intensified racially hostile attitudes among whites, who, as a result of these attitudes, established antiblack institutions such as Black Codes and Jim Crow laws. White children were born into this era of institutionalized racism and, accordingly, they became more likely to develop racially hostile attitudes themselves as a result of both these institutions and intergenerational socialization. For the next generation, the mechanism is the same: children grow up in a segregated environment, they develop racial attitudes that are similar to their parents', and they then have little incentive to abolish institutional segregation. This process continues: attitudes are passed down from parents to children and are reinforced by institutions. In chapter 7, we provide evidence for reinforcement mechanisms and argue for their importance in driving behavioral path dependence.

2.4 ATTENUATION DUE TO DECAY AND INTERVENTIONS

Between the time of slavery's collapse in the 1860s and today, many events have taken place that could potentially undo slavery's behavioral legacy. First, we would expect, naturally, for divergences created by the critical juncture of emancipation and Reconstruction to last for a long time, but perhaps not indefinitely. Moreover, the last 150 years have seen two world wars, the Great Depression and the policies of the New Deal that followed it, the civil rights movement, the Civil Rights Act of 1964 and the Voting Rights Act of 1965, desegregation of schools and public places, and even the election of the first African American president. Presumably these powerful intervening events—some of which have specifically targeted the Southern Black Belt—have attenuated those regional differences in Southern political attitudes created by the forces of slavery and its collapse. To put this another way, we might not expect differences sustained by behavioral path dependence to last indefinitely, so how, and why, would we expect them to attenuate?

We address these questions in light of what we refer to as "attenuation," which we take to be the softening of the divergence (and differences) in the development paths of political attitudes. Looking at the American South, we would see attenuation if, for example, the views of Black Belt whites began to look more similar to the views of whites living elsewhere in the South. We consider two important attenuating factors: (1) decay in attitudes across generations that differs across areas (a passive mechanism), and (2) active interventions, such as external involvement, legislation, and enforced changes on behavior (an active mechanism).

DECAY AND ATTENUATION

Decay speaks to the fact that, naturally, we would not expect attitudes to persist indefinitely—particularly if the institutions that support these attitudes or the social environment change. Underlying this point is the fact that behavioral path dependence does not require that successive generations have no agency to formulate their own independent worldviews. To the contrary, history shows that breaks occur as children rebel or push back (either implicitly or explicitly) against their parents' ways, making an intergenerational transfer of attitudes less than perfect. For example, work by Kent Jennings and Dick Niemi documents that contextual factors, such as the salience of the issue or how ideologically aligned parents are with others, influence the degree of intergenerational transmission.[41] While some individuals inherit much of their outlook from the previous generation, others inherit very little, and this could vary across both behavioral outcomes and the institutional environment.

Here, Boyd and Richerson provide a possible explanation for such decay by developing a model of "rule of thumb" decision-making, which is also an important foundation for the evolutionary models of economists Sam Bowles and Herbert Gintis. These authors developed models in which cultural norms appear as heuristic devices that support equilibria in complex environments according to which actions are most beneficial. (For example, racist institutions and practices are beneficial to white plantation owners because they suppress black wages.) The key idea is that when historical shocks and technological changes make the existing equilibrium unviable, the norms and attitudes that were produced under the equilibrium will gradually decay.[42]

An important point here is that attitudes in places could decay at different rates, leading to attenuation in regional differences. For example, there has been a widespread decline in the "old-fashioned" racism over the second half of the twentieth century, both outside and inside the South. But the decay in this type of racism will only attenuate the long-term effect of slavery if old-fashioned racist attitudes in the high-slave parts of the South decay *faster* than those in the low-slave parts. The relative gap between regions would remain the same, although the levels of old-fashioned racism would overall be lower. In extreme cases, differential decay could even lead to growth in the effect of long-dormant institutions.

Behavioral path dependence research has uncovered several examples of such attenuation due to decay in political attitudes. Saumitra Jha shows that medieval Indian port cities saw less conflict between Hindus and Muslims not only several hundred years ago, when these cities were lively multicultural centers of trade, but even today and even in cities that are no longer major commercial centers. However, he also finds that the cooperative equilibrium in port cities has been gradually eroding and that these cities—even though they are more peaceful than similarly matched non-port cities—are becoming less peaceful over time.[43] In yet another study of behavioral path dependence, Alberto Alesina and Nicola Fuchs-Schündeln found that Germans living in parts of former East and West Germany continue to hold different beliefs about the benefits of redistribution and government intervention even fifteen years after reunification. However, the beliefs of the two groups have been converging and, under certain assumptions, the authors estimate that the two groups will hold similar beliefs in around twenty to forty years from the time of their study.[44] Nunn and Wantchekon's study on the slave trade's effects on Africans' mistrust also hypothesizes that the effects among targeted ethnic groups will dissipate, but it could take a very long time; if Alesina and Fuchs-Schündeln found that effects of the Cold War (which lasted forty-five years) will take two to four decades to dissipate in Germany, then it should be no surprise that the impact of four centuries of African slave trade continues to be felt one hundred years after it ended.

One might ask whether we can measure the "half-life" of racist ideology that can be traced back to slavery. Just how persistent are the effects of slavery? This is *the* question of interest to those who want to know just when those effects might finally dissipate (and when, in this sense, America will finally become a "post-racial society"). Data scarcity prevents us from being able to estimate the half-life of these effects with any accuracy—public opinion data with sufficient geographic coverage stretching back far enough in time are not available. And even if we did have these data, there are the obvious challenges with extrapolating into the future. (Who is to say that future events will not redirect us toward *increasingly* racially charged politics?) Nevertheless, we make the best use of the available data to address these important questions in chapter 8.

INTERVENING FACTORS

In addition to naturally occurring decay, intervening factors moderate the relationship between slavery in the past and attitudes in the present day. With respect to the American South, the twentieth century is full of obvious cultural and political examples—the civil rights movement, the Civil Rights Act of 1964, and the Voting Rights Act of 1965 are just a few. All of these had the potential to influence the transmission of political attitudes and its regional variation across the American South. Other local, more subtle forces may also have attenuated slavery's effects. For example, some agricultural counties in the American South were early adopters in the 1920s and 1930s of mechanization technology (such as tractors), which reduced the demand for inexpensive black labor. This reduced need fundamentally changed the economic relationship between elite whites and black farmhands; whites no longer needed racist institutions (such as laws restricting black mobility) to maintain control over black labor.

These illustrations provide examples of how intervening factors can attenuate behavioral path-dependent differences over time. But the example of the South in the twentieth century is not idiosyncratic. For example, Voigtländer and Voth's study on Nazi voting in Germany finds that the relationship between Black Death pogroms and anti-Semitism during the interwar period in the twentieth century is moderated by exposure to trade and commerce. Specifically, the effects are weaker in towns that were part of the commercial confederation known as the Hanseatic League than in towns that were exposed to less commerce. The study of medieval Indian cities mentioned above also provides evidence that exposure to commerce can moderate intergroup hostility.

These examples provide some generalizable guidance as to when we can expect institutions to matter in attenuation. Specifically, if the institutional environment serves as a *reinforcement mechanism* that drives behavioral path dependence, then changes in the institutional environment can also moderate the transmission of attitudes. This makes it possible to intuit what will, or will not, be an effective intervention. For example, the mechanization of cotton farming that we discussed above is revealing. Southern white landowning elites had taken many steps to keep the farm wages that they paid to their black farmhands low, the most important of which was using racially targeted violence and hostility. (This violence reduced the outside options of black farmhands, thus lowering their wages.) In places where machines began to replace agricultural labor, demand for workers dropped and so did the need for the racist attitudes and institutions that supported low wages. On the other hand, in places where black labor was still important, these racist attitudes and institutions persisted. This is an example of an intervention (mechanization) that removed a reinforcement mechanism (the desire of white elites to have low-waged black labor); thus, as we show in later chapters, we can detect attenuation in antiblack attitudes in counties that were early adopters of mechanizing technology.

On the other hand, even the most effective interventions may not lead to absolute attenuation in behavioral path dependence. For example, as we discuss in chapter 8, the Civil Rights Act of 1964 was effective in reducing inequalities between blacks and whites across certain outcomes, including in black children's attendance in desegregated schools. However, despite this important intervention, and the fact that it addressed an important reinforcement mechanism (segregated schooling), the Civil Rights Act did not fully attenuate differences in antiblack views across the South. That is, even though the Civil Rights Act has been remarkably successful at addressing institutional outcomes, it has been comparably less successful at addressing behavioral outcomes, which have persisted via behavioral path dependence.

2.5 ALTERNATIVE EXPLANATIONS AND VIEWPOINTS

Our theory builds on the idea that behavioral path dependence, nurtured by intergenerational socialization and also, we believe, institutional reinforcement, can lead to divergence in behavioral outcomes over time. To identify instances of behavioral path dependence, however, we have several challenges. For example, how do we uncover evidence for behavioral path dependence? How do we make sure that any differences in attitudes are due to behavioral path dependence and not other factors such as demographic change or mobility over time? And how do we make use of the rich qualitative evidence that the study of political history provides?

These are particularly challenging questions because, as we noted in the previous chapter, the study of behavioral path dependence tends to focus on particular places (as opposed to individuals).[45] This is mostly due to data availability; we have data for places over time, but not necessarily for individuals (or for individual families). This concern leads to two interrelated challenges: (1) demographic persistence (or change) and (2) population mobility or sorting.

DEMOGRAPHIC PERSISTENCE

A key challenge to providing evidence for behavioral path dependence is demonstrating that the results are not driven by demographic or economic continuity. In our context of the American South, the share of a county that was enslaved in 1860 is highly correlated with many present-day economic and demographic indicators, such as black population shares, black incarceration rates, public school enrollment, and black-white income gaps.[46] To the extent that slavery influences political attitudes, these correlations suggest that slavery's legacy shapes outcomes like income inequality, incarceration, and educational attainment, which contemporaneously shape present-day political attitudes within a place. It would be these regional economic and demographic outcomes, rather than the mechanisms of behavioral path dependence (such as intergenerational socialization and institutional reinforcement), that influence today's political attitudes.

In contrast to this alternative mechanism, behavioral path dependence predicts that slavery and its demise produced an *independent* cultural and behavioral impact on American politics. The fact that there are high black concentrations in the Southern Black Belt is obviously a consequence of high historical slave shares in those areas, a fact that we address in detail in chapter 4. In that chapter, we argue that it is not the present-day high concentrations of blacks or contemporary antiblack laws that alone made the "whites of the black belts who have the deepest and most immediate concern about the maintenance of white supremacy."[47] Although these are important factors, racial attitudes that were hardened during slavery and its abolition formed a separate pathway that continues to persist in the ethos of Southern Black Belt communities. This is the case, as the theory of behavioral path dependence would predict, despite the fact that the current generation of Southerners were not alive during the politically and economically tumultuous periods of the Civil War, Reconstruction, and Redemption.

A separate question involving demographic persistence concerns the nature of the local black population, rather than its size. For example, if high-slave areas have poorer or less educated black populations compared to black populations elsewhere, then this could lead whites in these areas to have worse views of African Americans. This would be another case where demographic persistence—in this case, of the socioeconomic status of blacks—would be driving white attitudes in each time period, rather than the intergenerational transmission within the white community. We address this possibility in chapter 8, in which we argue that this mechanism is difficult to square with the attenuation in the relationship between slavery and the characteristics of local black populations. Simply put, black populations in the high-slave South are currently quite similar to black populations elsewhere in the South.

GEOGRAPHIC SORTING OR POPULATION MOBILITY

Finally, another important alternate explanation relates directly to the fact that studies that examine behavioral path dependence tend to use local communities as opposed to dynasties or lineages as the units of analysis. Because of this, a serious possibility is that findings attributable to behavioral path dependence are, instead, driven largely by population mobility over time. That is, any findings are not due to intergenerational socialization within a community, or such socialization operating in tandem with institutional reinforcement, but are instead due to the fact that people move around frequently and tend to want to live in proximity with like-minded people—what social scientists have called homophily. We note that such behavior could be considered to be a component of behavioral path dependence, and that in fact sorting is not an alternate explanation but simply part of the mechanism of behavioral path dependence. But, even so, population sorting operates separately than the pathways we have identified above (intergenerational socialization and institutional reinforcement).

In our context of the American South, population mobility across the twentieth and twenty-first centuries could serve to explain regional divergence in behavioral outcomes. For example, one possibility is that racially conservative whites are moving to former slaveholding areas while racial liberals are moving out of these areas. This would result in former slaveholding areas seeming more conservative and nonslaveholding areas more liberal, perhaps particularly on racial issues; however, the pathway explaining these differences would be population mobility and not the components of behavioral path dependence that we have laid out here. As we explain in chapter 4, we find very limited evidence that such population sorting is driving our results. Moreover, if sorting is taking place based on factors that are unrelated to racial attitudes, then high levels of population sorting may cause the dilution of the forces we discuss above and make it actually more difficult to detect a legacy of slavery. (Put differently, our estimates of the effect of slavery on present-day attitudes may in fact be conservative estimates of the behavioral path dependence mechanism.) The fact that we detect such a legacy at all *despite* population sorting and geographic sorting is worth noting.

2.6 CONCLUSION

Our goal in this chapter has been to show that the central concept of path dependence in the fields of historical sociology, American political development, and political history is also relevant to the study of political behavior. Where these ideas meet is in the idea of *behavioral path dependence*. By behavioral path dependence, we simply mean path dependence in behavioral outcomes such as partisanship, political attitudes, concepts of morality, and individual-level cognitions.

Behavioral path dependence has several components. The first is that divergence in behavioral outcomes and attitudes usually starts at a critical juncture, a historically significant moment in time that sets society down a specific path. Second, and moving temporally from that critical juncture, behavioral outcomes are often carried forward by path-dependent mechanisms. These can be cultural, such as the important pathway of intergenerational socialization. But behavioral outcomes can also be reinforced by institutions and laws. Often, both elements work in tandem with one another, as we discuss throughout this book. Lastly, when institutions and incentives cease to support certain behaviors, they begin to naturally decay. Sometimes intervening factors hasten this decay, particularly when they lower the underlying political or economic incentives that sustained the behavioral outcomes.

In the chapters that follow, we provide evidence demonstrating that behavioral path dependence provides a compelling explanation for the present-day regional patterns of political and racial attitudes we see across the U.S. South. Specifically, as we document in the remainder of this book, slavery's collapse at the end of the Civil War was a critical juncture that led political and racial attitudes in high-slave areas and low-slave areas to diverge. Both intergenerational socialization and institutional reinforcement have sustained these differences over time. However, we also show in later chapters that some of these differences have attenuated over time, thanks in part to important interventions such as the civil rights movement and federal legislation.

We conclude this conceptual discussion by noting that behavioral path dependence is not limited to the American South. Studies have documented behavioral path dependence in contexts as diverse as anti-Semitism in Europe, levels of trust and mistrust among Africans, and voting patterns in Ukraine, all of which experienced behavioral path dependence triggered by historical events. The concept can be used to analyze other critical junctures such as wars, geographic rifts, and pivotal elections, and it provides a framework for thinking about how important political and attitudinal patterns evolved and endured over time. Ultimately, behavioral path dependence is a powerful idea for understanding the origins and persistence of political and cultural attitudes.

PART I

SLAVERY'S CONTEMPORARY EFFECTS

CHAPTER THREE

HOW SLAVERY PREDICTS WHITE POLITICAL ATTITUDES TODAY

"We may say that this law of [racial] separation is written in the blood of the whites and is ineradicable."

William D. Jelks, Governor of Alabama (1901–07)

"Our Negroes, who constitute 35 percent of our population in Alabama—are they getting 35 percent of the fair share of living?"

"Big Jim" Folsom, Governor of Alabama (1947–51, 1955–59)

One of the most politically interesting places in the Alabama Black Belt is Barbour County (fifty-two percent enslaved in 1860), located about two hours southeast of Montgomery on the Georgia border. Formed from preexisting Pike County and also from Creek lands, Barbour County had a strategic location on the boundary between Alabama and Georgia and on the banks of the Chattahoochee River, a major trading route. Like many of its Black Belt cousins, Barbour County, and Pike County before it, was heavily reliant on black labor. In fact, the region was so tied to slavery that an antebellum group of white elites—known as the "Eufaula Regency"—formed in the 1840s with the goal of agitating for secession over the issue of slavery. Although the Civil War battered the county's economy, the post-Reconstruction period saw the intensive use of black laborers to build a massive transportation and railway infrastructure, which moved the county forward economically. Today, the remnants of area plantations and mansions—statements to the wealth that black labor generated for the mansions' occupants—still remain in places such as Eufaula, Alabama (2010 pop. 13,137).

Barbour County's political culture echoes this history. The county has produced eight state governors, the most of any county in Alabama, with the list including some of the most prominent segregationists in the entire South.[1] For example, the first Alabama governor from Barbour County, William Dorsey Jelks (1855–1931), was a white supremacist who

Jelks, "The Acuteness of the Negro Question: A Suggested Remedy," p. 389.
Folsom, *Speeches of Governor James E. Folsom, 1947–1950*, p. 184.

presided over the Alabama Senate in 1901, the same body that ratified the 1901 Alabama state constitution. As we discuss below, this constitution—which is still Alabama's governing document—brought with it a host of provisions intended to disenfranchise freedmen and limit their economic mobility. Jelks was, moreover, a peddler of white supremacist rhetoric, writing that he believed that the black man was an "ignorant devil ... a foul blot, a blight upon the land [and] a little short of savage"[2] and "[i]t would be far better if the two races could be separated."[3] More recently, another famous Barbour County native, George Wallace, famously promised his supporters at his 1963 gubernatorial inauguration that he would support "segregation now, segregation tomorrow, segregation forever."[4]

Barbour County contrasts with nearby Coffee County (fourteen percent enslaved in 1860). Like many other counties in the Black Belt, Barbour County was heavily reliant on slavery, postemancipation black labor, and large-crop agriculture. Coffee County, on the other hand, is part of Alabama's southeast region, known as the Wiregrass. Historically, this area was more forested and less suitable for growing crops; for much of the eighteenth and nineteenth centuries it was settled by mostly white subsistence farmers and Creek and Choctaw Native Americans. Although large-scale agriculture production eventually replaced the area's forests, this area of Alabama retained a distinct cultural outlook that also extended to some of its politics and politicians.[5] This included Governor "Big Jim" Folsom, who was born in Coffee County and later lived in Cullman County (six percent enslaved in 1860) and was one of the more progressive Southern politicians on the issue of race. Indeed, in a famous radio address on Christmas morning, 1949, Folsom gave a impassioned call for helping the black citizens of Alabama: "As long as the Negroes are held down by deprivation and lack of opportunity, the other poor people will be held down alongside them .... Let's start talking fellowship and brotherly love and doing unto others. And let's do more than talk about it; let's start living it."[6]

In this chapter, we start to explore the strong connection between slavery and the divergent attitudes of whites such as William Jelks, George Wallace, and Big Jim Folsom. How does the historical context of their home counties predict their politics? Can the same be said for other whites living in these areas? We address these questions by presenting several core empirical findings that show a direct historical connection between slavery in 1860 and political attitudes of these areas today—that is, the path dependence of political attitudes. Specifically, we show that those whites who live in counties that were more reliant on the institution of slavery (for example, Barbour County) are *today* more conservative, more likely to oppose policies that many think could help African Americans (such as affirmative action), more likely to admit to attitudes that political scientists describe as racially resentful, and more inclined to report cooler feelings toward African Americans. These results are tremendously consistent across different kinds of statistical tests, which suggests this pattern is not arbitrary: whites who live in parts of the South that were historically reliant on chattel slavery are more conservative on racial issues today. These findings suggest that men like William Jelks and Jim Folsom are not historical anomalies but are, instead, representative of the political cultures of the different areas of the South—political cultures that are predicted by historical forces.

We organize our discussion as follows. We start by explaining the contours of our historical data on slavery, which include county-level records of the enslaved Southern population at a time when slavery was at its peak, in 1860. We then discuss the sorts of data that provide our measures of contemporary attitudes. Drawing primarily on survey data, we focus primarily on four measures: (1) vote choice and election results, (2) self-reported partisanship, (3) attitudes on race-related policies such as affirmative action, and (4) measures of racial resentment or attitudes toward African Americans. We then show that the historical prevalence of slavery is predictive of these present-day attitudes. We show, furthermore, that these differences are not simply attributable to antebellum differences between nonslaveholding and slaveholding areas. We also show that, by contrast, there are fewer (or no) differences with regard to opinions on non-race-related questions. Our substantive conclusion is straightforward: whites who live in the Southern Black Belt in the present day are more conservative than whites living elsewhere, and these differences are especially salient when it comes to race and racial issues.

3.1 HISTORICAL DATA ON SLAVERY

We look to the 1860 U.S. Census for measures of the historical prevalence of slavery. We do so for three reasons. The first is the quality of the data. Only two U.S. Censuses included the kind of information on "slave schedules" that we need here—the 1850 and the 1860 U.S. Censuses. Slave schedules list the names of slaveholders and also the number of enslaved people, their ages, and their genders. Second, the census that took place in 1860 was the last U.S. Census that captured the height of chattel slavery's importance. Third, the 1860 U.S. Census captures the westward expansion of slavery after the Louisiana Purchase in 1803 and into what later became politically influential parts of Mississippi, Louisiana, and Alabama—areas that eventually became extremely reliant on slave labor for agricultural production. For that reason, we view the 1860 U.S. Census as the logical place to start.[7]

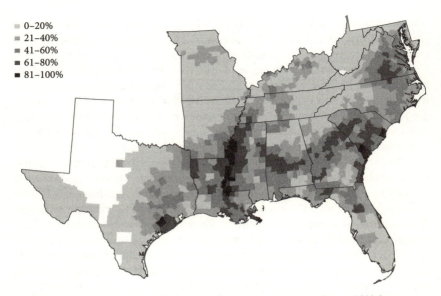

0–20%
21–40%
41–60%
61–80%
81–100%

Figure 3.1. Map of slavery in 1860 using modern county boundaries. Source: 1860 Census.

The 1860 U.S. Census data allow us to calculate the main variable that we use to explain contemporary outcomes: the proportion of a county's total population that was enslaved in 1860. (As we describe in Appendix A, we use an adjusted version of this variable that maps the historical data onto modern county boundaries, taking into account the fact that county boundaries have shifted over time.) Figure 3.1 demonstrates the 1860 Census data mapped onto modern-day counties. The figure shows that there are a number of distinct clusters of antebellum slavery in the South. The first, which follows a hook-shaped pattern from Virginia to Mississippi, is what scholars of the South have traditionally called the Black Belt. The second major cluster follows the Mississippi River from Memphis to the Gulf Coast of Louisiana. There are other, smaller pockets of slave prevalence in southeastern Texas and northern Florida.

To give some historical context, in the average Southern county, 36.7 percent of the population was enslaved in 1860. As is evident in figure 3.1, however, there was a great deal of within-state and within-region variation in the prevalence of slavery. In Benton County, in the northwest corner of Arkansas, for example, 4.1 percent of the population was enslaved, whereas in Chicot County, in the southeast corner of Arkansas, 81.4 percent of the population was enslaved. The South was thus hardly uniform in how enslaved populations were distributed, with some counties relying far more on slavery and slave-based labor than others. This is the variation we exploit in detecting behavioral path dependence in attitudes across regions.[8]

As many scholars have noted, the nature and character of slavery also varied greatly within and between each of these regions, depending on the time period, the local climate and growing conditions, and the demand for crops. For example, slave labor on many rice fields—large numbers of which were concentrated coastal areas of South Carolina—was mainly organized under the task system, which afforded enslaved people more autonomy and thus influenced the demands that they could make after emancipation.[9] Even within these areas the nature of slavery varied, including domestic work, farming, and other kinds of labor. Although variations in the nature of slavery are important to the historical development of these areas, we group all forms of Southern slavery together for much of our statistical analyses. In doing so, we trade historical detail for statistical power—that is, grouping all forms of slavery together gives us a more precise estimate of the relationship between slavery and attitudes today.

We also note the strong presence of slavery outside of the South, particularly earlier in American history. In the North, slavery was an important component in providing inexpensive labor through the eighteenth century.[10] By 1804, all Northern states had outlawed the institution of slavery, although some enslaved people continued to live in Northern states through the 1840s and 1850s due to inconsistencies in how slaves were emancipated.[11] By the time of the Civil War, the period that concerns us and represents the height of Southern slavery (and also the economic reliance of the South on slavery), there were minimal counts of enslaved populations in the Northern states, as documented in the 1860 U.S. Census. For example, in New Jersey, the 1860 U.S. Census reports only eighteen enslaved people in the entire state. For these reasons, we focus our analyses on the South, noting throughout how these potential patterns could explain, or be complicated by, interactions with the North.[12]

3.2 MEASURES OF CONTEMPORARY ATTITUDES

Our goal is to examine how contemporary attitudes vary across different areas of the South. In this section, we consider various measures of those attitudes. An ideal situation would be to use contemporary election returns and modern-day voter registration files. As we note below, however, these sources of data suffer from substantial measurement problems, meaning that we rely on them only when we have additional information, such as voter turnout data by race, or when historical circumstances allow us to do so. For the most part, though, we instead use outcome measures that do not suffer from these systematic problems. These data include survey responses to questions on partisanship, attitudes on race, and beliefs about race-related policies.

CHALLENGES WITH USING ELECTIONS AND VOTER REGISTRATION DATA

If slavery affects political attitudes today, then perhaps the most obvious starting point would be voting outcomes—that is, either how Southerners voted in national, statewide, and local elections, or how they registered. However, even though counties report the share of votes that went to the Republican or Democratic candidates, they do not report whether whites or blacks voted differently, which would be important in understanding whether white voters in the Black Belt differ from other white voters. This is an example of something called the ecological inference problem, which occurs when it is impossible to use aggregated data (such as voting outcome data) to understand individual-level behavior (such as the voting preferences of black versus white voters).[13]

For our purposes in examining the U.S. South, the ecological inference problem is especially vexing. A high correlation between historical patterns of slavery and present-day racial demographics exists, a fact that V. O. Key noted in his book, *Southern Politics*. That is, those areas where slavery was more prevalent in 1860 are also places where large numbers of African Americans have lived in the twentieth century and where they continue to live. In addition, and no doubt related to the economic and political incentives that we discuss throughout this book, a strong relationship between race and vote choice exists today: African Americans today vote for Democratic candidates at high rates. This makes the Southern Black Belt one of the most Democratic areas in terms of voting (see figure 3.2), even though whites living there may be some of the most conservative voters in the South and, therefore, the entire country. We therefore use voting outcomes sparingly, only when historical circumstances, such as the massive disenfranchisement of African Americans through the twentieth century, make it straightforward to infer the race of voters. We do note that, with the help of large surveys that we describe below, we can avoid many of the problems with analyzing election returns. For example, we can estimate from surveys the local vote share for particular candidates by race, at the state or even county level. When combined with election returns data, this allows us to estimate, for example, the white vote-share for Barack Obama in 2008.

Another option might be to consider voter registration data—or, how individual voters register (Republican or Democrat) in their particular

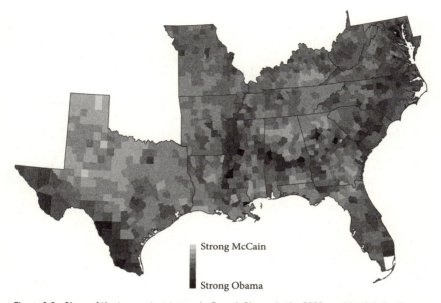

Figure 3.2. Share of the two-party vote won by Barack Obama in the 2008 presidential election.
Source: Leip, *Atlas of U.S. Presidential Elections.*

state. However, several problems prevent us from using such data. The
first problem is that only three Southern states (Florida, Louisiana, and
North Carolina) collect *both* racial and partisan voter information, both
of which are necessary components for our analyses. The second is the
South's history of partisan realignment, a shift we discuss more fully in
chapter 8. Once a solidly Democratic Party stronghold, the South—and
in particular Southern whites—began moving away from the national
Democratic Party in the 1930s, a process that only accelerated in the 1960s
with the national Democratic Party's support of the Civil Rights Act (1964)
and the Voting Rights Act (1965). By the time that Ronald Reagan was
elected president in 1980, Southern whites were consistently voting for
Republican candidates.[14] However, for much of recent Southern history,
many whites (and particularly older whites) who are registered Democrats
are in fact voting for the Republican Party. This disconnect could bias any
analyses that use voter registration as a way to assess core political attitudes.
The third reason, related to the second, is that many primaries in Southern
states (e.g., North Carolina) are open, which lessens the need for voters to
switch their party registration over time. For these reasons, an analysis of
voter registration data is of limited value.

USING SURVEY DATA

As an alternative to these sources, we rely more extensively on self-reported survey data to measure contemporary political and racial attitudes. Survey data, which are usually recorded at the individual level, do not suffer from the ecological inference problems associated with election returns data. They do, however, suffer from measurement problems that require some care in handling.

Until the last few years, most surveys included at most a few thousand respondents who were geographically clustered in order to minimize the cost of data collection. (Unfortunately, some of these smaller surveys are popular among scholars, including the General Social Survey [the GSS] and the American National Election Studies [ANES].) Given that there are approximately 1,400 counties in the U.S. South, the geographic coverage of such surveys was largely insufficient in terms of exploring county-by-county variation in attitudes, especially within states. We turn instead to larger, more recent surveys. One such survey is the Cooperative Congressional Election Survey (CCES), which includes roughly 14,000 to 55,000 respondents per year, about ten times the size of a typical GSS or ANES sample. To gain an even larger sample size, we pool CCES surveys from different years: 2006, 2008, 2009, 2010, and 2011. This yielded over 40,000 respondents across 1,345 counties out of 1,459 counties. In most of the analyses below, we aggregate the results of these surveys to the county level.[15] This approach gives us an estimate of the average political attitudes in a particular county on a host of important issues.[16]

For other kinds of questions, we turn to the American National Election Studies (ANES), a long-standing poll of Americans that has taken place every few years since the 1940s. Although smaller than we would like, the ANES includes questions on not only race and racial attitudes but also presidential approval, contemporary topics, and policies. It is typically fielded every two years, usually before and after an election. We use individual-level data from waves of the ANES from 1984 until 1998, a time period when the ANES both used a consistent sampling frame and included county-level identifiers for respondents. After again restricting the sample to Southern whites, we have an ANES sample of 3,123 individuals across sixty-four counties in the South. As we noted above, the geographic coverage of the ANES is more restricted and therefore not ideal for broader questions, but it contains valuable direct questions on the subjective evaluation of racial groups.

PARTISANSHIP

As we noted above in our discussion of Southern realignment, the parties have changed over time in ways that influenced Southern whites' party affiliation.[17] For example, the Republican Party—today the more conservative of the two American parties—was, in the period of the Civil War and after, the more racially progressive party. Indeed, the Republican Party was founded in 1854 by a mixture of antislavery activists, former Free Soil and Whig party members, and others unified against the expansion of slavery. Abraham Lincoln, the president who issued the Emancipation Proclamation in 1863, was a Republican, and Republicans made negligible inroads into Southern politics through much of the early twentieth century.[18] In the middle of the twentieth century, however, the Republican Party began to oppose federal civil rights legislation and the expansion of the welfare state. Today, most agree that the Republican Party is the more ideologically conservative party, aligned with interests favoring limited government, expansive individual freedoms (including the exercise of religion), and more modest redistributive policies.

The trajectory of the Democratic Party is different. During the Second Party system of the early nineteenth century, two parties fought for control of the government, the Democrats and the Whigs, both with sizable support in the North and South. Originating from the Jeffersonian anti-Federalists and the Democratic-Republican parties of the early nineteenth century, the Democratic Party, like the Whigs, was divided across regions over slavery, but generally endorsed a proslavery platform in the time period just before the Civil War. After the end of Reconstruction, the Democratic Party dominated the South: between 1877 and 1944, only sixteen of the over two hundred gubernatorial elections were won by a Republican, and half of those were in a single state, West Virginia (which broke away from Virginia during the secessionist debates of 1861).[19] Southern Democrats played hugely influential veto roles in limiting the impact New Deal era policies had in aiding African Americans.[20] Southern Democrats also attempted, with less success, to block the Great Society programs of Lyndon Johnson's administration, including attempts at blocking the Civil Rights Act of 1964 and the Voting Rights Act of 1965.[21]

Where does this leave us today? We focus on present-day politics and therefore on the contemporary positioning of the two parties—with the Democratic Party being more progressive on race and race-related issues (including crime, welfare, and affirmative action) and the Republican Party being more conservative on these same issues. We are mindful, however, of the interesting histories of both parties in fomenting their current ideological identities, and so we return to these histories in parts II and III of this book. Ultimately, while racial considerations are obviously not the entirety of a voter's decision to self-identify in a partisan manner, they clearly inform it. Returning to the CCES, we measure partisanship as whether or not the respondent identifies with the Democratic Party at all, even if they only "lean" in that direction. We discuss the exact wording of all outcomes in Appendix A.

RACIAL RESENTMENT

Although party politics and racial issues have long been intertwined in the United States, partisanship is also a reflection of attitudes beyond those on race and race-related issues.[22] The Democratic Party has different stances than the Republican Party, and these differences surround not just policies that affect minority groups disproportionately but also issues like the environment, gender (and reproductive rights), religion, international relations, and defense and national security. If our expectation is that slavery has had a differential impact on race-related issues, then examining attitudes specifically about race is essential.

Today, however, assessing Americans' racial attitudes is difficult. For much of American history, people freely expressed racist and racially hostile attitudes—even to scholars or members of the press. However, the civil rights movement and other grassroots organizing has significantly changed the contours of American racial discussions. Today, owing in large part to these movements, it is widely considered socially unacceptable to use racial slurs or racist language publicly; it is also considered unacceptable for political candidates or private companies to make overt racial appeals in political or commercial advertisements.[23] This general phenomenon is known as social desirability bias.

This social desirability bias raises a challenge: How do we detect the behavioral path dependence of racial conservatism when it is socially undesirable for respondents to express publicly such views? One approach used in the public opinion literature is to focus on a set of attitudes that measure a respondent's latent level of "racial resentment" (or "symbolic racism").[24] Work by Michael Tesler and David Sears describes these attitudes as "a blend of early socialized negative feelings about blacks with traditional conservative values, such as individualism or moral traditionalism."[25] However, these sorts of racially tinged sentiments are couched in ostensibly race-neutral language—language that possibly invokes the universal American principles of hard work, such as pulling oneself up by "one's bootstraps," and not asking for help. Put simply, someone who is racially resentful would not necessarily say that African Americans (or members of other minority groups, perhaps) are "unintelligent," "lazy," or "worse than whites," but they would be more likely to agree with the statement that "other groups have been able to overcome previous obstacles and that blacks should do the same."

A rich literature shows the predictive power of racially resentful attitudes. For example, Tesler and Sears argue that the 2008 election of Barack Obama turned significantly on the racial resentment of white voters and that those whites who scored highly on racial resentment scales were less likely to support Obama than his white Democratic opponents (Hillary Clinton and John Edwards).[26] Other literature extends this to specific policy positions. For example, those who rate highly on the racial resentment scale are less likely to support African American political actors, less likely to support welfare or other kinds of redistributive programs, and less likely to support other kinds of progressive policies.[27] At its narrowest interpretation, this kind of racial resentment appears to be an important predictor of other kinds of policy views. At its broadest, racial resentment could capture meaningful variation in racial attitudes and possibly uncover racial attitudes that are seldom openly expressed. On the other hand, a number of scholars (and also popular commentators) have cautioned that the racial resentment variables capture classical, ideological differences between liberals and conservatives rather than racial attitudes. Some of these studies have shown that the particular wording of these types of questions can impact responses, even for respondents who express support for racial equality.[28] Still other literature cautions that white liberals and conservatives interpret questions about racial resentment in different ways, suggesting that the same questions trigger racial versus ideological reactions.[29]

Our goal here is not to sort out the these questions. We let our data on Southern white attitudes, and how our data vary according to geography and slavery's historical presence, guide our inquiry, combining racial resentment measures with other race-related attitudes. Perhaps the racial resentment questions pick up some form of ideological conservatism or perhaps they meaningfully measure some kind of racial antagonism.

To measure racial resentment, we draw on two questions from the CCES, the first of which uses a five-point scale to ask whether respondents agree with the following statement:

> Generations of slavery and discrimination have created conditions that make it difficult for Blacks to work their way out of the lower class.

Here, larger values indicate stronger disagreement; that is, increased values to the question indicate more racial resentment. We combine this with another question, which is a five-point score of agreement with the following statement:

> The Irish, Italians, Jews and many other minorities overcame prejudice and worked their way up. Blacks should do the same without any special favors.

We take the simple average of the five-point scales of disagreement with the first question and agreement with the second question. This averaging helps us reduce the amount of measurement error in estimating these latent opinions. We note that, despite the debate surrounding the idea of "racial resentment," the first of our two questions—which specifically cites slavery—lends itself well to our historical inquiry.

BLACK-WHITE THERMOMETER SCORES

A concern with using racial resentment is that perhaps this measure captures differences in ideology rather than on race. In light of this potential criticism, and to further explore the nuances of racial attitudes throughout the U.S. South, we consider what are known as "thermometer scores." Thermometer scores are frequently asked in large, nationally representative surveys, such as the ANES. These questions operate by asking respondents how they feel about certain groups on a zero-to-one-hundred-point scale, known as a "feeling thermometer" scale. A rating of zero on such a scale represents a "very cold or unfavorable feeling," while a rating of one hundred indicates a "very warm or favorable feeling." Such thermometer questions register respondents' feelings toward a variety of different groups, including the Democrats and Republicans, Protestants, Catholics, women, African Americans, Congressional representatives, immigrants, and others. Although not without their critics, these thermometer scores provide an interesting vantage point into how various groups are viewed by others. To capture views toward blacks, we look at the way that whites score both whites and blacks on these scales. We also look at the difference between these scores, which is a compact measure of whites' perceived superiority.

SUPPORT FOR AFFIRMATIVE ACTION

Although the CCES asks a variety of questions related to different kinds of policy issue areas, one in particular appeals to our central question—the question on affirmative action.

The term affirmative action refers, loosely, to a set of policies that are designed to promote the candidacies of minorities (and occasionally women) in employment or admissions. However, affirmative action is divisive. For many Americans, affirmative action represents the improper use of race. For others, affirmative action represents a move toward compensating individuals for generations of previous discrimination and systematic denial of opportunities. A 2013 Gallup poll showed that a large majority of Americans believed that "only merit" should be taken into account when considering admission for colleges or universities, with three-quarters of whites and around half of blacks siding against affirmative action.[30] Thus, respondents' opinions about affirmative action could reflect either their liberal/conservative views or their beliefs about race and ethnicity.

We sidestep some of these unresolved ideological questions by focusing on the geographical variation in attitudes toward affirmative action, distinguishing them from attitudes on clearly non-race-related policy issue areas later on. The question we use appears on all of the CCES surveys. It reads, with slight variation from year to year:

> Affirmative Action programs give preference to racial minorities and to women in employment and college admissions in order to correct for discrimination.

The responses scale from "strongly oppose" to "strongly support," but we collapse the outcome to a binary measure where any support is coded as a one. As we see in the following sections, support for affirmative action is, among whites at least, fairly weak across the South.

3.3 HOW SLAVERY PREDICTS SOUTHERN WHITES' ATTITUDES

We now turn to seeing how these contemporary measures vary according to Southern geography and specifically how slavery in 1860 predicts these measures. Figure 3.3 provides a basic representation of the relationship between slavery in 1860 and our four race-related outcomes, measured among self-identified whites and all estimated with counties as the units of analysis. The share of the county that was enslaved (a figure that ranges from zero to nearly all) is on the x-axis while the y-axis on the top panels is the county-level share of Southern whites who (1) identify as Democrat and (2) oppose affirmative action. The same axes on the bottom panels show the county-level (3) average level of racial resentment and (4) the average difference in thermometer ratings for whites versus blacks in the county, once we've limited the subset to Southern whites. The size of the circle indicates the number of respondents in the county—that is, the number of people that the survey sampled in each county. Some counties have more respondents than others, which explains the fluctuations in circle sizes.

Figure 3.3 shows a clear relationship between the share of the population that was enslaved in 1860 and these important attitudes expressed by Southern whites in contemporary times. For partisanship, as the share of the population that was enslaved in 1860 rises, the share of the white population that today identifies as a Democrat falls—a relationship that is statistically significant at conventional levels. Simply put, we can be fairly sure that this relationship is highly unlikely to be due to chance alone. The same is true for affirmative action: as the share of the population that was enslaved in 1860 increases, the share of the white population today that expresses support for affirmative action falls (again, a relationship that is statistically significant at conventional levels). The pattern also holds, but in reverse, for our other measures of racial attitudes (again, these are

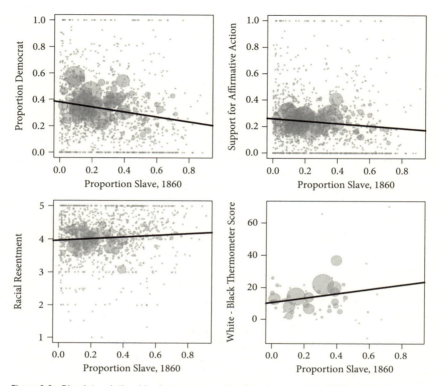

Figure 3.3. Bivariate relationships between proportion slave in a county in 1860 and the four outcome measures (partisanship, support for affirmative action, racial resentment, and differences in thermometer scores), with a linear trend displayed. Size of the circles correspond to the number of people in the sample from that county, weighted by the sample weights.

statistically significant). As the share of the population that was enslaved in 1860 increases, the average contemporary level of racial resentment among whites in the county rises; so too does the modern-day gap grow between how whites view other whites versus blacks. That is, the greater the share of the population that was enslaved in 1860, the more "cool" Southern whites feel toward African Americans in modern times.

Do these survey measures of attitudes translate into actual electoral outcomes among whites? As we described above, estimating the relationship between slavery and whites' voting is severely hampered by the fact that we generally have no individual-level voting data that allow us to determine a voter's race. (That is the ecological inference problem that we discussed above.) However, the 2008 general election provides some inroads into voters' racial backgrounds. First, we have county-level election returns for

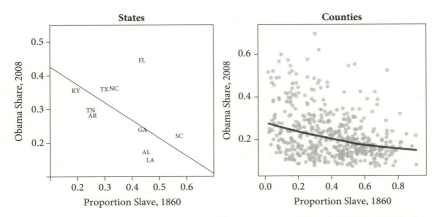

Figure 3.4. Estimated nonblack county-level vote-share for Barack Obama in 2008 by state (left) and county (right). Individual-level CCES data only used to estimate black support for Obama by state, combined with vote totals from voter file. Line in left plot is a linear fit line, while the line in the right plot is a LOESS (smoothed) curve. Source: Leip, *Atlas of U.S. Presidential Elections*; CCES; Catalist.

Barack Obama and John McCain in the 2008 general election. Second, we have voter turnout data for African Americans in the 2008 general election from voter files (collected by the company Catalist). For a handful of states, we therefore know the number of African American voters in each county even if we do not know for whom they voted. Finally, the CCES allows us to estimate the state-level vote share for Obama among African Americans, which is high across the South. We combine the last two sources of data to calculate an *estimated* number of black Obama votes, which in turn allows us to estimate the number of nonblack Obama votes as a proportion of the total two-party (nonblack) vote. Given the limited availability of turnout data by race, we can only perform this analysis for a subset of the Southern states: Alabama, Florida, Georgia, Louisiana, North Carolina, and South Carolina. These are all rough estimates; the true voter shares are unknown (again, due to ecological inference problems).[31]

From this analysis, we find that very few of the nonblack votes in the South went in Obama's favor. In the average county in this sample, roughly twenty percent of the nonblack population voted for Obama. In addition, as is evident in figure 3.4, the historical prevalence of slavery yields a substantial amount of variation: for counties at the lowest levels of slavery, Obama won about thirty percent of the nonblack vote, while in those at the highest levels of slavery Obama only won around ten percent of the nonblack vote (see right plot). We also note that we may be overestimating *white* support for Obama since these figures may include Latinos/as and Asian Americans, whom we expect to support Obama at higher rates.

One potential issue is that racial tensions surrounding the election of the nation's first black president in 2008 could have driven, or at least have exacerbated, the results. For example, Tesler and Sears suggest that race and ethnicity were at the forefront of people's minds after Obama's surge in popularity in early 2008, which perhaps primed racially hostile attitudes. There are two reasons why we think these results are not unique to this political era. First, our analyses on the difference in white-black thermometer scores predate Obama's 2008 election, which indicates that differences between former slaveholding and nonslaveholding areas existed in the late twentieth century. The second reason comes from the CCES fielded in 2006. At that time, Obama was the junior senator from Illinois, a national hopeful, perhaps, but certainly not squarely in the national spotlight, and not someone whose race or ethnicity was extensively discussed in the context of the nation's highest office. However, we find no statistically significant difference between these relationships in 2006 and in later years.[32] Again, this suggests that these differences did not become salient only after the election of the first African American president. To the contrary, for reasons we explore in depth in later chapters, these differences appear to be long-standing and persistent.

3.4 IS SLAVERY CAUSING THESE DIFFERENCES?

The previous analysis showed four simple relationships: counties that had a higher prevalence of slavery in the antebellum period tend to be places where whites today are (1) more Republican when it comes to their partisanship, (2) more opposed to affirmative action, (3) more likely to express agreement with what many scholars believe constitute "racially resentful" statements, and (4) more likely to express cooler feelings toward African Americans. However, these findings do not establish a causal connection. Did slavery cause these attitudes to develop? Or have the counties with historically high levels of slavery been distinct in other ways that made and continue to make them more conservative? In other words, how do we know that slavery had any "effects" at all?

In this section, we use three techniques to uncover whether the relationship between slavery and white attitudes today is truly causal or whether it is simply a predictive correlation—a statistical accident that whites who live in areas dominated historically by chattel slavery are more conservative on racial issues. First, we take into account historical factors that may have affected both the development and prevalence of slavery and contemporary attitudes today. Second, we employ a matching analysis that compares neighboring counties that are quite similar except for being either high-slave or low-slave in the antebellum period. Lastly, we use a statistical technique known as instrumental variables, which leverages the fact that cotton suitability was a strong predictor of the prevalence of slavery. As we show below, these three techniques provide evidence that the relationship between slavery and contemporary political attitudes is indeed causal.

TAKING INTO ACCOUNT ANTEBELLUM DIFFERENCES

Perhaps the most plausible explanation behind our findings is, quite simply, that areas of the South that came to rely on chattel slavery differed from those that did not, and our analyses reflect these preexisting differences. For example, it could be the case that the South's more rural and wealthy areas were more likely to develop slavery-based economies and it is the persistent wealth of these areas, not their legacy of slavery, that drives the political differences we observe today. In more technical language, such a situation would be an instance of omitted variable bias (or confounding), which would mean that we are finding results that are spurious or due to other factors.

To overcome these problems, we take several steps. The first is that we control for, or take into account, features of Southern counties in 1860 that might be related to the local development of slavery. Note that we do not control for any variables that might be a consequence of slavery in 1860 since that could bias our estimates of the long-term effect of slavery. For example, we do not control for education levels later in the twentieth century, since the political and economic environment created by slavery substantially affected government spending and educational segregation. We address these issue in greater depth in chapter 4.[33]

Economic and Geographic Differences. Perhaps the biggest difference among counties in the antebellum period was economic, with economic factors predicting whether counties became reliant on slavery or not. Some areas of the South had large enslaved populations for cultivating labor-intensive crops, such as cotton, tobacco, indigo, and rice, as well as for domestic labor. However, other areas of the South were also agricultural, populated by white farmers on smaller farms oriented toward self-sufficiency. Many nonslaveholding areas also tended to be clustered in "upland" and Piedmont areas, such as in the areas of Georgia, North Carolina, South Carolina, and Virginia that had higher elevations and cooler climates (and were in some instances in the mountains). Could these differences—and not the historical prevalence of slavery—speak to the varying regional patterns we see today?

To address these questions, our analyses include several key county-level economic and demographic indicators in 1860: size (in acres), population, average farm value per acre of improved land, total acres of improved farmland, presence of railways, and presence of waterways. The last two measures could also indicate how easy it was to travel to and from a county, which could affect both its economic development and its potential to become cosmopolitan. For example, we would think that a county with access to a railway would probably be more easily accessible to travelers and traders, thus exposing residents to different ideas and cultures—ideas that could also include antislavery attitudes. Steamship and railroad access also allowed for cheaper marketing of cash crops such as cotton. (As we shall see, we also leverage another ostensibly economic indicator—the county's suitability for growing cotton—later on in the discussion.) Given the spatial nature of the data, we also consider the geographic similarities and differences between counties by flexibly controlling for their latitude and longitude. In addition, because the shape of the terrain could also impact the development of slavery, we include a measure of its ruggedness.

Another economic indicator that we include is the proportion of small farms (as opposed to plantations) in each county. Economists Robert Fogel and Stanley Engerman argue that one of the key mechanisms by which slavery changed the nature of the South was through the concentrated development of plantations and of the incentives and business interests that these plantations engendered.[34] Large farms produced labor-intensive cash crops, leading these areas to be more likely to rely on high shares of enslaved workers. Small farms, on the other hand, required less hired labor because they tended to be worked by a single family for self-subsistence. To account for these differences in land holdings and the relative inequality they created within counties, we include a measure of land inequality developed by Nunn.[35]

Social and Political Differences. Slaveholding and nonslaveholding areas of the South differed in other ways beyond their economic organization. One worry is that antebellum attitudes on race and race-related issues may have driven some nonslaveholding areas to avoid slavery. Even though the historical record casts doubt on large differences in social attitudes about race across the South, we still would like to compare counties that had roughly similar attitudes in the antebellum period. We consider these social and political differences in more depth in chapter 5.

In terms of nineteenth-century political and racial attitudes, we do not have the benefit of the CCES, Gallup polls, YouGov, FiveThirtyEight, or other measures to assess nineteenth-century public opinion. Instead, we rely on other kinds of measures as proxies for potential differences in social attitudes within parts of the South. Among the factors that we include are the proportion of county population reported to be "free black" in the 1860 U.S. Census, which we hypothesize may be positively correlated with more racially progressive attitudes. That is, free blacks were likely to have lived in areas where whites were more comfortable with the idea of African Americans operating as free, emancipated people (even if, perhaps, not coequal citizens). Where slavery was extremely prevalent, whites were in general very hostile toward the free black populations, even going so far as to pressure free blacks to enslave themselves.[36]

State-by-State Differences. The last issue we consider is that the states themselves varied. Louisiana, for example, relies on a civil law system, a legacy of early French settlements. Mississippi and Alabama relied extensively on the cultivation of cotton, Virginia on tobacco, and South Carolina on rice. In sum: different states had different kinds of traditions, laws, and economic histories. These circumstances could affect not only the prevalence of localized slavery but also political attitudes today.

Because our argument rests on the idea that counties with high shares of enslaved populations differed from others, we believe that state-by-state variation (though interesting and discussed throughout) is something that we should adjust for, or take into account in the analyses. In the analyses that follow, we therefore include a control for each county's state—that is, fixed effects for each state. Functionally, this has the effect of comparing counties within states: counties in Mississippi are compared to other counties in Mississippi, counties in Georgia are compared to counties in Georgia, and so on. This strategy resolves many potential differences across states (e.g., political climate, laws, and customs), which allows us to more crisply isolate the importance of the localized prevalence of slavery—that is, slavery at the county level.

MATCHING NEIGHBORING COUNTIES

Even after controlling for a number of historical and geographic covariates, it remains possible that our results are driven by differences between slaveholding and nonslaveholding areas that are not fully captured by these covariates. Such differences could potentially be driving the effects we see here. For instance, the upland regions of northern Alabama and Georgia may have differed systematically from the Black Belt.[37]

To test the robustness of our results to potential omitted variables, we create matched pairs of *neighboring* counties that differ by more than twenty percentage points in the population that was enslaved in 1860 and compare the average difference in outcomes within these two groups. This enables us to compare the effects of slavery across neighboring counties, which are likely geographically, politically, economically, and culturally similar.[38] It also drops certain high-slave counties that are in

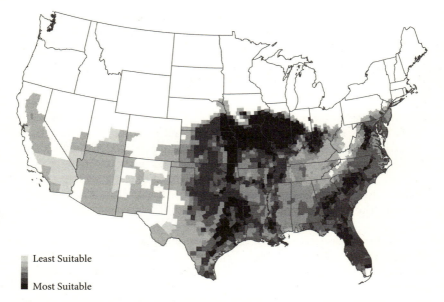

Figure 3.5. Map of cotton suitability in the United States. Darker shading indicates greater suitability. Source: U.N. Food and Agricultural Organization.

regions where all of the neighbors are also high-slave areas—for example, in the Mississippi Delta.

EXPLOITING COTTON SUITABILITY TO ASSESS CAUSALITY

Another strategy for trying to distinguish between correlation and causation is to use a technique called instrumental variables.[39] The general intuition is as follows. Ideally, we would want variation in slavery to be randomly assigned by nature to counties so that the high- and low-slave areas are comparable—similar in terms of their geography, culture, and white population. This is far from true in the real world, however. Those places that invested heavily in a slave economy differed in several ways from places that did not. Instrumental variables can help us around this problem if a variable—called an *instrument*—is randomly assigned across counties and is causally predictive of the outcomes we care about (partisanship, attitudes on affirmative action, etc.) only through its effect on slavery.

The instrument we use here is cotton suitability.[40] We do so because the type of cotton that is widespread in the U.S. South (*Gossypium hirsutum*, or upland cotton) can grow only in certain climates and kinds of soil. This kind of cotton requires a mild climate, with at least six months of frost-free

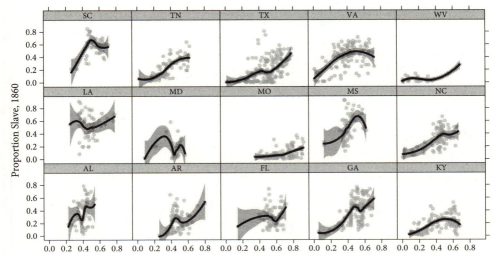

Figure 3.6. Relationship between cotton suitability and proportion slave in a county, 1860. Lines indicate LOESS (smoothed) curves while the shaded regions indicate confidence bands. Source: U.N. Food and Agricultural Organization.

temperatures (a fact that rules out much of the Northeast and certain parts of the West Coast). Cotton also requires a good amount of sunlight, which further rules out other parts of the country. Lastly, cotton thrives in soil that contains some sand or silt, so it particularly thrives in riverside areas. All of this means that cotton is well suited to grow in warm, moderately dry areas with good soil and with very few days of frost. Within the United States, the American South is particularly well suited to grow cotton, specifically the Black Belt areas of South Carolina and Georgia, parts of Mississippi and Alabama along the Mississippi River, and East Texas. Other parts of the United States are also well suited to grow cotton; these include parts of Illinois, Indiana, Ohio, New Mexico, Arizona, and California—all of which were nonslave states during the nineteenth century. For the analyses here, we use a measure of cotton suitability taken from the United Nations Food and Agricultural Organization (FAO).[41] The FAO measure is a 0 to 1 measure that captures holistically those variables that would make a place suitable to grow cotton (with 1 being very suitable to grow cotton, and 0 not).[42]

To explain what we do in the following analyses, we first analyze the relationship between the proportion of the county that was enslaved in 1860 and cotton suitability, which allows us to examine whether cotton suitability is a strong predictor of slave prevalence. If there is a strong correlation, then this suggests that cotton suitability might be a good instrument to use. As we show in figure 3.6, an area's suitability for cotton is

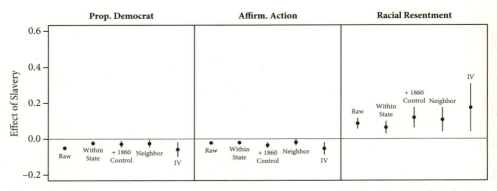

Figure 3.7. Slavery's effects on contemporary white attitudes. Each point is the estimated effect of a 25-percentage-point increase in the share of a county that was enslaved in 1860 on each of the county-level outcomes: proportion Democrat (left), attitudes on affirmative action (middle), and racial resentment (right). Lines represent 90% confidence intervals. From left to right, each plot shows results from analyses using (1) only the simple bivariate relationship ("Raw"); (2) state fixed effects ("Within State"); (3) state fixed effects plus the full battery of 1860 controls ("+1860 Control"); (4) our matched neighbors approach ("Neighbor"); and (5) cotton suitability as an instrument ("IV").

indeed a good predictor of slave prevalence (suggesting a strong first-stage relationship in terms of the instrument). This is not surprising. As many historians have noted, those who established the early cotton plantations and cotton farms understood that the climate and the soil in the Black Belt were favorable for growing cotton. This strong statistical relationship provides assurance that cotton suitability is a good instrument for analyzing the effect of slavery on political attitudes today.[43]

3.5 SLAVERY'S EFFECTS ON WHITE ATTITUDES

How do the simple bivariate relationships that we presented earlier in this chapter change once we use the more complicated and rigorous methods outlined in the previous section? Here we present these more sophisticated results, which confirm the basic findings. This is the case even after controlling for a host of historical factors, restricting our attention to neighboring counties, and even instrumenting for slavery with cotton suitability.[44]

To show this, figure 3.7 compares the estimated effects of slavery on political attitudes using the various causal techniques. As before, these are at the county level, meaning we are examining (1) the shares of whites in each county who identify as Democrats, (2) the shares of whites who support affirmative action, and (3) the average level of white racial resentment in the county. The y-axis on the figure represents the estimated effect of a twenty-five-percentage-point increase in the prevalence of slavery in 1860 on these outcomes today. Thus, these are roughly the average differences in each outcome between Barbour County, Alabama (fifty-two percent enslaved in 1860), in the Alabama Black Belt, and Clay County, Alabama (twenty-four percent enslaved in 1860), in the Alabama Piedmont. The first point in each panel of figure 3.7, model 1, presents the simple relationship between slavery and white attitudes with no controls and thus recreates the earlier bivariate relationships. Model 2 in each panel includes state-level fixed effects to create within-state comparisons, while model 3 includes these as well as the 1860 covariates described above. In model 4, we compare the matched neighbors, and in model 5, we show the effect estimated by instrumental variables, with cotton suitability as our instrument.

Across all of these modeling specifications, we see that the effect of slavery is fairly consistent: areas with more slavery in 1860 today are more conservative in terms of partisanship, more opposed to affirmative action, and more likely to score highly on racial resentment questions. In fact, in the instrumental variables analysis, perhaps the most credible of our analyses, the effect is even stronger than when controlling for covariates. To illustrate, according to the instrumental variables analyses, the effect of moving from Clay County to Barbour County (a twenty-five-percentage-point increase in slave proportion) is associated with a 5.56 percentage-point decrease in the share of whites who currently identify as Democrats, a 7.8 point decrease among those who currently support affirmative action, and a 0.19 point increase on the racial resentment scale (which runs from 1 to 5), which represents 0.27 standard deviations. The conditional effects of slavery are significant at conventional levels of statistical significance for all three outcome variables, meaning that these relationships are very unlikely to be due to chance alone.[45]

As we discussed above, a potential concern is that partisan identification, support for affirmative action, and agreement with "racially resentful" statements capture some articulation of ideology rather than underlying attitudes concerning race and race-related policy positions. We therefore replicate these analyses by looking at the thermometer scores from above. Because of the smaller sample size (around three thousand survey respondents), figure 3.8 presents the results of an individual-level analysis of these outcomes, with uncertainty estimates that take into consideration the clustering of respondents into counties.[46] Here, the points represent the effect of a twenty-five-percentage-point increase in proportion slave on the thermometer scores that white respondents reported.[47]

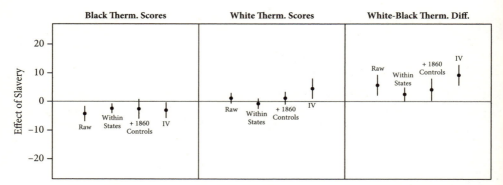

Figure 3.8. Slavery's effects on contemporary white attitudes. Each point is the estimated effect of a 25-percentage-point increase in the county-level slave share on whites' average thermometer scores evaluating blacks (left), thermometer scores evaluating whites (middle), and the difference in thermometer scores evaluating whites versus blacks (right). Lines represent 90% confidence intervals. From left to right, each plot shows results from analyses using (1) only the simple bivariate relationship ("Raw"); (2) state fixed effects ("Within States"); (3) state fixed effects plus the full battery of 1860 controls ("+1860 Controls"); and (4) cotton suitability as an instrument ("IV").

Figure 3.8 shows that whites in the Southern Black Belt continue to have cooler feelings toward African Americans as a group, across all specifications. Furthermore, these results hold when we benchmark their evaluations with the differences in whites' thermometer ratings of whites versus blacks. A larger gap in this measure suggests stronger feelings of superiority among whites. The figure shows that former slave areas are places where the divide in how whites view these two groups is the largest. The effects are all sizable—if a county were to shift from having twenty-five percent to fifty percent of its population being enslaved, we would see a statistically significant increase in the white-black thermometer ratings gap as high as ten points.

3.6 SLAVERY'S MIXED EFFECTS ON POLICIES UNRELATED TO RACE

While we have shown that the effect of slavery extends to race-related outcomes, a more powerful test of the connection between slavery and racial attitudes comes from issues that are largely *unrelated* to race. If differences between high-slave and low-slave areas in terms of their modern-day political and racial views are largely attributable to the legacy of slavery in the South, we should expect to see very small or no differences between high and low-slave counties on issues unrelated to race and ethnicity.

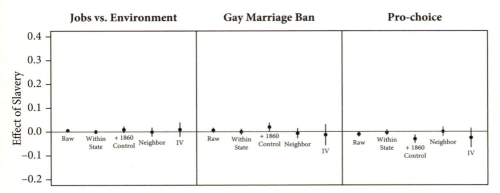

Figure 3.9. Effect of slavery on whites' attitudes on non-race-related issues. Each point is the estimated effect of a 25-percentage-point increase in the county-level slave share on whites' attitudes on the environment (left), gay marriage bans (middle), and pro-choice views on abortion (right). Lines represent 90% confidence intervals. From left to right, each plot shows results from analyses using (1) only the simple bivariate relationship ("Raw"); (2) state fixed effects ("Within State"); (3) state fixed effects plus the full battery of 1860 controls ("+1860 Control"); (4) our matched neighbors approach ("Neighbor"); and (5) cotton suitability as an instrument ("IV").

To address this, we consider potential variance in whites' attitudes across other important policy questions. Here, we consider three publicly salient topics: (1) prioritizing jobs over the environment, (2) bans on same-sex marriage, and (3) pro-choice views on abortion. We derive binary measures of these views from questions on the CCES, which makes these questions analogous to the ones on affirmative action and racial resentment. For these measures, a one indicates a more conservative position on jobs versus the environment and bans on gay marriage, whereas a one on the pro-choice measure indicates a more liberal position.

If there are differences across the race-related questions as well as these three questions, then our core finding would seem to be that slavery's effect is to push whites in an overall more conservative direction, not just on race specifically. If there are differences across the race-related questions, but *not* across these questions, then slaveholding and nonslaveholding areas have meaningful differences with regard to race specifically, no matter how questions about affirmative action and racial resentment are construed.

Figure 3.9 presents the results for these non-race-related outcomes, once again showing the estimated effects across a number of estimation strategies. The figure shows only slight differences within the South on these questions, and the differences are not robust to different statistical checks. For example, consider the environmental policy question on whether respondents would favor sacrificing jobs if it would help the environment. The high-slave South is only slightly more conservative on this question (in a jobs-leaning direction) than low-slave areas, *but none of these differences are statistically significant*, meaning that chance alone could explain any differences. With the question on opposition to same-sex marriage, there is strong disagreement across estimation strategies about both the strength and the direction of the effect. In the IV approach there is a *negative* relationship between slavery and conservative views on gay marriage. Views on abortion are similarly weak and dependent on modeling choices.

What can we glean from this? Comparing figure 3.9 with figure 3.7 shows that the race-related questions reveal differences within the South whereas non-race-related questions do not. Combined with the evidence on thermometer scores, this finding suggests to us that there is something meaningful and different about the *racial* attitudes of whites who live in areas of the South that were heavily reliant on enslaved labor. In other words, the evidence suggests that the legacy of slavery lies in shaping whites' attitudes on race specifically.

3.7 CONCLUSION

The findings presented in this chapter suggest that counties with high shares of enslaved people just before the Civil War are places where whites today are more conservative, more opposed to affirmative action, more likely to agree with statements that indicate racial resentment, and more likely to express cooler feelings about blacks. This is the case even when comparing counties that were similar in terms of economic, geographic, and political factors in 1860. The results on black-white thermometer scores and attitudes unrelated to race indicate that these patterns are driven in part by racial attitudes specifically. But *why* do these differences exist? Are they due to the demographic consequences of slavery? (Not likely, as we will see in the next chapter.) Are they due to different institutions in the high-slave counties? Or are these direct cultural legacies of this slaveholding history? So far, our results have established the long-term effect of slavery, but we need more analyses to trace the mechanisms behind this behavioral path dependence.

We conclude this chapter by stepping back from the quantitative methodology. What do these results tell us? On one level, they confirm what many historians, political commentators, and political scientists have observed: the parts of the South known as the "Black Belt" are, on average, more Republican, more solidly against policies that could promote racial equality (such as affirmative action), and more racially resentful than other parts of the South.

On the other hand, these results present something startling. It's not just that these parts of the country are simply more racially conservative than others. The results are not due to a random pattern, unrelated to the ebbs and flows of history. Our analyses instead show that those areas where the institution of slavery was a cohesive part of their culture, economy, and political life are more likely *today* to be conservative, especially on issues related to race. The past clearly matters to today's politics. It's not simply that more conservative people live in these areas—these are more conservative areas *because* of their past.

This is all troubling. The United States has made tremendous strides since the civil rights movement, in both dismantling formal institutions that were barriers to the American Dream and promoting an American creed of equality. Rulings like *Brown v. Board of Education* and important federal legislation like the Civil Rights Act of 1964 and the Voting Rights Act of 1965 has made great progress in eradicating unjust institutions. Many of these national initiatives have had the greatest effects in the South, where African Americans today attend schools along with whites, and where 18 of 147 House Representatives in this region are members of the Congressional Black Caucus. What, then, does it mean that something that happened centuries ago can predict attitudes and political behavior? Are these differences the consequence of the historical persistence of attitudes? Or could they be simply due to the lingering demographics of nineteenth-century America? We turn to these issues in the next chapter.

CHAPTER FOUR

AN ALTERNATIVE ACCOUNT: CONTEMPORARY DEMOGRAPHICS AND RACIAL THREAT

> "If the whites of the black belts give the South its dominant
> political tone, the character of the politics of individual states
> will vary roughly with the Negro proportion of the population."
>
> V. O. Key

Just as places like Leflore County, Mississippi, and Barbour County, Alabama, represent the past of the Southern Black Belt, places like Richland County, South Carolina, could possibly represent the future. Although not without urban problems, Richland County's seat and South Carolina's state capital, Columbia, is a dynamic, educated, and relatively affluent city. The city has over the years invested heavily in the arts, culture, and education, and it is home to the flagship state university, the University of South Carolina, which brings in thousands of students and millions of dollars in tuition and research grants. The revitalized city center has new restaurants, boutiques, and art galleries. These cultural and economic investments have for the most part paid off: Columbia is the largest city in the state, and Richland County is among the richest and most well-educated counties in South Carolina.[1]

However, like other Black Belt counties, Richland County had a turbulent racial past. The county's name—"Rich Land"—comes from the surrounding area's rich soil, which was well suited for cultivating large-scale agricultural crops, including cotton. (By contrast, areas of the South Carolina lowlands, closer to the coast and to Charleston, were mostly devoted to growing rice and indigo.) Urban slavery was prominent within the city of Columbia, which meant that thousands of slaves worked in city homes and establishments, including at the university.[2] In fact, shortly before the Civil War, Richland County was nearly sixty percent enslaved, evidence of the strong economic and political importance of the institution to the area's development and economic strength.

In some ways, however, the city's slave past has left less of an imprint, particularly when it comes to demographics. For example, unlike other areas in the Black Belt in which whites continue to be in the minority,

Key, *Southern Politics in State and Nation*, Knoxville: University of Tennessee Press, 1984, p. 5

whites constitute the largest racial group in Richland County: Richland residents are 48.1 percent white and 46.8 percent African American. This racial profile contrasts with places in the Deep South that remain majority African American, such as Leflore County, Mississippi (24.9 percent white, 72.2 percent black in 2010), and Wilcox County, Alabama (26.8 percent white, 72.5 percent black in 2010).

Despite this demographic difference, Richland County is similar to other Black Belt counties in that whites living in Richland County skew in a solidly conservative direction. For example, although Barack Obama won the county in the 2008 and 2012 presidential elections, he overwhelmingly lost its white vote—with approximately eighty percent of Richland County's whites voting each time for Obama's Republican opponents. In addition, its capital city, Columbia, has faced significant racial turmoil. In December 2009, Columbia's City Hall was defaced with graffiti containing racial slurs directed at two black mayoral candidates.[3] Earlier that year, a local representative compared then-First Lady Michelle Obama to an escaped gorilla.[4] In July 2015, Ku Klux Klan organizers skirmished with black protesters over a show of support for the confederate flag.[5] And in October 2015, a video of a white male school security officer pummeling a black female high school student went viral, shocking Americans across the country.[6]

These issues, taken in tandem with population shifts over the twentieth century, lead to the questions that we explore in this chapter. Is the ideological distinctiveness of the Black Belt and of places like Richland County due to the slaveholding histories of these areas? Or are the patterns better explained by *contemporary factors*, such as the share of the current population that is black? If the evidence for the former question is persuasive, then we would expect places like Richland County, which was heavily reliant on slavery in the antebellum period, to exhibit many of the same racially conservative characteristics as do other places in the Southern Black Belt. If political differences hinge more on *contemporary* demographics, then we would expect Richland County to have moved on from its past: after all, Richland County is no longer majority African American and population mobility—including both outward and inward migration—has fundamentally changed the county's demographics.

These differences are conceptually important: seeing a difference rooted in contemporary demographics would be one based on *demographic path dependence* and *demographic change*. This would mean that the primary legacy of slavery lies not in the institutional or behavioral changes that slavery (and its collapse) may have triggered, but, instead, in the fact that there are nearly forty million people of African descent now living throughout the United States, with particularly large numbers still living in the Southern Black Belt. Under this logic, the legacy of slavery lies primarily in permanently affecting the racial and ethnic composition of the United States, including in the Southern Black Belt. It would be these differences, and not the differences in attitudes, that persist.

Why might this kind of demographic heritage affect contemporary attitudes? And why might it affect attitudes in such a way that varies across areas of the country? The first possible explanation, as a number of scholars have convincingly argued, is via a concept described as *racial threat*. The idea is simple. A minority group (for example, African Americans) has the potential to threaten a dominant group (for example, Southern whites). The larger the disadvantaged group, the more of a threat it poses to the dominant group, leading the dominant group to respond with racial or ethnic hostility, repression, and attempts at segregation. This explanation originates out of the persistence of *demographics* rather than historical attitudes. This phenomenon may help explain why whites in the majority African American Mississippi Delta (including Leflore County, Mississippi) are more conservative. These are, after all, places where more African Americans live today.

The second plausible explanation concerns population mobility and sorting, both among white and black populations. Many areas of the South, including in the Black Belt, had large black out-migrations. Under the theory of racial threat, these should be areas in which the "threat" posed by minority populations receded first. In addition, and possibly working in tandem, the racial environment may have propelled white mobility into or out of the Black Belt, driving more racially liberal whites away. There is plenty of evidence for both forces: thousands of Southerners moved in the twentieth century—not just within the South but also to the North and Midwest and out west toward New Mexico, Arizona, and Southern California. And, in more recent times, the new economy of major cities in the South—including places like Columbia—has lured people pursuing work and study. Can these forces explain the patterns we have seen?

As we show in this chapter, we find little evidence to support the argument that contemporary demographic characteristics, or changes in those demographics, have been the primary driver of the patterns we find in chapter 3. With regard to the racial threat hypothesis, we show that adjusting for localized shares of black populations both in the present and over time does little to attenuate the independent effects of slavery. The racial threat hypothesis is, ultimately, unable to explain the empirical findings in chapter 3. In addition, studies that focus exclusively on contemporary minority populations overlook the historical and dynamic forces that influence attitudes today. With regard to population mobility, we show that the mobility of both blacks and whites out of the rural South does not substantially influence contemporary patterns. Put simply, the institution of slavery and its aftermath appear to have *independently* affected whites' attitudes, aside from changes in contemporary demographics and population mobility. This sets the stage for our exploration in later chapters, in which we set aside demographic explanations and instead focus on the historical and cultural link between the South's political past and its contemporary politics.

We organize this chapter as follows. We first provide a brief examination of how slavery transformed the demographic profiles of the Southern states. We then offer a more precise explanation of what scholars mean when they refer to "racial threat." Next, we explore what contemporary black populations do or do not tell us about our results. We show that, while contemporary demographics may be important, slavery continues to provide a separate, historically rooted explanation for regional variation in contemporary political attitudes. We next turn to the question of population mobility. Looking again at our contemporary measures, changes in the black share of the population did little to attenuate whites' attitudes, and white mobility does not explain the Southern Black Belt's distinctiveness. We conclude this chapter by exploring what these findings mean for long-standing theories concerning the contemporary "threat" posed to dominant communities by large shares of minority groups. Our conclusion is that relying on only contemporary demographics potentially overlooks more important, historically based channels of public opinion formation.

4.1 SLAVERY'S EFFECTS ON AMERICAN DEMOGRAPHICS

How did slavery influence America's racial demographics? The United States was hardly exceptional in its reliance on the labor of enslaved people.[7] If anything, North American colonies imported a *smaller* number of enslaved people than other colonies in the Caribbean and Latin America. According to the Trans-Atlantic Slave Trade Database,[8] around 400,000 enslaved people disembarked in North America—in Virginia and other parts of the American South. In contrast, around 2 million disembarked in the British Caribbean, 1.1 million in the French Caribbean, 1.2 million in the Spanish colonies, and around 4.8 million in Brazil. Overall, U.S. slavery accounted for around four percent of all slave ship disembarkations in the Western hemisphere.

However, the importation of enslaved people of African descent substantially changed the character of the U.S. colonies in ways that differed from Caribbean and Latin American nations. Much of the labor on Caribbean plantations was difficult and dangerous. Some accounts show that the population of enslaved Africans in the West Indies decreased from two to five percent per year due to various causes: poor nutrition, heat and humidity, disease, exhaustion, low birth rates, or some combination.[9] These unhealthy conditions meant that importing new enslaved labor was less expensive than simply taking care of existing populations. In the United States, working conditions were comparatively less harsh, the temperatures were cooler, and the communicable diseases were less deadly, which meant fewer enslaved people died initially and the fertility rates of American slaves grew over time. Thus, American slavery evolved around the economic importance of a "homegrown" enslaved population, which was quite different from Caribbean slavery.[10]

Due to both internal and external pressure, the involuntary importation of people as slaves formally ended with the Act Prohibiting Importation of Slaves, passed at the earliest opportunity under the U.S. Constitution in 1807.[11] However, the institution of chattel slavery, in which slaves were the personal property of their holders, only expanded in prevalence and geographic scope. Enslaved people were a form of captured labor that could be moved around to maximize profits, and the acquisition of the Louisiana Purchase in 1803 opened up new lands to cultivation.[12] This land was cheap and fertile—not suitable, perhaps, for growing tobacco or rice, but suitable for growing another increasingly important crop: cotton. Young white farmers took their slaves and followed the trail of cotton suitability into Mississippi, Alabama, Louisiana, and even eastern Texas, shifting the landscape of slavery from the eastern seaboard westward and further inland.[13] Figure 4.1 represents the county-level prevalence of slavery in the 1790, 1810, 1830, and 1850 U.S. Censuses, which clearly shows this westward expansion.

By the onset of the Civil War, large enslaved populations lived in the Black Belt—the swath of land extending southward from Memphis toward New Orleans and eastward from Birmingham up through Georgia and into South Carolina. Along with parts of Virginia, the South Carolina lowlands, the Florida panhandle, and parts of eastern Tennessee, these areas constituted the core of American slavery. In addition, Fogel and Engerman report that by 1850 the distribution of the farm population of slaves included some 73 percent on cotton plantations, 14 percent in tobacco plantations, 6 percent in sugar harvesting, 5 percent in rice cultivation, and 2 percent in hemp cultivation.[14]

POSTBELLUM POPULATION MOBILITY

How did this historical population dispersion translate into contemporary demographics? The post–Civil War period saw a time of significant restraints on the mobility of newly freed blacks. Firstly, states' Black Codes instituted punitive measures against African Americans and aimed to keep

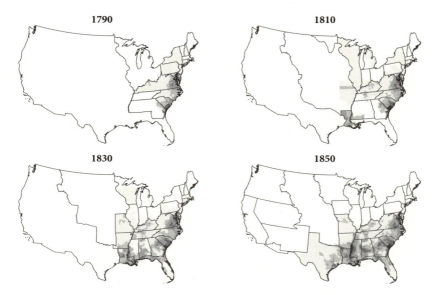

Figure 4.1. Maps showing the concentration of slavery (by county) from the 1790, 1810, 1830, and 1850 U.S. Censuses.

black labor cheap and immobile.[15] This meant that African Americans faced significant difficulties in leaving their former places of enslavement. Secondly and relatedly, as Wright argues, racial discrimination against black advancement in skilled labor led much of that labor back into the agricultural sector and, thus, back into the Black Belt.[16] Even as labor market pressures improved (to some extent) the wages and conditions of black workers over the late nineteenth and early twentieth centuries, these same market pressures mixed with invested racial norms to keep the relative distribution of the black population fairly consistent in the decades after abolition.

Not all African Americans, of course, stayed in the Black Belt. Thousands of blacks left the South during the Great Migrations of the first half of the twentieth century. In 1900, eighty-eight percent of African Americans lived in the South; in 1970, that percentage was down to fifty. Many of these migrants moved to industrial areas in the Northeast and Midwest. Within the South, other African Americans moved in large numbers to cities such as Memphis, Atlanta, and New Orleans, and also to smaller cities within the Black Belt, such as Selma, Alabama, and Albany, Georgia. Nonetheless, despite these migrations, the Southern Black Belt retained substantial numbers of African Americans (shown in figure 4.2), suggesting strong persistence in racial demographics.

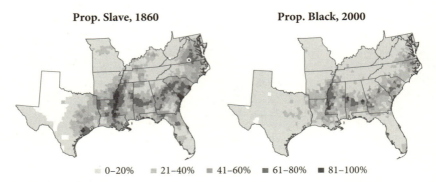

Figure 4.2. Left: Map showing historical slave data from the 1860 U.S. Census. Right: Map showing where African Americans live today, using data from the 2000 U.S. Census. Source: 1860 and 2000 U.S. Censuses.

Millions of whites also migrated out of the South, including many poorer whites. As W.E.B. Du Bois wrote, the "revolt of the poor whites, just as the revolt of the slaves, came through migration. And their migration, instead of being restricted, was freely encouraged."[17] The end result, according to Du Bois, was that "poor whites left the South in large numbers. In 1860, 399,700 Virginians were living out of their native state. From Tennessee, 344,765 emigrated; from North Carolina 272,606, and from South Carolina, 256,868."[18] Most well known are the Dust Bowl migrants of the 1930s, who departed the western parts of the South for New Mexico, Arizona, and California. Others moved both westward and northward, populating not just parts of the Southwest but also the industrial Northeast and Midwest. Many whites, often poor and from rural communities, moved to the same cities (if not the same neighborhoods) as the Southern blacks.[19]

TODAY'S BLACK POPULATIONS

This history illustrates the important demographic legacy of slavery: counties that had a high prevalence of slavery in the antebellum period continue to have the highest shares of African Americans today. We see this pattern in figure 4.2, which compares historical census data with current data on African American populations. The left plot shows our historical county-level data depicting the share of the population that was enslaved in 1860. The right plot shows where African Americans live today.

The similarities are immediately obvious. Although there has been substantial dispersion across time, and despite the movement of blacks into cities like Memphis, Atlanta, and New Orleans (as well as northern cities), the Black Belt still has a substantially higher share of the black population than other Southern counties. In fact, the correlation between the percent enslaved in 1860 and modern-day African Americans is 0.77, which is staggeringly high given that slavery was abolished over 150 years ago. This correlation strongly suggests that one of slavery's legacies, and perhaps its most important one, is the long-term demographic effect it has had on the American population and its distribution. All of these could potentially cloud the arguments we make about the historical persistence of politics and of political attitudes, and could potentially explain differences between places like Richland County, South Carolina, and Leflore County, Mississippi.

4.2 THE THEORY OF RACIAL THREAT

Why would the present-day distribution of African Americans across the U.S. South have importance for the attitudes of whites today? Why would living amongst a larger share of African Americans affect whites' political and racial attitudes? The theory of racial threat, which we described briefly in chapter 3, is one plausible answer. This theory developed in part out of the research of a scholar of Southern politics, Key, who observed that "the whites of the black belts ... have the deepest and most immediate concern about the maintenance of white supremacy." Linking these attitudes to the concentration of African Americans, Key—who wrote *Southern Politics* in the critically important period of the 1940s—further noted that "[t]hose whites who live in counties with populations 40, 50, 60, or even 80 per cent Negro share a common attitude toward the Negro," one that was the most concerned with "white supremacy" and antiblack policies. He wrote that "[i]f the whites of the black belts give the South its dominant political tone, the character of the politics ... will vary roughly with the Negro proportion of the population."[20] Underlying this argument was a simple descriptive observation: as the relative number of African Americans rose, so too did white hostility toward the black population.

Key never used the term "racial threat," but he did expand on this "black concentration hypothesis" by highlighting the common economic and political interests of the white elite in the Black Belt. He noted that the politics of these regions were fundamentally about the "maintenance of control by a white minority." Key discussed the interaction between race, class, and sectionalism in Southern politics:

> The planter may often be kind, even benevolent toward his Negroes, and the upcountryman may be, as the Negroes say, "mean"; yet when the political chips are down, the whites of the black belts by their voting demonstrate

that they are most ardent in the faith of white supremacy as, indeed, would naturally be expected. The whites of the regions with few Negroes have a less direct concern over the maintenance of white rule, whereas the whites of the black belts operate an economic and social system based on subordinate, black labor.[21]

Thus, even though he never used the language of "threat," Key certainly did highlight in his exhaustive analysis the fundamental logic of how large black populations could influence white attitudes. Even so, Key's focus was less on the development of attitudes in the Black Belt and more about how sectional battles played out in each state (often along planter-upcountry lines) and how the elite whites in the Black Belt used their influence to create a "Solid South" in the national arena based on racial politics.[22]

Key's observation engendered numerous other studies of Southern politics documenting the correlation he observed: whites' attitudes became increasingly conservative and, in earlier analyses, more pro-segregation the more African Americans there were living in an area. Among the first of these are a group of studies showing that high concentrations of blacks predicted white support for segregationist candidates such as George Wallace.[23] Other early studies also found correlations between high concentrations of African Americans and racially hostile white attitudes, negative attitudes on school desegregation, resistance against black voter registration, and higher incidences of lynching.[24]

To explain these patterns, scholars developed the theory of "racial threat" (also sometimes called "power threat"), which builds on some of the insights about the economic structure that Key highlighted. The idea is straightforward: as the numbers of minorities increase, they begin to pose a "threat" to the political and economic standing of the dominant group. As Hubert M. Blalock argues, the subordinate group threatens the dominant group by either limiting its access to economic resources or undermining its political power.[25] To combat these threats, the dominant group seeks to protect its status by developing exclusionary antiminority attitudes, policies, and social norms.

A number of more recent studies report findings consistent with racial threat, including evidence that increased concentration of blacks (or other minority groups) is strongly correlated with whites' partisanship, suggesting that whites more often self-identify or vote in a more Republican or conservative direction as the local concentration of blacks rises.[26] Other studies show that increased geographic concentrations of minorities are correlated with whites being more likely to support antiminority policies and less likely to support policies that would benefit minorities.[27] For example, Glaser finds support for racial threat within the South on questions related to civil rights or African American politicians.

(However, he finds no support for racial threat's relationship to racial prejudice.) Giles and Buckner find a strong relationship between high concentrations of blacks and whites' support for extremely conservative candidates, such as David Duke.[28] In addition, other studies demonstrate that high concentrations of minorities are predictive of whites' attitudes about racial minorities.[29] The conclusion from this literature is that where there are high concentrations of African Americans, whites are most likely to be conservative and more racially hostile or resentful, primarily because of the "threat" posed by the minority group.[30]

However, the literature on racial threat (and in particular the literature on racial threat in the South) has focused on black concentrations, or the *contemporary* presence of African Americans—as opposed to historical institutions or norms. We believe that this represents a conceptual soft spot. The Black Belt, where studies have shown the strongest link between black concentrations and more conservative white attitudes, are areas where a significant economic and cultural climate surrounding the subjugation of one group of people developed. These were also areas where the dominant white elite had, in the historical time period, much to lose from the political enfranchisement and the economic mobility of African Americans. If anything, blacks needed to be "reigned in," so that their labor could be leveraged into economic productivity. While V. O. Key recognized this fundamentally materialist aspect of the black concentration hypothesis, the subsequent racial threat literature has often overlooked the origins of the possible "threat," instead taking the size of the black population as its direct source. This version of the theory of racial threat posits that minority groups are viewed as undesirable and to be segregated from white society, but this stands in sharp contrast to the historical patterns (that we explore at great length in the chapters that follow) in which the white upper class sought to control and dominate black labor resources in order to keep them immobile and restrained. In other words, the white elites in the post-Reconstruction era and in the early twentieth century did not want blacks to leave; far from it. They wanted blacks to stay and be policed and controlled, and to remain the bedrock of the Southern economy.[31] Ultimately, the literature on racial threat tends to overlook these historical forces and, indeed, provides little explanation about the origins or historical developments of the potential "threats."

The story of racial threat also struggles to account for the population changes in the rural South during the Great Migrations of the 1930s and 1960s, which included both black and white out-migration. This movement out of the South impacted the geographic distribution of blacks across the South, which should have consequences for the geographic distribution of "threat" toward local white populations. To return to an example that we highlighted at the start of the chapter, South Carolina's

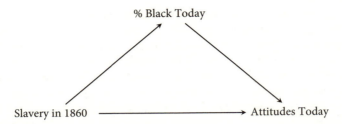

Figure 4.3. Representation of slavery's possible effects on contemporary attitudes and demographics.

Richland County had significant outward black mobility—thousands of blacks left the county over the course of the twentieth century, ultimately leading to a large decline in the relative black population share. The theory of threat (or the black concentration hypothesis) would predict that white hostility toward African Americans should be lower in those areas, particularly over the last part of the twentieth century. As we show below, this is not the case. We believe the inability of racial threat to explain these basic patterns presents not just empirical but also conceptual weaknesses.

4.3 IS THE CONCENTRATION OF AFRICAN AMERICANS TODAY EXPLAINING SLAVERY'S EFFECTS?

However, when it comes to what the data tell us, our questions are straightforward: Do contemporary black concentrations explain our findings? Or does slavery have separate, historically connected effects on attitudes today? These questions not only speak to our conceptual concerns but also illuminate potential differences between places like Richland County, South Carolina (high slave, but relatively lower in terms of contemporary shares of the black population), and Leflore County, Mississippi (high slave, but also high share black). If the theory of contemporary racial threat is a persuasive explanation, then we would expect to see differences between Leflore County and Richland County. If, on the other hand, a location's historically grounded political culture—including its history of slavery and coercive black labor—drives differences, then we would expect places like Leflore and Richland Counties, both of which had a high prevalence of slavery, to have fewer differences.

Figure 4.3 shows a simple, stylized example of these possible relationships. In the plot, a direct arrow links slavery in 1860 to attitudes today (in this case, white attitudes), and two diagonal arrows link slavery to white attitudes today via the share of the current African American population. (There are, of course, significant intervening factors that we could include in this very simple graph, including Black Codes, Jim Crow, the civil rights movement, the Civil Rights Act of 1964, and the Voting Rights Act of 1965, to name a few. We discuss these in far more detail in chapters 6 and 8; for now, we focus on contemporary demographics—here, the share of the population that is black.) It's possible that the lower arrow, which shows a direct connection between slavery in 1860 and attitudes today, doesn't really exist because slavery's influence on white attitudes operates mostly via contemporary shares of the African American population—that is, slavery's primary effect is through its *demographic* impact. At first glance, this is a very appealing explanation for our findings: a large and important literature documents the relationship between contemporary black concentrations and white attitudes, and, as we noted, African Americans continue to live in the Black Belt in large shares. This could explain potential differences in contemporary white attitudes in places like Richland County and Leflore County.

Our approach in trying to disaggregate these issues is simple: we check how much of our main findings can be explained away by taking into account contemporary shares of the black population. That is, we estimate the magnitude of the effect represented by the bottom arrow, which directly links slavery and outcomes today. We do this in two ways. First, we simply include proportion black in the year 2000 as an additional control variable in our analyses. Second, and to avoid any potential issues with what is called *post-treatment bias*, we estimate the direct effect of proportion enslaved by fixing proportion black today using a statistical method called "sequential g-estimation."[32] Post-treatment bias is a type of selection bias that occurs when a statistical analysis conditions on a consequence of the main independent variable of interest.[33] Here, the contemporary share of the population that is black is a direct downstream consequence of an area's slaveholding past (as we have discussed); for that reason, if we include the contemporary shares of the black population in an analysis, the potential for inducing this type of bias is high. Note, however, that the logic of both approaches is the same—if demographics explain the entirety of slavery's effects, then we should see no remaining effect associated with slavery once we account for contemporary black concentrations.

We present the results of these analyses in figure 4.4, with the (direct) effect of slavery estimated using both approaches compared to the overall, total effect of slavery from our earlier analyses in chapter 3. (As before, we examine whites' attitudes on (1) partisanship, (2) affirmative action, and (3) racial resentment.) The figure demonstrates that, under either approach, the effect of slavery on white attitudes continues to be strong and in the same direction. These results show that contemporary shares

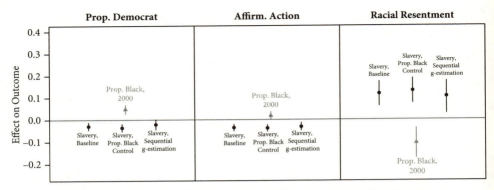

Figure 4.4. Effect of slavery on white attitudes. Each point is the estimated effect of a 25-percentage-point increase in 1860 slavery on each of the outcomes. "Baseline" is the results with 1860 covariates from chapter 3, "Prop. Black Control" adds proportion black in the county in 2000 as a control variable, and "Sequential g-estimation" uses an alternative direct effects estimation strategy. Gray triangles represent the equivalent effect of proportion black in 2000. Lines represent 90% confidence intervals.

of black population have little influence in attenuating slavery's effect on any of the outcomes. Indeed, the direct effects of slave proportion are similar to those in chapter 3 and are still highly significant. Substantively, this means that *we see no evidence that slavery's effects operate exclusively via contemporary black concentrations.* Even when we fix the share of today's African American population, the localized, historical presence of slavery continues to powerfully predict white attitudes today. In other words, the black concentration hypothesis does not explain all of the effects that we see here or in chapter 3.

In this same figure, we also report the relationship between proportion black in 2000 and white attitudes. (This is reported with the light gray bars.) This effect is estimated to be the opposite of what racial threat would predict: once we take slavery into account, whites living in high-black counties report *more* liberal attitudes.[34] This finding poses an intriguing question: Why do our results on contemporaneous black concentrations differ from those in the previous racial threat literature? One reason is that once historical slave shares are taken into account, contemporary shares of minority populations do little to explain contemporary attitudes. In a direct comparison, in other words, historical forces are more important than contemporary demographics. This is the crux of our argument in this book, and it is also the foundation of behavioral path dependence, which we find to be a compelling mechanism by which attitudes persist over time.

To provide a stronger, more direct examination of demographic persistence juxtaposed with historical explanations rooted in slavery, we undertake

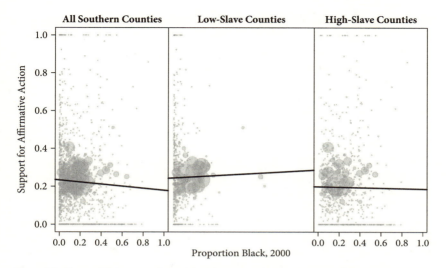

Figure 4.5. How racial threat can be explained by slavery. County-level scatter plots of proportion supporting affirmative action on proportion black in 2000, according to the CCES and the U.S. Census. First panel is all counties and the negative relationship is statistically significant. Second and third panels are the same relationship within levels of slavery, low and high, respectively. In these panels, there is no relationship at all. Regressions used to calculate effects include county-level measures of log of total population in 2000, the log of the median income in 2000, and the unemployment rate.

an additional analysis looking at contemporary black concentrations. We take all counties in the U.S. South (approximately 1,300 of them). We divide these counties into two groups: (1) formerly high-slave counties (where the proportion of the county that was enslaved was above the overall median of 0.25); and (2) formerly low-slave counties (where the proportion of the county enslaved was below the median). We then examine within each group how the share of the population that is black today affects or predicts whites support for affirmative action in a county.[35] This is a straightforward test of the predictive power of simple present-day demographics, conditioning roughly on a county's former slave past. The theory of racial threat would predict that as the percentage of African Americans increases, white attitudes about affirmative action grow more conservative *regardless of slaveholding history*.

We present these results in figure 4.5. The plot on the left represents the relationship between the share of the population that is African American and white attitudes today (i.e., white support for affirmative action) for all Southern counties. This plot, which does not control for the share of the county that was enslaved in 1860, shows a slight negative (and statistically significant) relationship—the more African Americans living in a county today, the more conservative is the white population regarding affirmative action. However, when we look at the plots in the center and on the right, which divide counties into (a) low-slave counties and (b) high-slave counties, and look at the effect of African American population share on white attitudes, *the previous negative relationship disappears*. Similar results hold for our other measures of racial attitudes.

This point is worth emphasizing, as it challenges the empirical and conceptual underpinnings of previous scholarly findings: *Once we take into account an area's historical slave dependence, larger present-day African American populations in a county actually result in warmer feelings among whites with regard to race.* Our findings are limited to the South because slavery was not a legal institution in this time period in the North, and so we do not aim to explain all scholarly findings involving racial threat. However, our results suggest that historical and behavioral path dependence is extremely important in shaping contemporary attitudes. Moreover, exclusively focusing on contemporary demographics masks how history and institutions are real forces at play in influencing attitudes and beliefs. This is very strong evidence against the explanation that contemporary political attitudes are rooted exclusively in contemporary demographics.

One concern could be that these beliefs about affirmative action are somehow skewed by the fact that these data originate during the election of the nation's first black president, Barack Obama. To investigate this, we analyze additional data from the American National Election Studies (ANES) over the 1980s and 1990s, when many canonical results in the racial threat literature were discovered. We estimate the relationships between various measures of racial liberalism and the proportion black in 1980 to see if respondents in counties with higher levels of African Americans were more racially conservative. Figure 4.6 shows these relationships under various estimation strategies. The first is the simple bivariate relationship between each outcome and proportion black; for example, the "Raw" estimate for black thermometer scores implies that a twenty-five-percentage-point increase in the share of the population that is black leads to a five-point drop in Southern whites' thermometer ratings of blacks.[36] Similar results hold for the other measures, including thermometer scores for Jesse Jackson, a question on whether the government should help blacks (seven-point agreement scale), and a question about whether blacks "get less than they deserve" (five-point agreement scale). Taken together, and with other results not presented here, the raw results appear to support the racial threat hypothesis. And, indeed, these are very similar to the results presented in the literature.[37]

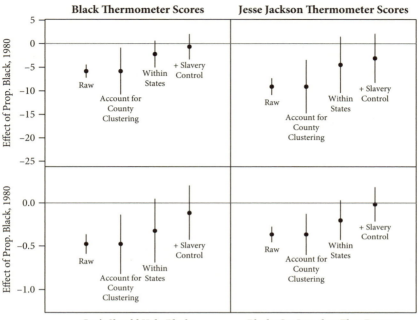

Figure 4.6. Effect of proportion black in 1980 on white attitudes in the ANES pooled from 1984–96. Each point is the estimated effect of a 25-percentage-point increase in proportion black on each of the outcomes. The first estimate ("Raw") is without controls; the second ("County Clustering") uses standard errors clustered at the county level; the third adds state fixed effects ("Within States"); the last adds proportion enslaved in 1860 as an additional control ("+ Slavery Control"). For all outcomes, higher values are more racially liberal. Lines represent 90% confidence intervals.

However, once we appropriately address the statistical problems with these models, the support for racial threat becomes at best unclear and at worst nonexistent. First, simply adjusting our uncertainty estimates for the clustering of respondents in counties significantly increases the uncertainty of each estimate.[38] Second, when we evaluate the racial threat hypothesis within states (by including state fixed effects in the analysis), all of the estimates move sharply closer to zero and we cannot rule out the possibility that there is no relationship between black concentrations and white attitudes. And finally, when including the historical prevalence of slavery as a control, many of the results move even further from the standard racial threat story. This indicates that past results on racial threat may be highly sensitive to changes in the modeling strategy. Furthermore, the large change in the estimated effects when including state fixed effects indicates that much of the racial threat findings in the South were picking up differences between, rather than within, states.

Taken together, our analysis of contemporary black concentrations leads to two conclusions. The first is that there is very little evidence that the effects of slavery are exclusively due to contemporary racial threat. The second is that there is actually very little evidence of contemporary racial threat in the South once historical forces (and statistical realities) are taken into consideration, suggesting an important role for an area's political and historical context.[39]

4.4 COULD BLACK MIGRATION CONFOUND BEHAVIORAL PATH DEPENDENCE?

A potential problem with our analysis is that it looks at only a demographic snapshot—that is, *contemporary* shares of the black population—and thus fails to account for effects of slavery on demographic dynamics that have been felt over the last 150 years (at least). It might be the case that contemporary shares of the black population don't explain our findings, but historical population changes do.

WHITE RESPONSES TO BLACK MIGRATION

This kind of dynamic explanation of ongoing threat is perhaps more appealing because it engages the fact that many parts of the South had significant population mobility over the course of the twentieth century. For example, under a simple reading of the theory of racial threat, those places where African Americans left in larger numbers as part of the various waves of the Great Migration would be the places where the "threat" posed by the large black population should be diminished and where (in the South at least) any kind of white racial hostility generated among whites by black concentrations should have attenuated.

We check this in figure 4.7. The figure shows how the relationship between the proportion enslaved in 1860 and political outcomes today varies as a function of the drop in the black population between (1) 1920 and 1940, which would capture part of the first Great Migration (1916–30), and then again (2) between 1920 and 1970, which would capture both the first and second Great Migration (1940–70), including very important post–World War II mobility. If the racial threat story holds, then we should see weaker effects of slavery where there were large declines in the black population. The results are inconsistent with this interpretation: areas with greater black out-migration are not meaningfully different in terms of the effects of slavery. Once again, our evidence is at odds with a simple theory of racial threat.

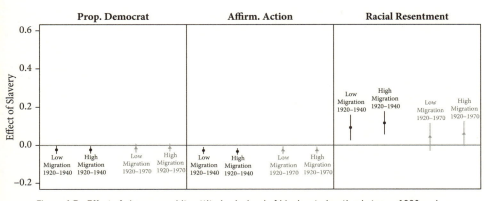

Figure 4.7. Effect of slavery on white attitudes by level of black outmigration between 1920 and 1940 (black dots and lines) and between 1920 and 1970 (grey triangles and lines). Each point is the estimated effect of a 25-percentage-point increase in 1860 slavery on each of the outcomes. High and low values of black outmigration are the 25th and 75th percentile of those variables. Lines represent 90% confidence intervals.

DOES RACIAL THREAT EXPLAIN PATTERNS IN THE PAST?

A slightly broader (but related) question is whether racial threat has been a driver of Southern political opinion in the past. That is, although slavery's effects today cannot be explained away by the black concentration hypothesis or by racial threat (as we saw in the earlier analyses), perhaps the theories can explain white attitudes *earlier in the twentieth century*. Perhaps what we are uncovering is the fact that whites' exposure to blacks and racial threat created antiblack attitudes *within*, not across, generations (as would be predicted by behavioral path dependence), and that it has done so for consecutive generations moving forward from emancipation. This would both link historical forces and provide support for the idea that black concentrations are significant contributors to the fomenting and promotion of antiblack white attitudes *in any given time period*. Looking at patterns over time would also highlight the potential within-generation impact of population mobility (for example, the Great Migrations).

To see if African American concentrations and the idea of racial threat can explain the entirety of our results in earlier time periods, we look at historical presidential elections as a proxy for white public opinion, using as the outcome the share of the county-wide vote that went to the Democratic candidate between 1900 and 1944. Note that this was a period in which black voters were effectively disenfranchised in the South, meaning that these voting outcomes are almost certainly capturing *white* political preferences.[40] (We leverage this research design again in chapter 5.) Figure 4.8 plots these findings. It shows, for each election year,

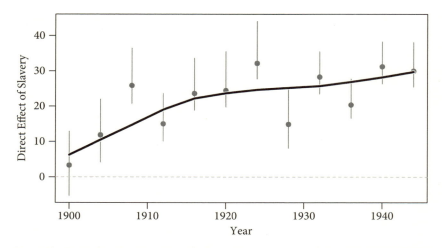

Figure 4.8. Direct effect of slavery over time. The x-axis is year of the presidential election and the y-axis is the direct effect of proportion slave on presidential vote share, net the effect of proportion black in the most recent U.S. Census. The dots represent point estimates while the vertical bars represent 90% bootstrapped confidence intervals. The red line represents a moving average (LOESS smoother) across the years.

the (controlled) direct effect of slavery on Democratic county vote shares fixing the proportion black, as measured by the most recent U.S. Census to the election. For example, the 1924 presidential election would fix the proportion black at 1920 levels. These results condition on all of the 1860 covariates from chapter 3.[41]

Substantively, the figure represents an estimate of the effect of slavery on Democratic vote share in each of these presidential elections *that is not due simply to the share of the population that is African American in that time period*. That is, this is the effect of slavery net the separate effect of contemporaneous black concentrations. For example, in 1900, a twenty-percentage-point increase in the share of the population that was enslaved is linked to roughly an eight-percentage-point increase in the share of the county vote going toward the Democratic candidate, holding as fixed the share of the county population that was black in 1900. More illustratively, in 1932, after the first Great Migration of the 1910s and 1920s, a twenty-percentage-point increase in the share of people enslaved in 1860 is linked to around a thirty-percentage-point increase in the share of the county vote that went to the Democratic candidate (Franklin Roosevelt), holding as fixed the share of the population that was black in 1930.

Taken together, this analysis leads to two substantive conclusions. The first is that, even in the early part of the twentieth century, slavery had a significant direct effect on earlier political outcomes—and this effect wasn't simply due to the demographics of the day. The second substantive conclusion is that, as the figure shows, the direct effect of slavery grows in strength over time. (That is, looking at the upward trajectory of the line, the effect of slavery goes up in magnitude over the years.) Why might this be the case? As we discussed earlier, there were several waves of black migration out of the South, including the first Great Migration of the 1910s and 1920s and the second Great Migration of the 1940s through the 1960s. In fact, the correlation between proportion slave and proportion black in 1900 is 0.93, suggesting that many African Americans stayed in areas where slavery was once prevalent—a testament to how effectively Southern blacks' mobility was curtailed in the post-Reconstruction period. However, this correlation drops to 0.87 by 1940; despite this, white attitudes still lean in a more Democratic direction (where the Southern Democrats were the racially conservative party). This would point us to the idea that, despite demographic shifts and blacks moving northward and westward, white attitudes continued to remain more racially conservative in former slave areas. Thus, for newer generations, the direct effect of slavery net proportion black is larger, since the contemporary black population has decreased. This analysis helps explain places like Richland County, South Carolina, where whites have remained conservative, despite the fact that the share of the population that is black has decreased over time.

4.5 COULD WHITE MIGRATION CONFOUND BEHAVIORAL PATH DEPENDENCE?

We have discussed the potential effects of black concentrations and black migration on our patterns (and we do so in greater length in subsequent chapters, in which we discuss attempts to restrict African American mobility and political power). However, the question of *white* demographics and mobility so far remains open. Perhaps it was the case that more racially tolerant whites left during the twentieth century (possibly at the same time as the Great Migrations of African Americans or possibly in more recent periods), or that more racially conservative whites chose to move into the Black Belt in subsequent years—for example, into places like Leflore County, Mississippi, or Barbour County, Alabama. Either of these, or both at the same time, could explain our findings, and both would operate within the racialized environment cultivated by the presence of large black concentrations and economic and political racial threats. It might be the case, for example, that the whites who left the Black Belt were those who feel, or have felt, the most racially threatened by living in a majority-black area.

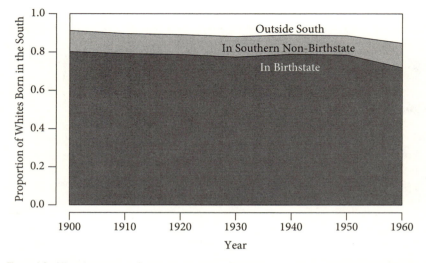

Figure 4.9. Migration patterns for whites born in the South. Source: U.S. Census, Public Use Micro Sample, 1900–60.

MID-TWENTIETH CENTURY WHITE MIGRATION

Data on migration at the individual level are difficult to come by, making it very challenging to assess whether whites who left former slaveholding areas in the twentieth century differed substantially from those who stayed behind. Data from various years of the U.S. Census, plotted in figure 4.9, show that the overwhelming majority of residents of the South still live in their state of birth, and a small minority left the South entirely before 1960. But can we say something about the migrants themselves? Partial answers are provided by focusing on the 1940 U.S. Census. This census is rare in that it asked people where they lived five years prior to its enumeration. This critical piece of information enables us to track which individuals migrated between 1935 and 1940, a time period that approximately falls within the scope of the Great Migrations (which took place in waves from 1910 to 1970), and to determine how they differed from those who remained in the same counties over the same time period.

Looking at these data, roughly twelve percent of all whites in the South moved to a new county (either in-state or out-of-state) between 1935 and 1940, and 4.5 percent moved to a new state. This high rate of internal migration could explain our main findings if there were differential patterns of migration in high-slave counties versus low-slave counties—for example, if more racially tolerant or progressive whites moved away. To make these comparisons, we look at (1) how migrants

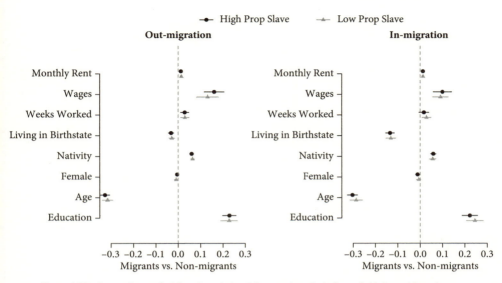

Figure 4.10. Comparisons of white migrants to white nonmigrants in formerly high- and low-slave areas, 1935–40. The similarity in the two groups suggests that migrants (both in- and out-migrants) looked similarly depending on whether they left/entered formerly high- or low-slave areas. Source: 1940 U.S. Census, Public Use Micro Sample. This figure reproduced from Avidit Acharya, Matthew Blackwell, and Maya Sen, "The Political Legacy of American Slavery."

out of formerly high-slave areas compare to nonmigrants who live in high-slave areas and (2) how migrants out of formerly low-slave areas compare to nonmigrants who live in low-slave areas. We compare if patterns of *out-migration* differ between formerly high- and low-slave areas. Second, we do the same comparison for migrants *into* high- and low-slave areas, which will determine if patterns of *in-migration* differ between these areas. Our goal with this analysis is not necessarily to determine if migrants are different from nonmigrants, but, instead, to see if migrants into or out of formerly high-slave areas are uniquely different.

We present results from this comparison in figure 4.10. Each point on the figure represents the average difference in the outcome between migrants and nonmigrants for both formerly high- and low-slave counties, further separated by in- and out-migration.[42] For example, looking at age, this figure shows that both out-migrants and in-migrants are significantly younger than those who remained in their original county during this time period. However, the pattern is the *same for low- and high-slave counties*. Thus, although migrants are younger overall than those who stayed behind, migrants into or out of formerly high-slave counties are no younger than migrants into or out of other counties.

This pattern holds more generally: migrants in the 1935–40 period are distinct from nonmigrants, but those differences are fairly constant across formerly high-slave and formerly low-slave areas. Migrants are higher earners, younger, more likely to be male, more highly educated, and more likely to have both of their parents born in the United States. These differences are consistently present across both formerly high-slave and formerly low-slave counties. Across all of these observable characteristics, migrants into and out of high-slave areas were statistically indistinguishable from migrants into and out of low-slave areas. Thus, we see no evidence of the type of differential sorting that would be necessary to create the political geography that we see today. Although these results are specific to a five-year period in American history, and although migration was a significant force both before and after this period, this does present some evidence against the argument that white population mobility is the key driver of our findings. Indeed, what these findings show is that the distinction between migrant and nonmigrant is far more important than the distinction between migrants from formerly high- versus low-slave counties.

LATE TWENTIETH-CENTURY WHITE MIGRATION

We also present some more evidence against the white migration hypothesis—albeit also only suggestive—using data on between-county migration from 1995–2000 from the 2000 U.S. Census. These data help us investigate the extent to which *contemporary*, as opposed to historical, migration explains our findings.[43] This analysis is well suited for exploring the argument that places like Asheville, North Carolina, and Charleston, South Carolina, are places where whites' attitudes have been tempered both by recent white out-migration and by the more recent arrival of whites from Northern states, including college students and retirees. For example, both Columbia and Asheville have attracted thousands of university students over the last part of the twentieth century; many have chosen to stay permanently.

In order for contemporary white mobility to explain our results, two conditions must hold. The first is that there must be some migration from low-slave areas to high-slave areas (or vice versa); otherwise, there is no meaningful population sorting of any kind. To test this condition, we use this recent county-to-county migration data to calculate dyads (or connections) of where people move to and from, measuring the absolute difference in the proportion 1860 slave between the departing and receiving county; this enables us to assess how much migration takes place between low-slave and high-slave areas. In previous work, however, we show that the vast majority of contemporary migration is within low-slave areas or within high-slave areas, not between.[44] To put things more concretely, we are much more likely to see migration from places like Greenwood, Mississippi, to Eufaula, Alabama (both cities in solidly Black Belt counties), as opposed to migration from Greenwood, Mississippi, to Asheville, North Carolina (one in the Black Belt, the other not).

SURVEY DATA EVIDENCE

The second condition for population mobility or sorting to explain our findings is that racially conservative whites are moving into high-slave areas, racially liberal whites are moving out of high-slave areas, or some combination. Even if there is very little migration between low- and high-slave counties, the distribution of political beliefs among these migrants could be so highly skewed so as to produce our results. For example, perhaps all of the out-migrants from high-slave counties are racially liberal and all of the in-migrants to high-slave counties are racially conservative. With regard to the first possibility, this seems unlikely: the reasoning relies on racially hostile whites moving to areas with extremely large proportions of African Americans. This would mean that more racially conservative whites have migrated into places like Greenwood, Mississippi—certainly possible, but somewhat unlikely, given that (1) these are also places with large black populations and (2) these are areas that have seen significant, across-the-board population losses. This is also a pattern whose existence is questioned within the academic literature. To give one example, Farley et al. show that antiblack attitudes correlate with stronger preferences for geographic segregation, suggesting that, if anything, racially intolerant whites would seek to live elsewhere.[45]

A likelier source of geographic sorting comes from movement of racially liberal whites out of former slave counties. This could partially explain our results if, for example, racially liberal whites became fed up with race relations in Greenwood, Mississippi, or Birmingham, Alabama, and departed—possibly to places like Asheville, North Carolina, but perhaps also to places outside of the South. As a final investigation on whether white migration can account for our results, we turn to a unique study: the Youth-Parent Socialization Panel Survey, which followed a cohort of American students in 1965 into their adult years, interviewing them again in 1973, 1982, and 1997. What makes this study unique is that it collected data on the racial views of these students in each wave of the survey, which also recorded county of residence, with only one exception (1997). The measures of racial views we have from this survey are the same questions on thermometer scores we used in the previous chapter. From this data, then, we can determine the impact of the local context of historical slavery between, say, 1965 and 1983, when the students were roughly in their mid-thirties. If sorting on the basis of racial views is indeed occurring, then we should see white students with negative views toward black people systematically moving into former high-slave areas or white students with positive views moving into former low-slave areas.[46]

What we find fails to support this account: there is no correlation between black thermometer scores in 1965 (or the white-black difference) and changes in the proportion enslaved in the county of residence between 1965 and 1982.[47] Thus, with a panel study of students in the crucial period after the Civil Rights Act, migration appears to be unrelated to the type of geographic sorting discussed above. This, combined with our above data, provides strong evidence that population mobility is an unlikely explanation for the differences in attitudes between places like Richland County, South Carolina, and Leflore County, Mississippi. Certainly white migration has introduced some random noise into the equation, but we have no evidence that it is a primary driver of contemporary white attitudes.

4.6 CONCLUSION

To return to the question that we started with in this chapter, what do our findings here mean for the potential differences between places like Richland County, South Carolina (high proportion enslaved in 1860, but relatively fewer African Americans today), versus places like Leflore County, Mississippi (high proportion enslaved in 1860 and high share black today)?

Our analysis shows that high contemporary black concentrations may explain some things, but they explain far less when placed in the appropriate historical and institutional context. Holding constant high black concentrations today, there appears to be something distinctively conservative about places that had high concentrations of enslaved peoples historically, and black concentrations by themselves don't appear to explain very much once an area's history and traditions are taken into account. These findings therefore cast doubt on existing studies making links between contemporary levels of the African American population and various political outcomes, especially those related to race. Previous studies have pointed to black concentrations and racial threat as being a strong predictor of these sorts of outcomes; however, black concentrations—and also the contemporary threat posed by these populations—can lose their predictive power once we take into account an area's past. On a technical front, this would suggest that something like slavery, its history, and its abolition could function as a kind of omitted variable across many studies on the U.S. South.

This leads us to what our findings have to say about racial threat. Recall that the theory of racial threat centered on the economic and political "threat" posed by the minority group, and that these threats generally increase as the share of the minority population goes up. Here, we have no evidence that the fluctuations in the share of the minority population—either today or historically—explain why whites who live in areas where slavery was more prevalent are today more conservative. Instead, we have far stronger evidence—which we discuss in greater depth in later chapters—that it was slavery and its collapse that influenced white attitudes. Specifically, the institution of slavery and its sudden collapse created very strong incentives for Southern whites to wield black labor in ways best suited to their interests. Paradoxically, rather than wanting to reduce or drive away black concentrations (as the theory of racial threat would imply), antebellum and postbellum whites wanted and sought *larger* black labor populations in order to maintain and promote white interests. These sorts of economic and political incentives—which led to segregation, restrictions on black mobility, and policing—are different to the sorts of "threats" underlying the theory of racial threat; however, we think they represent a much more convincing portrayal of the political and economic forces that drove and sustained white attitudes. In short, our findings suggest that demographic context clearly matters; it shapes our surroundings, affects who people interact with, and sheds light on ongoing tensions and resolutions. However, these sorts of contemporary demographic contexts are a direct product of historical and path-dependent forces, and looking only at demographics can obscure the potentially pivotal roles played by historical institutions and behavioral path dependence. Contextual effects like racial threat can often be traced to, and better explained by, their own historical roots.

We conclude this chapter by reemphasizing the key empirical takeaways. First, the areas of the American South that used to have high concentrations of enslaved people at the dawn of the Civil War are today also those areas where Southern blacks live in high levels—an interesting tale of demographic persistence across generations. Second, despite this high correlation, we still can discern a tangible effect of slavery on Southern whites' political attitudes, and this effect operates independently of these high black concentrations. Even holding constant these high numbers of African Americans, the effect of slavery is still detectable. Third, we see little evidence that mobility—either African American or white mobility—has substantially affected our findings. Taken together, these findings lead to one of our major themes, which is that historical forces appear to have independent effects that we can still see today, suggesting an important pathway of behavioral path dependence. We now turn to exploring when and how these historical forces took shape.

PART II

THE ORIGINS OF DIVERGENCE

CHAPTER FIVE

ANTEBELLUM POLITICS OF SLAVERY AND RACE IN THE SOUTH

> "We came honestly by our slaves at the South, we are treating them as the law of God directs, and before we will have them seized and carried off by Abolitionists, we will pour out our blood as freely as we would water."
>
> *William Brownlow, Governor of Tennessee (1865–69)*

As its name implies, East Tennessee, one of Tennessee's three Grand Divisions, is located in the eastern third of the state. The region is situated in the Great Smoky and Cumberland Mountains and is separated from Middle and West Tennessee by the Cumberland Plateau, a geographic boundary that makes East Tennessee appear geographically and culturally more like Appalachia than the Deep South. But the differences between East Tennessee and the rest of the state are more profound than just geography and also more longstanding. For example, in the antebellum period, East Tennessee's Knox County (10.4 percent enslaved in 1860) was significantly less reliant on slavery than other counties in other parts of Tennessee, including Shelby County (35 percent enslaved), Davidson County (23.9 percent enslaved), or Haywood County (57.3 percent enslaved). Even so, despite these differences, support for slavery in East Tennessee was strong in the decades before the Civil War. In the immediate years leading up to the war, however, the tide turned, and the economic divides between East Tennessee and its counterparts in West and Middle Tennessee became increasingly salient. These factors led East Tennessee to emerge on the union side against secession.[1] Since these times, counties in the region have mostly voted Republican, even when the rest of the state was controlled exclusively by the Democratic Party.

A good example of East Tennessee's political vicissitudes comes from the biography of William "Fighting Parson" Brownlow, a prominent nineteenth-century Knoxvillian and, after the Civil War, Tennessee governor. As a newspaper editor and speaker, Brownlow flipped constantly on the issue of slavery. An early opponent in the 1830s, Brownlow's thoughts

---

Epigraph quote from "Ought American slavery to be perpetuated?: A debate between Rev. W. G. Brownlow and Rev. A. Pryne." p. 270.

on the subject took a 180-degree turn by the 1850s, growing more in line with proslavery sentiments in Memphis and Nashville.[2] Himself a slaveholder, Brownlow at that time argued that "God always intended the relation of master and slave to exist" and that church and state "provided for the rights of owners, and the wants of slaves."[3] However, Brownlow's support for slavery conflicted with his strident pro-Union sentiment in the years leading up to the Civil War, during which he campaigned vigorously across the state trying to unite Tennesseans against secession and to cast slavery as an economic wedge issue. "The honest yeomanry of these border States, four-fifths of whom own no negroes and never expect to own any," he incredulously complained, "are to be drafted, forced to leave their wives and children to toil and suffer, while they fight for the purse-proud aristocrats of the Cotton States."[4] After the war, Brownlow's position on slavery changed yet again, and he aligned with abolitionist interests, condemning slavery as "incompatible with the perpetuity of free and republican institutions."[5] Brownlow eventually became a Republican governor of Tennessee, developing an extremely testy relationship with the cotton interests from the eastern parts of the state. His attitude throughout was representative of that of many upcountry whites: once defenders of the institution of slavery, they later came to oppose secession over the issue, all the while holding firm racist beliefs.

The example of East Tennessee and of "Fighting Parson" Brownlow speaks to a key question about the political legacy of slavery: When did differences between low-slave areas (like the areas around Knoxville) and high-slave areas (like the areas around Memphis and Nashville) begin to emerge? To use the language that we developed in chapter 2, was there a critical juncture that began, or jump-started, the process of behavioral path dependence in political attitudes? When did the attitudinal paths followed by the low-slave and high-slave South *diverge*? This chapter addresses these questions by exploring political and racial divisions across the U.S. South in the antebellum era.

For example, one possible explanation for the patterns that we see is that the racial and political attitudes of today actually predate slavery, to the earliest white settlers of the South. Under this argument, settlers—mostly from England and Scotland—brought with them racial attitudes and political cultures, and these informed subsequent support for slavery and its eventual prevalence. Slavery, in other words, is a symptom of this political culture, rather than a cause. We call this the *antebellum folkways hypothesis* after the pioneering work of David Hackett Fischer, who describes the cultural legacies (or "folkways," as he calls them) of different groups of British settlers to American colonies.[6] Is it possible that our findings about contemporary political attitudes predate slavery and instead were caused by seventeenth- and eighteenth-century migration?

As we show in this chapter, antebellum folkways cannot fully explain the patterns of political culture we see today. Before the Civil War, the high-slave and low-slave areas were distinct—culturally, economically, and politically—but their differences existed in spite of a broad agreement over the institution of slavery and the role of African Americans in society. Indeed, as we show below, high- and low-slave counties in the South broadly voted in similar ways, even in elections and on issues where slavery was the most salient issue. We also consider whether differences on racial topics could have been more deeply cultural, and not necessarily reflected by partisan preferences or policy positions. Although we do not have data on antebellum racial attitudes, we do have measures on how slaves were treated. Looking at two such measures—slave mortality and the relative density of slave dwellings—indicates no difference across high- and low-slave counties. This is further evidence against the antebellum folkways hypothesis.

Instead, the historical accounts suggest that slaveholders and nonslaveholders in the antebellum period were united in their political support for slavery: for their part, slaveholders had a vested interest in maintaining the institution of slavery, and, for theirs, many yeoman farmers (nonslaveholders) aspired to accumulate slave wealth. However, as slavery was challenged, and became increasingly out of reach for poorer white farmers, this unity collapsed—just like it did in East Tennessee in the years leading up to the Civil War. The substantive takeaway—and what we show in this chapter—is that the first true reflections of the political divergence outlined in chapter 3 appear in votes over secession in 1861. Indeed, the relative political homogeneity we find across the high- and low-slave areas of the South appears to break rather suddenly around this time, leading us to conclude that the time period around emancipation was a critical juncture for the behavioral path dependence we find in part I. We develop this argument more fully in the next chapter, where we discuss how the political economy of the postbellum South drove at least part of the political cultures that we see today.

We organize this chapter into two parts. The first begins by discussing the partisan configurations of the antebellum South, which suggests that slavery by itself was not necessarily a significant wedge issue—at least not until the cusp of the Civil War. We next present several analyses that support this conclusion and provide evidence against the antebellum folkways hypothesis. First, we examine support for Unionist candidates, finding no difference between high- and low-slave areas. Second, we examine how legislators voted on state measures aimed at expanding slavery, again finding no significant differences. Lastly, we present a historical analysis of the effect of slavery on presidential elections from 1844 to 1964, which suggest that the political divergence between high- and low-slave counties began to emerge in the years immediately after the Civil War, not before. The second part examines regional variation in racial, as opposed to partisan, attitudes. After reviewing the long history of racism in both high- and low-slave areas, we examine two measures that serve as proxies for antiblack sentiment: slave mortality and crowded slave dwellings. We find no difference in these measures across regions of the South—evidence, we argue, that racial attitudes across the antebellum South did not vary much. This sets the stage for our next chapter, in which we advance the argument that emancipation and Reconstruction presented a critical juncture that began the process of divergence in political attitudes in the South.

5.1 ANTEBELLUM POLITICS AND REGIONAL PATTERNS IN PARTISANSHIP AND POLICY

As the historian Barbara Fields has written, slavery was "the central organizing principle of society" in the South.[7] This fact was most plainly obvious for the enslaved, whose labor, physical safety, and family life were beholden to the slaveholder. But slavery also dictated much of white life in the South, perhaps most of all in terms of its relationship with the Southern economy. As historian Walter Johnson observed, it was the internal slave trade, not a common crop or "shared mode of production," that united the South into a "single slave economy" in the antebellum period.[8]

Indeed, just like capital today, slavery was a key conduit for Southern whites to acquire and hold wealth. Economic historians estimate that slavery constituted almost half of the total wealth held by all residents of Alabama, Georgia, Louisiana, Mississippi, and South Carolina. (Farmlands and buildings, on the other hand, only accounted for a quarter of wealth.[9]) As the economic historian Gavin Wright noted, "[A] man who owned two slaves and nothing else was as rich as the average man in the North."[10] This wealth, moreover, was not evenly distributed across the South. To give one example of the extreme accumulation of wealth into certain parts of the Black Belt, the estate of Joshua J. Ward in Georgetown District (later Georgetown County), South Carolina, had over one thousand slaves in 1860. Overall, the average farm in the South had two slaves, and in the Deep South farms had an average of 6.5 slaves.[11] Thus, although slavery was one piece of the Southern economy, it was an important one, and helped divide white society into "haves" and "have-nots."

Slavery had an impact on other parts of the American economy as well. Farms with many slaves not only represented significant accumulations of wealth, but they were also vital to the production of cash crops. For example, an estimated eighty-four percent of Southern cotton was produced on farms with more than ten slaves.[12] Furthermore, the slave economy was a primary driver of wealth across the South and therefore across the nation. Cotton exports accounted for over half the value of all American exports before the Civil War, and helped spur Northern industry.[13] Even nonslaveholding farms benefited from this system, as they saw their value double between 1850 and 1860 while the cotton economy boomed.[14]

Slavery also affected the political fabric in the South. Although the national-level politics of the United States revolved around dealing with the thorny "peculiar institution," many of the key political players from across the different parties actually sought to minimize its intrusion into national politics. For example, from the presidency of Andrew Jackson (1829–37) through the middle of the 1850s, two political parties vied for control over national politics as part of the "Second Party System." The Democratic Party, the party of Jackson and Martin Van Buren (1837–41), was broadly committed to agrarian interests and to limiting the role of the federal government. On the other hand, the Whigs, organized by Henry Clay in response to Jackson's politics, pushed an agenda of modernizing reform, including economic protectionism and what we would now call infrastructure projects.[15] Each of these parties, however, was competitive in the South. Each also had sectional divisions along a North-South axis that would threaten their stability once slavery arose as a national issue. In other words, slavery as a policy issue did not divide the national parties so much as it divided elements within the parties. And these within-party tensions grew in increasing salience through the middle part of the nineteenth century as the issue of slavery became more pressing.

The Whig Party experience provides a good illustration of how Southern party politics transcended region. Many Southern planters traded cotton with the North and with international markets. For that reason, many were supportive of efforts to improve infrastructure, banking, and trade—and thus many were supportive of the Whigs. The same interests also appealed to commercial elite interests in urban areas and other primarily commercial centers. As Cole put it, "Slaves constituted a large portion of the property of the successful planter, that of the capitalist of the city or large town was of a more readily convertible type; but their interests were essentially the same and they soon joined in political union to protect them."[16] Thus, Whigs were not, as scholars have noted, a Southern rights party that "mainly reflected the state rights proclivities of the great planters," but, instead, a party that drew support from both wealthy strongholds of slavery and centers of commercial activities, as well as from areas like Knox County that were politically mixed and hoped to gain from investments in infrastructure.[17] (For that reason, the Whigs drew support from men like Knox County's William Brownlow, who edited a well-known newspaper entitled *Tennessee Whig*.) This Southern Whig element joined with their colleagues in the Northern Whigs to protect the interests of property and capital, but this union would be difficult to maintain as slavery reemerged as a more urgent political issue throughout the nineteenth century. Indeed, while many Northern Whigs vigorously opposed the expansion of slavery, Southern Whigs included many wealthy, prominent slaveowners.

The Democratic Party, which had a more tolerant position to slavery at the national level, also drew approval across high- and low-slave areas of the South. Within the Black Belt, the Democratic Party enjoyed support, carrying over forty percent of the Black Belt vote through the Jackson era.[18] The party also drew much support from small farmers outside the Black Belt, especially those in the Southwest, who resented the concentration of wealth (including slaveholding wealth) and power among the eastern elite. The opposition to a business-oriented planting interest was driven by those trying to break into the slave-plantation economy, and it simultaneously rejected the concentration of wealth in the hands of the few and also accepted the basic tools of this concentration, including slavery.[19] As one author commented, the "vast majority of the southern white population ... consisted of small slaveholders and nonslaveholders who aspired to slaveholding status."[20] Thus, these small farmers found much to like in the Democrats' support of slavery's expansion, viewing the institution as a way for individual farmers to climb the socioeconomic ladder.[21]

This political history suggests that, while there were cleavages (particularly economic ones) between the slaveholding and nonslaveholding South, *slavery itself was not a wedge issue dividing voters or political parties*, nor were the partisan leanings of the South perfectly aligned along a map of slavery density. In terms of national policy, both Southern Whigs and Southern Democrats attempted to position themselves as defenders of slavery.[22] At a regional level, both the Whigs and the Democrats drew support from high- and low-slave areas.[23] There was, of course, considerable variation in the politics of high- and low-slave areas—but this concerned policy discussions over infrastructure improvements, tariffs, and banking, not necessarily the morality or legality of slavery.[24] We discuss racial attitudes in more detail below, but for now note that there existed "a widespread consensus among white Southerners, slaveholders and nonslaveholders alike, that slavery must be protected and sudden abolition prevented."[25] The picture of Southern politics before the Civil War, therefore, is that of economic tensions between the commercial interests of the Black Belt and the yeomanry of the upcountry, and perhaps less to do with differences in racial attitudes. Indeed, as we show below, even when slavery and secession became prominent issues in the aftermath of the Compromise of 1850, the low-slave areas of the South were at least as supportive of slavery as were the high-slave Black Belt counties.

5.2 ASSESSING THE ANTEBELLUM POLITICAL FOLKWAYS

The previous discussion provided some context for the Southern political landscape in the first half of the eighteenth century, suggesting that partisanship cut across high- and low-slave areas and that each had preferences that favored slavery. But can we detect these patterns statistically? Can antebellum political differences explain the results we find in part I? These are important questions that speak to both the origins of political differences between high- and low-slave areas as well as to the possible onset of critical junctures. For example, finding that antebellum political patterns vary across high- and low-slave areas would point to the antebellum folkways hypothesis, suggesting that the political culture differentiating these areas was simply always there. On the other hand, finding no antebellum political patterns that correlate with slavery would suggest that the differences we see in chapter 3 do not date back to this time period.

In this section, we investigate these questions by examining four empirical settings: (1) the prevalence of slavery in the antebellum period and voting for Unionist-oriented candidates in the aftermath of the Compromise of 1850; (2) roll-call voting by Georgia state legislators on slavery-related issues in 1849 and 1855; (3) secession votes in Tennessee; and (4) Southern voting in presidential elections. We find strong evidence that, while slavery and policy interests were intertwined, high-slave areas did not differ substantially from non- or low-slave areas on these important political questions. We also find, in our historical analysis, that significant divergence in expressed political preferences emerges after the war. Low-slave areas turned away from slavery, but only once it appeared that the institution's future was seriously threatened.

VOTING FOR UNIONIST CANDIDATES IN HIGH-SLAVE VERSUS LOW-SLAVE AREAS

As we have discussed, partisan politics in the antebellum South were structured more so around views toward commerce, infrastructure, and business than around views on slavery. To highlight this pattern, we focus on two antebellum state-wide elections in which slavery and sectional issues were acute: the 1851 gubernatorial elections in Georgia and Mississippi. To give some brief historical context, the Compromise of 1850 temporarily settled whether and how slavery would be extended westward following land acquisition in the Mexican-American War (1846–47). The deal, crafted by Whig Henry Clay and Democrat Stephen Douglas, admitted California as a free state and allowed for popular sovereignty to decide the slave status of the New Mexico and Utah territories. In the aftermath of this compromise, several states were divided over the deal's fairness to the Southern states and, ultimately, over the issue of secession from the United States.[26] More extreme states' rights advocates openly discussed plans to secede and form a Southern confederacy. Several moderate Southern politicians, some of whom had helped broker the compromise, formed Unionist parties in response.

Given this background, the gubernatorial elections in Georgia and Mississippi in 1851 provide a nice test of how slavery and politics interacted in the antebellum period: these are not only states for which we have quality local-level data, but these are also elections that pitted a strong Southern rights promoter against a more moderate Unionist candidate.[27] For example, in the 1851 gubernatorial election in Georgia, the moderate Constitutional Union candidate Howell Cobb ran against former governor and Southern rights candidate Charles McDonald. In the 1851 gubernatorial election in Mississippi, the moderate Senator Henry Foote, who helped shape the compromise, ran against former Senator (and future Confederate President) Jefferson Davis, who vehemently opposed it.[28] The Union candidates, Cobb and Foote, endorsed more moderate positions, advocating for the South to remain in the Union. This is not to say that the two men were antislavery candidates—far from it. The Constitutional Union party in Georgia, for instance, conditioned its endorsement of Unionism on the rights of slaveholders being respected by the federal government.[29] However, the elections did provide voters a choice on the national discussion over slavery and its expansion into the West.

Does the density of slavery in Georgia and Mississippi predict the vote shares for the Unionist candidates during a time period when the issue of slavery was highly salient? Figure 5.1 presents these relationships for both Georgia and Mississippi. Each plot shows the proportion slave on the horizontal axis and, on the vertical axis, the percent of the county voters supporting candidates who wanted to stay in the Union. The plots show a key fact: *the density of slavery in 1850 does little to predict the vote shares in these 1851 gubernatorial elections*. In Georgia, there appears to be no relationship at all, whereas in Mississippi, there appears to be, if anything, a positive relationship between slavery and support for Unionist candidates. (This relationship is, however, not statistically significant.) Substantively, these data suggest that the low-slave areas of Southern states were not necessarily bastions of antislavery sentiment, nor did they drag their feet on the issue of secession in the early 1850s. If anything, the planter counties of Mississippi stood in opposition to secession at this point, consistent with concerns over how disunion would worsen the "problem" of fugitive slaves or how a civil war might lead to complete emancipation—which was, to these areas, a fate

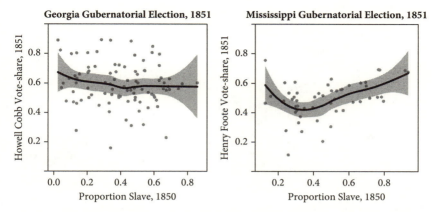

Figure 5.1. Within-state relationship between proportion slave in 1850 and percentage voting for Unionist candidates in 1851. Both Howell Cobb and Henry Foote were running against strong Southern rights supporters in the aftermath of the Compromise of 1850. This figure reproduced from Avidit Acharya, Matthew Blackwell, and Maya Sen, "The Political Legacy of American Slavery."

worse than the simple restriction of slavery.[30] Both of these findings run counter to the patterns we see today—with formerly high-slave areas more conservative—and they suggest that contemporary patterns might not trace to this time period, evidence against the antebellum folkways hypothesis.

STATE LEGISLATURE ROLL CALL VOTES

One possible criticism of the above analysis is that voters may have had many reasons to choose a political candidate, with attitudes on slavery or on blacks being only a small component of this bundle. This bundling may hide important patterns related to slavery, making a more direct measure of support for the institution of slavery preferable.

To this end, we investigate voting patterns by members of the Georgia House of Representatives on legislation regulating how slaves could be imported in the antebellum period. During the nineteenth century, many Southern states enacted restrictions on the domestic movement of slaves into their states, especially for sale or for hire. (The international slave trade had been banned by Congress since 1808.) Georgia first enacted such a law in 1816 and went through a series of repeals and replacements until it was permanently repealed in 1855.[31] Fortunately, we have roll call votes for a handful of these repeals in the Georgia House of Representatives, specifically 1849 and 1855. In both years, lawmakers voted on whether to remove restrictions on the importation of slaves from other slaveholding

Figure 5.2. Proportion of Georgia state legislators voting for the repeal of restrictions on the importation of slaves to Georgia in 1849 and 1855, by density of slavery in the counties they represent. Source: Journal of the House of Representatives of the State of Georgia, 1849 & 1855.

states. Substantively, a "yes" vote on these proposals meant endorsing slavery's expansion within Georgia, while a "no" vote was an endorsement of restricting slave-based commerce. We match each legislator to his county, which enables us to explore the relationship between the density of slavery in a county and its legislator's support for these bills.

Figure 5.2 shows the results of this analysis. It shows the proportion of state legislators that voted for removing restrictions on the import of slaves by the density of slaves in their counties. We divide the counties in Georgia into low-slave (below the median proportion enslaved) and high-slave (above the median proportion enslaved). The figure shows that low-slave counties in Georgia were actually *more* likely to support the expansion of the interstate slave trade than were high-slave counties, in both 1849 and 1855. Substantively, these votes would be difficult to reconcile with the low-slave counties of Georgia being more opposed to slavery or supportive of the rights of blacks. Instead, these findings are more consistent with representatives of the low-slave counties attempting to lower barriers to entry into slaveholding status and to lower the cost of purchasing slaves for their constituents. These votes are also consistent with legislators representing planters with large shares of slaves (in the high-slave counties) voting to keep slave prices high by regulating their purchase and sale. Regardless of the reason, both votes cast doubt on the antebellum folkways hypothesis.

SECESSION VOTES IN HIGH-SLAVE VERSUS LOW-SLAVE AREAS OF TENNESSEE

The political rifts between the high- and low-slave South started to deepen as the Civil War approached and Southern solidarity on the issue of slavery began to fray. One direct cause of such growing tension and division between places like East Tennessee's Knox County (low slave) and high-slave areas was the steep rise in the price of slaves, especially relative to other goods.[32] This steep rise, moreover, was partially due to fears over the future of slavery itself. As Genovese points out, "[p]lantation-belt yeomen ... aspired to become slaveholders," and the path to this outcome was becoming more and more out of reach for poor white farmers.[33] Combined with the yeomen distrust for the planters, the growing inaccesibility of slavery as a path to wealth meant that the slave system was on increasingly shaky ground. The strain of this tension came to the forefront on the eve of the Civil War as each state in the South grappled with the decision to secede while, in the North, the Republican Party began to gain ground on an antislavery agenda.[34]

The case of Tennessee in the years leading up to the Civil War—and the political and economic divisions between its three Grand Divisions—represents a microcosm of how the issue of slavery and the threat of abolition furthered the divisions in Southern society, at least between high-slaveholding and low-slaveholding areas. During the 1850s, Tennessee had two-party competition, with the Whigs winning every election from 1836 until 1852. By the mid-1850s, the Whig Party was collapsing due to internal party disagreement about slave expansion, and, in 1856, a narrow majority of Tennesseans supported the Democratic candidate James Buchanan over Know-Nothing Millard Filmore. By 1860, slavery and secession were at the forefront of partisan discussions with the rise of the Republican Party. Crofts describes that "the average southerner heard repeatedly that the Republican party constituted a grave menace, that its leaders wanted to annihilate the freedom, liberty, and equality of white southerners, slaveowner and nonslaveowner alike, and that Republicans encouraged reckless fanatics who were hell-bent on unleashing slave rebels."[35] In the 1860 election, Southerners for the most part had two options. John Bell, the former Whig running on the Constitutional Unionist ticket,[36] sought to preserve the Union and took a neutral position on the slavery issue, while John C. Breckinridge of the Southern Democrats took a stronger states' rights position.[37]

Does the prevalence of slavery predict how Tennessee counties voted in these tense elections? To investigate this, figure 5.3 plots the relationships between the density of slavery (measured in the most recent census) and the proportion of the county population voting in favor of the Democratic Party in the key elections of 1852 (top left), 1856 (top right), and 1860

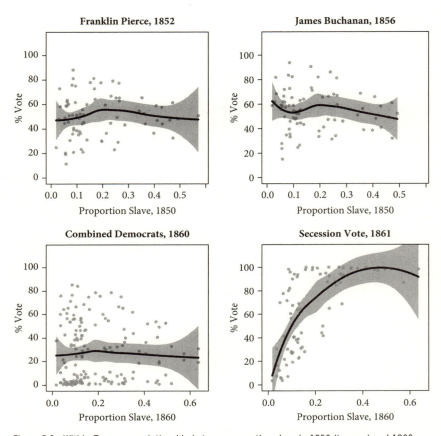

Figure 5.3. Within-Tennessee relationship between proportion slave in 1850 (top row) and 1860 (bottom row) and percentage voting for Democratic candidates in 1852–1860 and in the state-wide secession vote in 1861. Source: Clubb, Flanigan, and Zingale, *Electoral Data for Counties in the United States: Presidential and Congressional Races, 1840–1972*, U.S. Census Bureau, Nashville *Union and American*.

(bottom left), where the 1860 vote aggregates the votes for the two Democratic candidates, Breckinridge and Douglas. Each of these panels shows that there was *no relationship at all between the proportion enslaved and the presidential votes in any of these years*. These results mean we cannot rule out that white men living in slaveholding and nonslaveholding counties were voting in favor of (or against) the Democratic Party at more or less equal rates. Even in 1860, when Republican antislavery rhetoric was fairly strong, Tennessee high-slave counties like Shelby and Haywood Counties still voted at the same rates for the Constitutional Union (and at that time antisecessionist) candidate Bell than did the counties with a lower prevalence of slavery, such as East Tennessee's Knox County. Why might this be the case? As discussed above, one reason might be that the planter class had many commercial interests, leading planters to support many of the same candidates and policies as their urban counterparts.

The political alignment of the planter class came into stark relief, however, as the threat of Civil War and emancipation became increasingly salient, after the firing on Fort Sumter in April of 1861 and the subsequent call for seventy-five thousand Union troops by Abraham Lincoln. On June 8, 1861, Tennessee held a vote to secede from the United States and simultaneously join the Confederate States. The bottom right panel of figure 5.3 shows the relationship between county-level proportion slave in 1860 and this 1861 secession vote.[38] As opposed to the previous plots, which showed little or no relationships, the relationship here is strong: the *areas more dependent on slavery, mostly centered in Middle and West Tennessee, were at this point more in favor of secession.* This is worth emphasizing: in the seven months between the 1860 presidential election and this 1861 secession election, a dramatic shift took place between high-slave and low-slave areas, with low-slave areas voting against secession and high-slave areas voting overwhelmingly in favor.

EXAMINING HISTORICAL PRESIDENTIAL ELECTION RETURNS

If the example of Tennessee and its Grand Divisions is any indication, voting behavior and partisan alliances began to diverge on an issue directly related to slavery—Southern secession—in the immediate lead-up to the Civil War. But is Tennessee an outlier due to its variegated geography and (perhaps already existing) cultural and political divides? Or is it part of a broader regional tendency whereby political divisions between the high- and low-slave South intensified and increasingly turned on slavery in the years immediately leading up to and during the Civil War?

To investigate this further, we broaden our approach to examine county-level voting across the entirety of the U.S. South—specifically the county-level Democratic vote share in each presidential election between 1844 and 1964, a much longer time frame. An important point for these analyses is that the Republican Party was the more progressive party earlier in the time period, while the Democratic Party was the more racially conservative, especially in the South.[39] To take into account the possibility that former high-slave and low-slave counties could differ according to agricultural, economic, and geographical features, we again leverage our instrumental variables analyses that we discussed in the previous chapters, using a county's suitability for growing cotton as our instrument for slavery.[40]

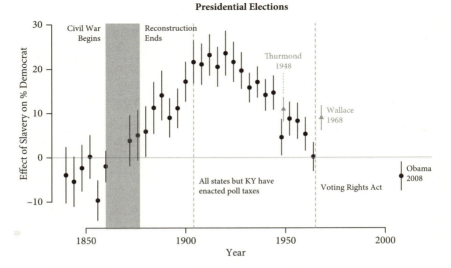

Figure 5.4. Effect of proportion slave on vote for Democratic presidential candidates in the South over time. Each point is the effect of a 25-percentage-point increase in proportion slave from separate IV models of county-level Democratic share of the presidential vote on proportion slave, using cotton suitability as an instrument. This figure reproduced from Avidit Acharya, Matthew Blackwell, and Maya Sen, "The Political Legacy of American Slavery."

In terms of the analysis, we look at each presidential election year separately. For each, we calculate the estimated effect of the county's proportion slave in 1860 on the percentage of the county voters that voted for the Democratic candidate, as estimated from the instrumental variables analysis.[41] We display these results in figure 5.4, where each point represents the effect of a twenty-five percentage-point increase in the proportion enslaved. We further illustrate the uncertainty associated with each analysis by putting vertical bands that represent ninety-five percent confidence intervals. To provide a substantive interpretation, a positive point estimate (that is, the point being above the figure's zero horizontal line) indicates that those in high-slave counties were *more* likely to vote for the Democratic presidential candidate, while a negative point estimate (below zero horizontal line) indicates that those in high-slave counties were *less* likely to vote for the Democratic candidate. (After the Civil War, a reasonable assumption is that the absence of a vote in a Democratic direction usually means a vote in a Republican direction.) When the vertical lines cross zero, it means that we cannot rule out the possibility that there is no relationship at all between a county's high- or low-slaveholding status and its vote share in that particular election. As a helpful benchmark, we delineate key points in this time frame, including the beginning of the Civil War (1861) and the end of Reconstruction (1877).[42]

As figure 5.4 shows, there is *little difference between high- and low-slave counties before the Civil War.* That is, statistically speaking, we cannot rule out that there is no difference between high-slaveholding and low-slaveholding counties in terms of Democratic vote share. In addition, and perhaps consistent with our above findings, many of the effects are below zero. This suggests that, if anything, high-slaveholding areas were *less* likely to vote in a Democratic direction (although these effects are mostly nonsignificant, meaning that we cannot rule out that there is no pattern at all here). The only prewar election where we see significant differences is in 1856, by which point the Whig Party had lost much of its base. For all of the other antebellum years, we see no statistically significant differences, indicating that the political geography of slavery that we see today had not quite coalesced before the war. We also see no difference in the 1860 election, the last before the Civil War, which makes these results consistent with our results on Tennessee. In figure 5.5, we show how slavery varies with the 1860 Breckinridge vote within states, which also shows no consistent pattern.

Returning to figure 5.4, these null findings appear to continue through the time of the Civil War (1861–65) and Reconstruction (1863–77), denoted with an overlapping shaded region.[43] Fascinatingly, however, as the South moved on from Reconstruction (ending in 1877), we see a strong move by the high-slave Black Belt toward the Democratic Party. This also coincides with increased attempts to suppress the black vote through fraud and ballot-stuffing in the early post-Reconstruction period.[44] Thus, as Redemption marched forward in the later parts of the nineteenth century, large differences emerged between high- and low-slave parts of the South.[45]

There are a few other historical patterns worth noting, which we return to in later chapters. For example, we see the difference between former slaveholding and nonslaveholding counties peak in the 1920s and 1930s and then attenuate, starting in the 1940s. Several reasons could explain this, which we explore further in part III. For now, we note that part of the attenuation could be due to the small but growing numbers of black voters—thanks to the effective registration efforts by organizations such as the National Association for the Advancement of Colored People (NAACP). We see the difference between slaveholding and nonslaveholding areas attenuate even more in the 1950s and 1960s. By 1964, we see a substantial shift by Southern Black Belt whites toward Republican Barry Goldwater, which, we believe, is indicative of the beginnings of Southern realignment, or the movement by Southern whites away from the Democratic Party and toward the Republican Party.

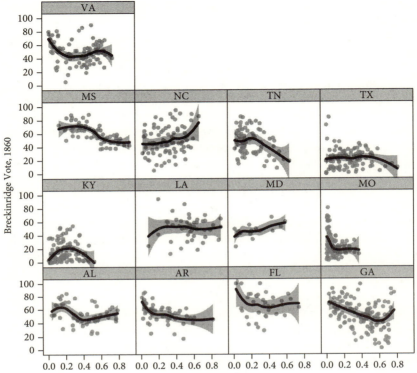

Figure 5.5. Within-state relationships between proportion slave in 1860 and percentage voting for Southern Democratic candidate John C. Breckinridge in the 1860 presidential election. Source: Clubb, Flanigan, and Zingale, *Electoral Data for Counties in the United States: Presidential and Congressional Races, 1840–1972*, U.S. Census Bureau.

5.3 WHITE ANTEBELLUM VIEWS ON RACE

Our findings in this chapter convey that regional differences in the South on political issues underwent a divisive transformation in the years leading up to the Civil War. Our results in part I, though, transcend partisan disagreements. They show that whites in former bastions of slavery are today more conservative on *racial issues*, not just in terms of their support for political parties. Given this, what do we know about racial attitudes in the antebellum period? Could an argument be made that the patterns we see in the modern day simply reflect antebellum folkways about race and not partisanship? Did the Black Belt areas of the South harbor distinct, perhaps more negative, views on race that could persist until today? These questions are worth exploring on their own. They also provide a potential explanation for the political divisions we saw in part I.

Historians and political scientists have long pointed out that white supremacy and racism were widespread in the United States.[46] This was true among planters, yeomen farmers, and even some antislavery forces.[47] For example, many slaveholders justified their "ownership" of other humans on the alleged inferiority of their race. Indeed, by the middle of the nineteenth century, slaveowners had developed a robust intellectual tradition justifying the racial nature of slavery through the supposedly "scientific" study of black people as biologically distinct. For example, the historian Walter Johnson describes the rhetoric of Samuel Cartwright, a Louisiana slave doctor and ardent proslavery theorist, as "rework[ing] enslaved residence, exhaustion, starvation into Negro-ness. Cartwright noted the unwillingness of slaves to work without being hectored, goaded, or beaten, and attributed it to biophysical inability."[48] Slaveholders like Cartwright simply believed that slavery was the only way to compel people of African descent into labor due to their biological inferiority; this fact alone was sufficient to justify the institution of slavery. Such sentiments were echoed by proslavery politicians (including those who eventually adopted antislavery positions, such as "Parson" Brownlow). For our purposes, whether these justifications were a cause or a consequence of slavery is less important than their reinforcement of the ties between slavery and racism. That is, there could exist a correlation between the prevalence of slavery and racism that could explain both antebellum differences on racial attitudes and also postbellum (and perhaps contemporary) differences as well.

What about the nonslaveholders and, in general, those in the low-slave places like Knox County? As our discussion of political behavior suggests, yeomen farmers and upcountry whites were resentful of the agricultural elite and their accumulated slave wealth—which in turn could be seen as a tacit opposition to the white supremacist foundations of the planter class. In fact, the historical record suggests strong antiblack sentiment in the upcountry areas, but one that was filtered through these economic and wealth differentials. As the historian Steven Hahn has noted, "racism and anti-planter sentiment ... could represent two sides of the same coin."[49]

Historians have pointed to at least two factors that may have contributed to antiblack sentiment in the low-slave South. First, although many white farmers in the antebellum South did not hold slaves themselves, this did not stop them from aspiring to own slaves. This led, interestingly, to these nonslaveholders borrowing political and social attitudes and behaviors from their wealthy, slaveholding neighbors. As Genovese described it, "It was, therefore, natural, as a matter of inclination and social conscience, to be ready to ride patrol, to help discipline the slaves,

and to take part in the political and police aspects of the slave regime—
in short, to think and act like slaveholders even before becoming one."[50]
The second reason that nonslaveholders generally supported slavery was the
widespread fear of a slave revolt and a more widespread slave revolution—
which would be highly threatening to whites living in both high- and
low-slave areas. The Haitian Revolution (1791–1804) saw enslaved Haitians
overthrow the white minority, a process that led to the massacre of many
former slaveholding whites.[51] The fear of this dynamic replicating itself
in the South deeply pervaded discussions of slavery and, as Denman
describes it, "the one great objection to abolition, common to virtually all
Southerners, was that several million irresponsible blacks would be turned
loose on the community ... [and] those who doubted the possibility of such
consequences were reminded of [Haiti]."[52]

5.4 ASSESSING REGIONAL VARIATION IN ANTEBELLUM RACIAL ATTITUDES

These historical accounts suggest a certain homogeneity in racial attitudes
among Southern whites before the war, with racism and antiblack attitudes
prevalent across high- and low-slave areas. But is there any way to quanti-
tatively assess what whites from different parts of the antebellum South
thought of black people? These are important questions. Our earlier results
from the modern day not only uncovered differences in contemporary
whites' partisanship but also across questions specifically related to race,
including attitudes on affirmative action, racial resentment, and overall
group feelings (via thermometer scores). Thus, perhaps any antebellum
differences attached only to attitudes on race, and not partisanship. This
would be a slightly different version of the antebellum folkways hypothesis,
one that suggests that whites living in different parts of the South always
adhered to different racial attitudes.

As we mentioned above, the historical accounts counsel against this
inference. Even so, we investigate these questions by examining several
possible indicators of how whites viewed or treated blacks, which gives
us some evidence on the antebellum folkways hypothesis with regard to
attitudes on race.[53] We do so using two novel data sources for attitudes on
race and on the treatment of enslaved people: (1) data on slave mortality,
which causally stems from forced fertility, nutrition, health care, and working conditions and serves as a useful proxy for health and living standards;
and (2) data on the number of enslaved people per slave dwelling, a proxy
for overcrowded or dangerous living conditions.[54] Neither is, of course, a
perfect measure of how whites viewed blacks. For example, these measures
focus on slaveholder and enslaved relationships, to some extent leaving
aside some whites who did not hold slaves. Nonetheless, we believe that
these measures are useful proxies—albeit imperfect ones—of antebellum
racial hostility.

VARIATION IN SLAVE MORTALITY

The 1860 U.S. Census collected data on mortality—all deaths of those living in a county in the year before the census, including slaves. One example from the mortality schedules we looked at showed the death of a one-year-old biracial ("mulatto") infant born into slavery, Henry, whose cause of death was marked as "teething" and who died after a four-day illness. We coded the overall mortality figures from original census manuscripts documenting deaths such as this one in order to compare the relative mortality of slaves to whites in 1860 and how this varied from county to county.[55]

We use this measure as a proxy for how enslaved people were treated by local whites since these deaths could be caused by poor nutrition, unsafe working conditions, a lack of medical attention, or excessive punishment.[56] Although not perfect measures, these could be an indication of negative white attitudes toward African American people, especially with regard to nutritional support and safe working conditions. In addition, because we take this variable relative to the white mortality rate, we effectively adjust for any between-county factors that raise or lower the death rate for all people (such as disease, drought, heat, rainfall, or other climatic conditions).

The results are presented in figure 5.6, which plots the county-level relative slave mortality against the county-level proportion slave (in 1860). The fact that the relative slave mortality is, on average, above zero indicates that slaves had higher mortality rates than whites, which is to be expected.[57] In terms of the substantive implications, if the white planters who owned slaves in the Black Belt were more cruel to the enslaved (which would perhaps be evidence of more racist attitudes), then we should expect to see a *positive* relationship between the density of slavery and relative slave mortality. However, as figure 5.6 shows, we do not see this: the smoothed line is mostly flat across the different kinds of counties. This means that we cannot rule out that there is *no relationship between the prevalence of slavery and relative mortality of enslaved people.* We take this as evidence that the treatment of enslaved workers, their health, and their mortality seems not to have been markedly worse in areas with a high prevalence of slavery, such as the agricultural centers of the Black Belt. And while this does not necessarily show that whites' attitudes toward blacks were homogeneous across the South, it does point to a lack of difference between high- and low-slave areas in terms of how slaves were treated.

REGIONAL VARIATION IN SLAVE DWELLINGS

Slave mortality is a complicated measure, confounded by factors such as the age and gender of enslaved workers.[58] We therefore supplement this

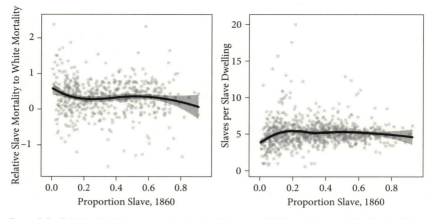

Figure 5.6. Relationship between county density of slavery in 1860 and the log of the black-white mortality ratio in the county in 1860 (left) and the average number of slaves per slave dwelling on county farms in 1860 (right). Source: 1860 U.S. Census, Population, Mortality, and Slave Schedules.

analysis by looking at another measure of how slaves were treated, which is how many slaves lived in a particular building on the average farm in a county—that is, the density of slaves within the slave quarters.

Slaves were often housed with immediate family members—fathers, mothers, and children—so larger families would mean more people living within the same quarters. However, this was not always the case, and substantial variation exists in how many slaves (on average) were housed per dwelling; fewer people per household would suggest more affluence and better living conditions. Thus, in terms of the final measures, seeing large numbers of enslaved people living per dwelling would suggest one of two factors (or both): (1) more density in each dwelling, perhaps a sign of more crowded conditions and less room and consideration of privacy; or (2) larger families or larger units of people living within familial networks, which would perhaps suggest more aggressive strategies to try to increase the number of enslaved people per farm.[59] As before, if the white planters who owned slaves in the high-slave Black Belt counties were more cruel to the enslaved, and more focused on rapidly increasing slave fertility (without investing in living conditions and housing), then we should expect to see a *positive* relationship between the density of slavery and the density of dwellings.

Figure 5.6 shows the relationships between the density of 1860 slavery (on the horizontal axis) and the average number of enslaved people living per dwelling in the county (on the vertical axis). Note that when there are fewer than five to ten percent enslaved in a county, the slaves per dwelling is slightly lower than the overall average; however, it is difficult to say whether this reflects the small numbers of slaves in these counties or actually better living conditions. However, and again surprisingly, there is basically no relationship between the prevalence of slavery and the resident density of slave quarters. This analysis reinforces the point made by the mortality analysis: in the antebellum period, the racism inherent in treatment of slaves was fairly constant across areas of the South with different densities of slavery.[60]

5.5 CONCLUSION

In this chapter, we considered the antebellum folkways hypothesis and its variants. This is the idea that any contemporary differences in political culture across regions of the South are long-standing and owe more to the types of white people who settled the various parts of the South. (For example, Fischer argues that settlers from different parts of Great Britain brought with them different cultures, which then inform the character of the places in the South that they settled.) This argument is consistent with our arguments about behavioral path dependence; the antebellum hypothesis simply posits that these differences are much more long-standing and predate slavery. However, the antebellum hypothesis would not view slavery and its collapse as a possible defining point—a critical juncture—that drives differences in political attitudes. That is, under the antebellum folkways hypothesis, slavery was itself a possible consequence of differences in political and racial attitudes, and not necessarily a catalyst in leading this divergence.

The findings in this chapter challenge this view. First, in terms of political attitudes and partisan affiliations, our analyses are consistent with the work of historians, and suggest that both high- and low-slave parts of the antebellum South had varying political and partisan preferences. Whigs drew support from Black Belt counties, yes, but they also drew support from upcountry counties. Likewise, Southern Democrats received support from low-slave areas and also from high-slave areas. We see similar patterns when it comes to legislation related to slavery. Specifically, both high- and low-slave areas across the South broadly supported policies that eased the expansion of slavery. High-slave areas did so because the agricultural elite supported the maintenance of slavery; low-slave areas did so because subsistence farmers and others believed they would economically benefit from the expansion of slavery. Thus, to the extent that political differences existed in the South, they were largely orthogonal to the actual prevalence of slavery. This is evidence against differences in contemporary political attitudes simply dating back to the antebellum political climate.

Second, our findings about Southern racial attitudes supports this argument. Although we might think that high-slave areas—because of both their intimacy with the institution of slavery and the intellectual justifications necessary to propagate it—may have developed more strongly held racist views, we see limited evidence of this. In our analyses, enslaved people who lived in high-slave areas—including the counties throughout the Black Belt that were home to the large plantations—died at the same rates as enslaved people living elsewhere. In another comparison, the number of enslaved people per dwelling—perhaps a proxy for poor or overcrowded conditions—also varied little from high-slave to low-slave areas. This suggests that hostility or indifference toward the living conditions of enslaved people was fairly uniform across the South in this time period—perhaps a reason why, as historians have argued, Southern upcountry whites aspired to owning slaves as a path for upward mobility. It was only the sharp increase in the price of slaves in the years leading up to the Civil War, combined with the threat of emancipation, that triggered a growing political gap between the Black Belt and the upcountry.

The patterns we have explored in this chapter leave us with a puzzle—if most of the South, whether slaveholding or not, was invested in slavery and immersed in a political and racial ideology that supported it, then why do we see differences across the South *today* in terms of political and racial views? If not in the antebellum period, when did this variation in the political culture of the South actually appear? The changed environment around the time of the Civil War and emancipation points us toward one clue. After emancipation, the Southern economy—and in particular, the Southern Black Belt economy—changed radically. As the historian C. Vann Woodward noted of this tumultuous time period, "the temporary anarchy that followed the collapse of the old discipline produced a state of mind bordering on hysteria among Southern white people."[61] As we discuss in the following chapter, this temporary anarchy gave way to a systematic subjugation of African Americans over the century at the hands of white political and economic elite—and it did so with particular force and severity in those areas of the South that had been previously reliant on slavery as an economic engine. Thus, our answer to why we see political differences today, whereas we do not see it in the antebellum period, draws in large measure on how this postslavery system of racial subjugation evolved and came to exist. This is when the process of behavioral path dependence appears to have started.

CHAPTER SIX

EMANCIPATION AS A CRITICAL JUNCTURE AND THE TIMING OF DIVERGENCE

"In those days, it was 'Kill a mule,
buy a mule. Kill a n*gger, buy another.' They had to have a license
to kill anything but a n*gger. We
was always in season."

Shelby "Poppa Jazz" Brown, Blues Musician

Elaine, Arkansas, is a modest rural city with a population of fewer than one thousand people (as of the 2000 U.S. Census) on the banks of the Mississippi River, about an hour's drive south of Memphis on the border with Mississippi. It is small and mostly poor, with close to forty percent of town residents living below the poverty line; around half of Elaine's residents are African American. In many respects, the town is typical of modern-day Delta poverty: although the town is in prime "King Cotton" land (Phillips County, 58 percent enslaved in 1860), just a handful of shuttered brick buildings dot the downtown, interspersed with empty lots and small dwellings. The town has dwindled to the point where its school district was folded in 2006 into the nearby Marvell School district, also serving Phillips County. These schools today are approximately eighty-five percent black and ninety-six percent of students are on free or reduced-fee lunch plans. A whites only "segregation" academy, the private Marvell Academy, opened in 1966 to serve Phillips County's white children in 1966; as of 2010, that school was still exclusively white.[1]

Many Americans may not have heard of Elaine, Arkansas, or of Phillips County. But the town of Elaine was, in 1919, the location of the largest mass lynching of African Americans in recorded American history. Like other massacres before it, the Elaine "negro uprising" started as a labor gathering. Many black sharecroppers from Phillips County had not received their settlements from white landowners and were considering participating in organized activities led by the Progressive Farmers and Household

Union of America, an African American labor movement.[2] On the night of September 30th, a group of black sharecroppers gathered in an Elaine church to discuss developing issues; hearing of this, two white men tried to enter to disrupt the gathering, but were stopped by guards. Shots were fired, one of the men was killed, and, within one day, whites from around the area began pouring in to put down the rumored "black insurrection."[3] Over the course of the next day, hundreds of blacks were dragged from hiding, shot, and killed, with some estimates putting the number of dead at over three hundred. Ultimately, the disorder was quelled with the arrival of five hundred federal troops, who blamed blacks for the unrest and immediately put dozens into stockades and under arrest. Several African Americans were eventually put on trial and convicted of murder, with the case rising all the way to the U.S. Supreme Court; it was only the governor's eventual (and very discreet) release of the defendants that spared their lives.[4]

In this chapter, we explore the economic and political environment in the Black Belt around the time of emancipation and through the first half of the twentieth century. Why it is that racial violence—like the Elaine Massacre and other labor-related mob activities—was not only tolerated but also promoted during this time? Why did these patterns of racial hostility appear to strengthen over time following slavery's collapse? What did this mean for the reinforcement of political and racial attitudes? Building off of the conceptual argument in chapter 2, our response to these questions is that emancipation was a *critical juncture* that dramatically changed the political and economic landscape of the South. Emancipation was a shock that reconfigured economic and political incentives and led Southern whites to make choices that altered the path of Southern society, triggering a set of rippling effects. As historians of the South such as C. Vann Woodward have argued, this time period after emancipation and leading up to the turn of the century marked a transition point for Southern society, one in which more racially tolerant paths—which Woodward refers to as "forgotten alternatives"—were set aside in favor of a trajectory that led the South, and in particular the Black Belt, toward Jim Crow.[5] This produced divergent paths in the development of Southern political and racial attitudes.

We develop these ideas by documenting how parts of the South varied locally in the degree of political, social, and economic oppression of African Americans during this time period. In the face of the political and economic changes brought about by the abolition of slavery, the Southern white agricultural and business elite became desperate to hold onto a large and cheap labor force to support the labor-intensive cotton economy, and—in the fallout of the South's defeat in the Civil War—were also desperate to maintain political power. Over time, motivated by these interests, white society began to respond to the abolition of slavery with local institutions, both formal and informal, as well as violence— political intimidation, lynchings, and racial terrorism (such as the Elaine

Massacre)—to meet these political and economic objectives. As evidence, we show that parts of the Deep South that were the most reliant on slavery—and on the labor provided by African Americans—were also those most likely to inflict particularly severe types of economic and political oppression during the Jim Crow era. For example, the former slaveholding bastions within states like Alabama and Mississippi were also those that most strongly supported enactments of regressive state constitutions; these early twentieth-century state constitutions codified many provisions that would go on to form the bedrock of Southern Jim Crow. We also document that these areas of the Black Belt were those most likely to have black farmers living in poverty. In addition, we show that these areas were locus points of racial violence and lynchings, which grew at significant rates during this period. As we show using quantitative data (as well as more anecdotal examples like the Elaine Massacre), the highest rates of lynchings took place where slaveholding had been the most prevalent.

We organize this chapter in the following manner. First, we discuss the radically changed landscape after emancipation, focusing on the new economic environment as well as the new political anxiety, setting the groundwork for thinking of this time period as a "critical juncture." Next, we focus on white responses to this new institutional environment. We organize this discussion around two themes: (1) violence, both politically and economically motivated, and (2) institutional responses, both formal and informal, which include Black Codes and early Jim Crow laws, the co-optation of the criminal justice system to be antiblack, and antiblack social norms such as segregation. Because our focus is on regional variation, we explain throughout—and also document with quantitative evidence—how these responses were more forceful in the former high-slave South of the Black Belt.

This evidence, taken together with historical accounts, points to the idea that the time period between emancipation and the turn of the twentieth century was pivotal, one in which the old racial order was overturned and, in its place, a divergence in attitudes and behaviors between the Black Belt and other parts of the South was established. This sets the stage for the analysis of behavioral path dependence in Southern white attitudes, which we take up in subsequent chapters.

6.1 THE POLITICAL ECONOMY OF EMANCIPATION

It is difficult for us living in the present day to imagine the kind of grave danger felt by the white elite—particularly agricultural and business elite—in the years following the Civil War. The emancipation of enslaved people was a major event that dramatically changed the economic and political landscape of the South.[6] These changes led to three sets of interlocking incentives that drove whites to subjugate blacks:

- Economic incentives: white planters and businessmen continued to demand cheap labor, which now had to be negotiated with freedmen.
- Political incentives: freed blacks had the votes to alter the balance of political power and, in some cases, completely rule local areas.
- Social incentives: the end of slavery had equalized the legal status of poor whites and poor blacks, leading to a large loss in relative status.

Each of these incentives operated to some extent throughout the South. They took on the greatest urgency, however, where the white community was reliant on the institution of slavery and the labor provided by formerly enslaved people. The more that the local white elite had to lose as a result of a free, mobile, and politically active black labor force, the more intense was their response to emancipation. We discuss the historical context surrounding the first two sets of incentives here and then return to the social incentives when discussing segregation and racial etiquette below.

THE NEW ECONOMIC LANDSCAPE

To understand the economic incentives of the white elite, it is important to understand how the Civil War and emancipation changed the economic landscape of the South. Simply put, the South was devastated by the Civil War. In 1860, the average value of an improved acre of farmland was estimated to be roughly $30 but was reduced to less than $15 in 1870, both in 1859 dollars.[7] In 1857, per capita income for whites was $125 but, by 1879, it was $80, again in 1859 dollars.[8] The average wealth of farms in the South in 1860 was around $22,819, but fell to $2,340 by 1870 (both in 1870 dollars), an astounding drop-off; much of this loss came from plantation farms, which had an average prewar value of $81,382 (again in 1870 dollars).[9] Southern Confederacy currency and bonds were rendered completely worthless by the war, making credit markets ineffective.[10]

These losses were, moreover, concentrated in the regions of the South most dependent on slavery, meaning that the need to secure cheap labor from previously enslaved blacks was most dire for plantation owners living in areas that had high slave concentrations. In figure 6.1, we show the relationship between the density of slavery and the percentage change in total farm value in a county between 1860 and 1870.[11] The figure shows, quite simply, that the economic threat from emancipation and by the freeing of labor was not uniform across the South. To the contrary,

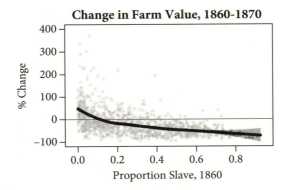

Figure 6.1. Proportion slave in 1860 and the percentage change in total farm value in a county between 1860 and 1870 (excluding Texas and one outlier county in Arkansas). Source: U.S. Census.

predictably—and consistent with the arguments made by economists—emancipation destroyed the value of the areas where slavery was the most prevalent.

Southern whites also lost what was perhaps their most valuable asset: over four million enslaved laborers.[12] In the immediate aftermath of the war, "[l]arge numbers of colored people left the plantations; many flocked to our military posts and camps to obtain the certainty of their freedom, and others walked away merely for the purpose of leaving the places on which they had been held in slavery."[13] The consequences of such actions were nothing less than devastating for Southern whites, who depended on high labor productivity as well as a steady supply of workers—a supply that had previously included women and children. As W.E.B. Du Bois later wrote about this time period, "[o]ne would not dream that the United States was on the verge of the greatest labor revolution it had seen."[14]

The labor system of the South had to change rapidly in response. Before the war, the system of gang-labor resting on forced (that is, enslaved) labor was widespread, but it was unclear whether the same institution could be successful after emancipation. In 1865 and 1866, after emancipation, many white landowners hired wage-laborers to work in gangs similar to the slave era; however, by the 1870s, with labor in comparatively low supply, newly freed black workers started to demand payment in the form of a share of the crops produced.[15] Thus, by 1870 hiring wage workers was very rare.[16] Sharecropping and tenant farming emerged quickly as an alternative system, wherein tenant farmers were leased a plot of land in exchange for a portion of the crops produced. The newly gained ability of black farmers to quit employment or leave a tenant arrangement after the crop season gave blacks a true, if often limited, ability to negotiate over their working conditions.

The economic reverberations of this "labor revolution" were felt with particular acuity in the slave-reliant Black Belt, where whites had an especially urgent economic need to maintain control of black laborers. In these counties, the coercion of the master-slave relationship would have to give way to the negotiation of an employer-employee relationship and consequently a greater share of the surplus to the black worker. White planters and businessmen had strong incentives to weaken workers' bargaining positions and prevent their ascension up the socioeconomic ladder. The intense labor demands of the various Southern industries meant that the wealth and profit of the white elite depended on maintaining control over the labor force. As Du Bois noted, "If all labor, black as well as white, became free—were given schools and the right to vote—what control could or should be set to the power and action of these laborers? ... [H]ow would property and privileged be protected?"[17]

THE NEW POLITICAL LANDSCAPE

Along with these economic concerns, whites throughout the South faced strong threats to their political supremacy. First, the ruling elites faced the threat from the changing balance in the relationship between the North and South. Prior to the war, each of the four million Southern blacks was counted as "three-fifths of a person" (per the Three-Fifths Clause of the U.S. Constitution). This had made the total number of seats allocated in Congress to Southern politicians proportional to the "10.5 million Southerners" they represented, but in reality these seats represented only the eight million whites who could vote. This meant that white Southerners were overrepresented in Congress. If blacks were given the vote and the full privileges of citizenship, the South would come to represent a total of twelve million people in Congress, but a significant number of these seats could presumably represent blacks. Not only would this reduce the representation of Southern whites, it would give Southern blacks a political voice in Congress, which they could use to influence policy, including the federal government's policy with respect to the South.

Second, in terms of the newly enfranchised freedmen, areas that were more reliant on slave labor were those where blacks could outvote whites by large margins. In some areas of the Black Belt—for example in Concordia Parish, Louisiana (ninety percent enslaved in 1860), and Sharkey County, Mississippi (eighty-two percent enslaved), blacks outnumbered whites by a ratio of at least nine to one. In other areas, for example, Leflore County, Mississippi (seventy-two percent enslaved), blacks constituted a significant majority.[18] Indeed, in around nineteen percent of Southern counties, blacks constituted greater than fifty percent of the population at the time of emancipation, meaning that enfranchisement very clearly called into question whites' political control, especially at the local level. In these areas, Black Belt whites might have had to submit themselves to local black authorities in the role of tax collector, sheriff, or board supervisor. As Morgan Kousser points out, doing so "would be inescapable symbolic reminders of the dominance of a race that all Southern whites believed to be inferior."[19] Although it is difficult to pinpoint with certainty how many of these eligible blacks actually voted during Reconstrution, by some estimates, "[a]t the high point of southern black voting during Reconstruction, about two-thirds of eligible black males cast ballots in presidential and gubernatorial contests."[20] In addition, in the decade following the end of the Civil War, approximately fifteen hundred blacks held political office in the South.[21]

The Black Belt white elite also faced the threat of a budding political alliance between newly enfranchised freedmen, poorer whites, and whites living in former low-slave areas. Before the Civil War, state legislatures in the South were largely malapportioned to the advantage of the Black Belt whites, due to the counting of slaves. The planter class of these areas used this power to dominate state politics, often to the bitter exclusion of poorer and upcountry whites. The enfranchisement of millions of freedmen provided the possibility of a new ruling coalition—biracial and interested in populist, redistributive policies that could benefit those with less wealth and fewer resources.[22] Indeed, through emancipation and early Reconstruction, it was far from clear whether the fate of poor blacks and poor whites would coevolve to unite around their shared economic interests to produce a "class-based" Southern politics, or whether their fates would diverge.[23]

THE EXAMPLE OF POSTBELLUM VIRGINIA

Postbellum Virginia provides an account of how black voting had the potential to undermine the uneasy political relationship between white voters across formerly high- and low-slave areas. In the late 1870s and early 1880s, two factions of Virginia's Conservative Party fought along lines that closely mirrored the national parties of the day. Virginia's Readjuster Party, a group that would eventually merge with the national Republican Party, sought to expand the scope of public spending in the state and fund a host of social programs; on the other hand, the Conservative Party sought to pay down the prewar debt. What is remarkable (and short-lived) about this division is how the Readjusters mobilized both black and white voters, going so far as to pay the poll taxes of black voters whom the Conservatives tried to disenfranchise. This led to high rates of

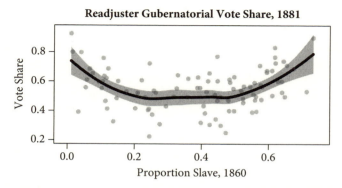

Figure 6.2. Proportion slave in 1860 and the vote share for the Readjuster candidate William Cameron in the 1881 Virginia gubernatorial election. Source: U.S. Census, Clubb, Flanigan, and Zingale, *Electoral Data for Counties in the United States: Presidential and Congressional Races, 1840–1972.*

black voting in the former slaveholding counties and a broad coalition that would challenge the white planter elite and fund a large increase in black schools in the early 1880s.[24] This black and upcountry white coalition can be seen in figure 6.2, which shows where Readjuster Governor William Cameron drew his support in the 1881 gubernatorial election. The nonlinear relationship hints that Cameron's support was high in formerly low-slave counties and also in formerly high-slave counties— suggesting support among whites in low-slave counties and blacks in high-slave counties. (Note that we do not address here the possibility of ballot-stuffing or voter intimidation.) By contrast, there is less support in areas in the middle range of the slaveholding distribution.

These data highlight the possibility of a biracial coalition between upcountry whites and Black Belt freedmen. From the perspective of the Black Belt white elite, this potential coalition represented a significant broader threat: if freedmen and white Republicans could join political forces, it might threaten the political control that the plantation and agricultural regions had enjoyed in the antebellum period.[25] Given the potential for these coalitions, it is not surprising that in both Virginia and the broader South, white elites responded with violence, intimidation, and electoral fraud.[26] However, it is clear that the inherent threat of these types of political coalitions were a direct consequence of emancipation and Reconstruction and were perennial thorns in the sides of the conservative elite of the South from the end of the Civil War until those elites were able to disenfranchise the newly freed blacks—a goal through the late nineteenth century.

6.2 WHITE RESPONSES TO EMANCIPATION AND THE RISE OF JIM CROW

How did Southern whites respond to these significant economic and political threats? By and large, the white elite attempted to recreate a racial hierarchy or reinstate features of antebellum life shortly after emancipation. During Reconstruction, however, the Southern white elite were thwarted in their response by the Union army, federal government, Radical Republicans, Freedmen's Bureaus, and newly freed blacks themselves.[27] As federal intervention waned toward the end of Reconstruction, Redeemers began to put into place the system of institutionalized white supremacy that came to be known as Jim Crow. Although that system took many forms, it was felt with particular force early in the twentieth century with regard to racial violence, political disenfranchisement, and social and cultural oppression. These responses were both a product of, and a mechanism to reinforce, the Southern racial hierarchy. In addition, these were patterns that *varied locally*, with the strongest forms of oppression in the Black Belt suggesting the increased importance of localized institutions and norms.

WHITE RESPONSES THROUGH RACIALLY TARGETED VIOLENCE

During Reconstruction, racial violence took on a more systematic, organized tone than it ever had with the rise of white supremacist vigilante groups like the Ku Klux Klan (KKK), founded by six ex-Confederate army soldiers in Pulaski, Tennessee (Giles County, forty-one percent enslaved in 1860), in 1865.[28] At its origin, the original Klan was particularly active in high-slave areas outside of the traditional Black Belt, but its "rides" soon took it deep into Mississippi, Alabama, South Carolina, and Louisiana.[29] Ultimately, "[t]he Ku Klux organization flourished principally in middle and northern Alabama, notably in Montgomery, Greene, Tuscaloosa, and Pickens counties," all relatively high-slave areas in the antebellum period.[30] In addition, there is evidence from various historical accounts that the Klan and other white supremacist organizations, though most active in high-slave areas outside of the traditional Black Belt, then made substantial inroads into formerly high-slave areas in Mississippi, Alabama, and Louisiana.[31] Over time, the Klan's influence receded somewhat, although the rate of lynchings was still high through the early twentieth century. As figure 6.3 shows using data from Beck and Tolnay, lynchings of blacks peaked in the post-Reconstruction period and then slowly tapered off through the Jim Crow period.[32]

Whether organized or not, racial violence had several objectives. One was economic: violence could intimidate blacks from organizing for better labor conditions or prevent them from advancing up the economic ladder.

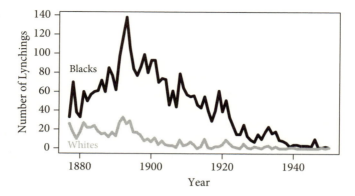

Figure 6.3. Number of lynchings of whites and blacks, 1877–1950. Source: Beck and Tolnay, "The Killing Fields of the Deep South: The Market for Cotton and the Lynching of Blacks, 1882–1930."

Both of these were a threat to the white elite (especially planters and merchants who profited from black agricultural labor) because they would increase the value of the outside option, and thus the wages, of black labor. If a black farmer could buy land and farm it for self-sufficiency, then he may demand quite a bit to forgo this opportunity to work the cotton fields for a white landowner with large holdings.

To this end, there is evidence that violence and threats of violence were directed with particular force toward African Americans looking to acquire or purchase land, which was seen by many at this time as being important for economic independence. By the time of Reconstruction, however, Southern credit markets were in shambles and, with no acquired or inherited wealth, freedmen had no means with which to acquire land. This gave whites a powerful position vis-à-vis blacks, and violence was used to maintain that advantage. Actual or threats of violence was levied against both blacks who attempted to buy land and whites who attempted to sell it. Roger Ransom and Richard Sutch recount one observer, who noted that "[i]n many portions of the Mississippi Valley the feeling against any ownership of soil by negroes is so strong, that the man who should sell small tracts to them would be in actual personal danger," while another observer noted that, in Mississippi's "Winston County [forty-three percent enslaved in 1860] a dozen men were whipped, and the only charge against them was that they had bought land."[33] Black education, another path out of poverty, was a target, with black and white teachers being lynched or threatened for trying to educate black students.[34]

In addition, and perhaps more cynically, rampant violence gave many whites the opportunity to offer blacks the benefits of their privately provided "protection" from the violence, usually in exchange for lowered wages or other labor agreements. This sort of arrangement, which was more prevalent in the Black Belt areas, had the tendency of tying black workers to specific white landowners, further suppressing blacks' bargaining power and economic mobility.[35]

Other qualitative accounts document that blacks who exhibited economic success or engaged in labor organizing were particular targets—as the example of Arkansas's Elaine Massacre of 1919 shows. As Eric Foner notes, "the most 'offensive' blacks of all seemed to be those who achieved some modicum of economic success, for, as a white farmer commented, the Klan 'do not like to see the negro go ahead.' "[36] One example of this was the practice of "whitecapping," or the targeted assassinations of prosperous blacks, sometimes carried out in a carnival-like environment but also often done quietly and in cold blood—a style designed to be maximally effective and instill the most fear among potential targets. The "Whitecaps" operated somewhat similarly to the Ku Klux Klan and were comprised of marginal white sharecroppers; their targets were often affluent or up-and-coming blacks, and they had the specific purpose of attempting "to force a person to abandon his home and property; it meant driving Negroes off land they owned or rented."[37]

In addition, quantitative studies have found support for a relationship between poorer economic conditions and incidences of lynching and other racial violence. For example, Beck and Tolnay find a substantial relationship between the market for cotton—specifically decreased market value for cotton combined with inflationary pressures—and increased incidences of lynching.[38] Their conclusion is that this kind of racially driven mob violence was caused by these poor financial conditions, which in turn flamed racial competition. The fact that cotton decreased steadily in price from 1881 to the turn of the century no doubt furthered these tensions.[39] Taken together, these forces actually gave white landowners—and increasingly, white industrialists as well—a strong incentive to promote (or at least not prevent) the violence that was being perpetrated against blacks, both by organizations like the KKK and by less organized interests. Of paramount importance was white farmers' ongoing need to secure and maintain control over a crucial supply of cheap labor.

Violence was also levied against blacks trying to exercise political rights, particularly in the Black Belt and toward blacks voting for the racially progressive Republican Party. At one level, organized violence was used as a straightforward weapon to prevent and intimidate blacks from exercising their suffrage. Foner notes, "[i]n effect, the Klan was a military force serving the interests of the Democratic party, the planter class, and all those who designed the restoration of white supremacy."[40] However, at another level, racial violence was deployed strategically to effectuate corruption and ballot stuffing; this ensured that black votes "counted" against their economic and political interests (when it was tolerated that they would vote at all). For example, Valelly observes remarkably high pro-Democratic voting in deep Black Belt areas after the enactment of the Fifteenth Amendment and before effective black disenfranchisement.[41] This puzzle suggests that blacks were either voting against their own economic and political interests or (more likely) that they were the targets of corruption and violent intimidation.[42] As others have noted, this kind of political corruption was particularly rampant in the former high-slave holding areas of the Black Belt, beginning as soon as interventions began allowing blacks to exercise any kind of suffrage.[43] Others have found that lynchings increased with not just depressed economic conditions but also populist challenges, and that there were more lynchings of blacks in election years.[44]

Lastly, violence was also used as a strategy both to unify whites and to maintain social control over blacks who overstepped certain unwritten boundaries. This was particularly so in the early twentieth century, after the organized efforts of the Klan receded somewhat. For example, in a detailed study of Southern lynchings, Tolnay and Beck write that, "[l]ethal mob violence for seemingly minor infractions of the caste codes of behavior was more fundamental for maintaining terroristic social control than punishment for what would seem to be more serious violations of the criminal codes."[45] Many of these lynchings were done in a "carnival-like" atmosphere, with cheering crowds and with displays of mutilations, followed by the selling of souvenir body parts for both entertainment and profit.[46] These public displays of violence point to the idea that the very act of lynching actually brought whites together in a shared mob mentality, reinforcing a sense of white dominance. Racial violence was, therefore, an important component of the development and path dependence of antiblack attitudes, even among poor whites who did not always share the incentives for labor coercion and disenfranchisement that the Southern white elite faced. In addition, this sort of racial violence—which often had strong community participation—was an important mechanism of intergenerational socialization. As authors like DuRocher and Ritterhouse document, white children were often present at displays of racial violence and, in some striking cases (for example, the lynching of Jesse Washington in Waco, Texas, in 1919, or the lynching of Rubin Stacy in Ft. Lauderdale, Florida, in 1935) they were also active participants.[47] We discuss this further in chapter 7.

SLAVE LEGACY AND LYNCHINGS

How do these lynchings relate to the legacy of slavery in the South? If economic threats led to increases in racial violence, we might expect that lynchings were higher in high-slave areas, which had a stronger reliance on black labor. On the other hand, other regional differences could push

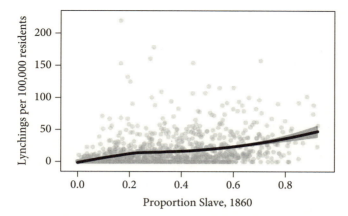

Figure 6.4. Relationship between proportion slave in 1860 and total black lynchings from 1877 to 1950 per 100,000 county residents in 1920. Source: Beck and Tolnay, "Confirmed Inventory of Southern Lynch Victims, 1882–1930."

in the opposite direction. For example, a well regarded early twentieth-century study argued that the blacks of the Black Belt were, ironically, among the safest from racial violence. In these areas, the author wrote, "the Negro tenants and wage hands are practically indispensable. Here the variant economic and cultural levels of the mass of whites and the mass of Negroes are well defined and far removed."[48]

To investigate this, we examine data on lynchings in the late nineteenth and early twentieth centuries.[49] We note that like many of the historical data that we work with, the lynchings data could be measured with error in ways that could call into question the veracity of the inferences. Lynchings were highly political, and implicit cooperation among white elites (including newspaper reporters, from which some of this data is gathered) appears to have resulted in the systematic undercounting of lynchings targeted at racial or ethnic minorities. By some estimates, the lynchings of Latinos or people of Latin American origins, Asian Americans, and Native Americans were severely *under* counted—perhaps by as much as fifty percent—because they were nearly always included in "nonwhite" categories.[50]

We therefore examine the relationship between the proportion of the county that was enslaved in 1860 and the rate of lynchings per capita. Figure 6.4 presents these results, with the proportion of the county that was enslaved in 1860 on the horizontal axis and the number of lynchings over the entire period of the data (1877–1950) per one hundred thousand residents in 1920 on the vertical axis. The figure confirms the hypothesis that the number of lynchings is *greater in counties that had high slave proportions in 1860*.[51] This result is in line with our other findings: there is more racial violence in areas previously more reliant on slave labor. This is also in line with the literature suggesting that economic concerns might play an important role in the expression of acts of violence: the more important black labor was to an area (as it was in the Black Belt), the more racial violence would be used as a tool to maintain, police, and secure that labor. As Raper noted as an aside in his study of lynchings, "[t]he Black Belt lynching is something of a business transaction," and the "whites, there, chiefly of the planter class and consciously dependent upon the Negro for labor, lynch him to conserve traditional landlord-tenant relations rather than to wreak vengeance upon his race."[52]

WHITE RESPONSES IN LOCAL LAWS AND INSTITUTIONS

In addition to violence, Southern white elites established local laws and institutions (both formal and informal) with the purpose of securing cheap labor to sustain the cotton economy and keeping blacks politically neutralized. As before, the urgency with which these measures were approached varied according to the economic and political necessity; for that reason, as we show below, Black Belt counties and Black Belt elites took the lead in promulgating these sorts of antiblack measures. Although there are a wide variety of laws and regulations that fell into these categories, we discuss the four most important: Black Codes and early Jim Crow laws, the local co-optation of the criminal justice system, voter disenfranchisement measures (such as poll taxes and literacy tests), and informal institutions or social norms that promoted the maintenance of the Southern racial hierarchy.

BLACK CODES AND JIM CROW

All states in the former Confederacy enacted and tried to enforce "Black Codes," many of which were enacted shortly after emancipation in 1865 and 1866.[53] The aims varied. Many Black Codes contained antivagrancy statutes or ordinances, which made it illegal for freed blacks to loiter or appear out of work. Mississippi's Black Code, enacted in 1865, decreed that "[e]very freedman, free negro and mulatto shall, on the second Monday of January, one thousand eight hundred and sixty-six, and annually thereafter, have a lawful home or employment, and shall have written evidence thereof."[54] Failure to have such "lawful employment" was punishable by arrest and imprisonment. Other Black Codes authorized or called for convict leasing, or the leasing out of imprisoned people (mostly men) to private companies at extremely low costs.[55] Still others limited African Americans' abilities to keep and bear arms, inflated punishments for theft (or alleged theft), and criminalized insolvency and the carrying of debt.

Although disparate in their immediate goals, the overarching aim of the Black Codes was to try to address economic issues, in particular blacks' perceived unwillingness to work and to labor. One backer of the Georgia Black Codes wrote in their defense that he simply had "seen how indolent and worthless the negro has become, in nine cases out of ten, since his elevation to freedom."[56]

Despite the intent (both implicit and explicit) of these Black Codes, many of them were rendered invalid by the federal government or unenforceable by federal institutions.[57] What the federal government could not do, however, was thwart whites' growing informal and socially rooted responses to emancipation. Indeed, the response of conservative white Democrats during Reconstruction was often to attempt local discrimination by adapting the local judicial system for white supremacist purposes. In some Democratic counties, blacks were excluded from juries, endured extreme punishment for small crimes, or faced local judges who ignored the state or federal laws.[58] The social consequences of such behavior cannot be understated. As an editor of the *New Orleans Tribune* observed in an 1865 editorial, the Black Codes in totality resembled in many ways the "old regime." Slavery, he wrote "is abolished; but the ordinances of police enacted to uphold slavery have not been revoked. And according to that reasoning a man may be whipped in the parish prison, at the demand of any other man, provided the victim be called not a slave, but a freedman."[59]

Following the withdrawal of the federal government from Southern affairs after the Compromise of 1877, Southern states became more aggressive in pursuing antiblack legislation. A number of these laws were enacted shortly after the Supreme Court's ruling in *Plessy v. Ferguson* in 1896 upholding the doctrine of "separate but equal," but many were also enacted later, on a rolling basis, as social customs changed and the federal courts decided how far white Southerners could go in instituting segregation, disenfranchisement, and violence. For example, Mississippi and Alabama enacted dozens of laws that could be described as "Jim Crow" statutes between the end of Reconstruction and the Supreme Court's decision in *Brown v. Board of Education* in 1954. Mississippi's Black Codes, passed in 1865, prohibited, among other things, interracial marriage and the owning of firearms by blacks. Moving forward past Reconstruction and into Redemption, the 1890 Mississippi constitution required separate educational institutions for blacks and whites, while laws in 1892 and 1906 called for "separate but equal" accommodations in railroads and streetcars, respectively. The Mississippi prohibition of the marriage between blacks and whites was furthered by laws in 1892, 1906, and 1930. Following Mississippi, Alabama banned interracial marriage in its own Black Codes of 1866 (which was reinforced by a subsequent 1923 law) and required segregated education for whites and blacks in the 1901 constitution.

(We discuss the topic of Alabama's 1901 constitutional convention, which was called specifically to enact white supremacist policies, below.) Jails were segregated by law in 1911, hospital care in 1915, and schools again in 1927. By the 1930s, Alabama had written into its statutes explicit racial classifications (in 1927) and by the 1940s had written into its constitution that any voters had to be able to read, write, "and explain every article of the U.S. Constitution" (1946).[60]

While many of these laws were enacted at the state level, a wide variety of Jim Crow laws were enacted at the city or county level, and these varied according to the political and economic interests of the local elite. Implementation of state laws varied locally as well. Looking at Alabama as an example, several cities moved forward more quickly than others in the enactment of early Jim Crow ordinances—among them Birmingham, Mobile, and Selma, all of which had fairly high concentrations of slaves in the prewar period. For example, Mobile enacted a 1900 ordinance segregating streetcars (which engendered a subsequent black boycott) and in 1909 enacted an ordinance that applied only to African Americans, who were prohibited from being outside past 10 p.m.[61] Such restrictions were mimicked across other Black Belt cities. Birmingham, for example, had a plethora of Jim Crow ordinances, including a 1930 enactment that white and black restaurant customers should not be served in the same place unless "effectually separated by a solid partition extending from the floor upward to a distance of seven feet or higher, and unless a separate entrance from the street is provided for each compartment."[62] The city also forbade blacks and whites from playing games together—including "cards, dice, dominoes, checkers, baseball, softball, football, basketball or similar games."[63]

LOCAL CONTROL AND CO-OPTATION
OF THE CRIMINAL JUSTICE SYSTEM

Black Codes operated in tandem with aggressive policing of newly freed blacks via the criminal justice system. Many laws enacted during this period also had the ulterior motive of suppressing blacks' economic mobility and political freedoms, making them intimately related to the twin economic and political incentives created by emancipation. Perhaps the most insidious form of criminal coercion came in the form of laws that criminalized, or tried to control, economic activity—for example, laws that criminalized the activity of being unemployed (or vagrant) and the recruitment of black workers.[64] Nearly all states in the former Confederacy had vagrancy laws of some sort that criminalized loitering or being outside at certain times, including during working hours. These were designed to be race-neutral, so as not to run afoul of the loosely enforced Fourteenth Amendment, but the laws were nearly exclusively applied against blacks.

Over time, these sorts of economically motivated laws made it even harder for blacks to leave their jobs, further lowering the value of their outside option.[65]

CONVICT LEASING AND THE PREVALENCE OF SLAVERY

Under this system, many blacks had to serve extraordinary punitive sentences for what today would be considered very minor infractions—and these sentences often included hefty sums that blacks simply could not pay off. Many African Americans were captured randomly by rural whites, who falsely accused them of failing to pay their debts and then used the court system to extract money or labor from them under a system called "peonage," or debt bondage, which had the effect of sharply increasing the number of people incarcerated, especially black men. Many incarcerated African American men were subsequently "leased" out by the state to private companies. This convict-leasing system had the ostensible purpose of bringing in money to the state and providing convicts with useful activities, but ultimately served private companies substantially. This tacit cooperation between private industry and the state resulted in the provision of black labor—again, part of the narrative that drove Southern institutions and politics in the post-War era.[66] This system of peonage (or debt bondage) was used extensively in the post-Reconstruction period more broadly as an additional tool of labor coercion.

Going back to the question of regional divisions within the South, how did this vary with the prevalence of slavery? Were former slaveholding areas indeed more likely to participate in this practice? Historical accounts imply that the regional patterns of convict leasing are mixed. As the nineteenth century progressed, increasing numbers of industries—including timber, mining, and steel manufacturing—competed with agricultural interests for labor. On the one hand, this meant that people were sent to mines as opposed to cotton fields. On the other hand, this shared interest united previously disparate interests, including existing wealthy elites and "new money" elites from other parts of the states, in pushing for more convict leasing and debt peonage. Perhaps it was the case that former slaveholding areas did not participate as heavily in the practice of debt peonage and convict leasing as other parts of the former Confederate states.

To investigate this, we examined data from an unusually detailed statistical report prepared by Carroll D. Wright, the first U.S. Commissioner of Labor (1885–1905). At the time, Wright was a supporter of the convict leasing system, and this report was used in support for the proposition that prison labor was by far less expensive than other sorts of labor.[67] For our purposes, the Wright report is useful for its detailed county-level reporting

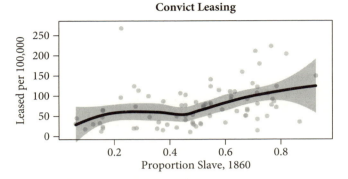

Figure 6.5. Proportion slave in 1860 and rate of convict leasing per 100,000 residents in 1886 in Alabama and Mississippi counties. Source: U.S. Census, Wright, *Second Annual Report of the Commisioner of Labor, 1886: Convict Labor.*

on the number of convicts in Mississippi and Alabama who were leased out via this system.[68] Figure 6.5 represents a scatterplot of counties in Mississippi and Alabama in 1886, as recorded in Wright's report; on the horizontal axis is the proportion of the population that was enslaved in 1860 and on the vertical axis is the proportion leased out (per one hundred thousand total population in 1886).[69] The figure shows precisely that it was the formerly high-slave areas that were more likely to engage in this practice, indicated by the smoothed line's upward trend. Note that this figure does not definitively answer the question of where the convicts who were leased out were sent (nor does it provide information on the race of the convicts), and so it is possible that convicts were sent to upcountry areas within the states. However, we can say that the use of convict leasing by local governments was correlated with the previous prevalence of slavery.

STATUS OF BLACK FARMERS IN THE BLACK BELT

Laws criminalizing black vagrancy and other loitering had the objective of restricting the economic mobility of blacks. What was the result of these efforts? How did these efforts vary regionally? Seeing a stronger effect of these repressive measures in the Black Belt would lend credibility to our argument of path dependence, suggesting stronger antiblack norms within these areas. However, blacks in these areas were certainly worse off than whites, but was their lot worse compared to blacks outside the Black Belt?

We examine this by looking at the status of black farmers after Jim Crow had firmly been established. Specifically, we examine the extent to which black farmers were (compared to white farmers) tenant farmers or actual land owners. Seeing a higher share of blacks owning their own

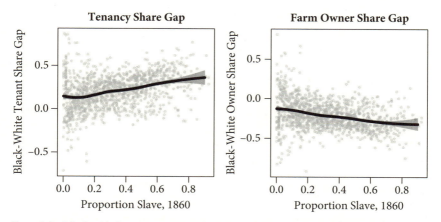

Figure 6.6. Relationship between slavery and the gaps between black and white tenant shares (left panel) and black and white owner shares (right panel), both measured in 1925. Source: U.S. Census.

farms would suggest greater economic independence and mobility; seeing less (and correspondingly more tenancy) would suggest a more dependent status, one that was more tenuous as a result of the economic repression of the early twentieth century. Indeed, across the South, tenancy was considered the lowest rung on the economic ladder, and it was the least promising in terms of upward mobility.

For data on this topic, we look to the U.S. Census of Agriculture, which is a census of American farms and ranches that usually takes place every five years. Here, we look at the 1925 Agricultural Census to compare the county-level gap between blacks and whites in former high-slave counties versus those same gaps in low-slave counties.[70] In the left panel of figure 6.6, we plot the difference between the share of black farmers in the county that are tenants minus the share of white farmers that are tenants (on the vertical axis) as a function of proportion slave in 1860 (on the horizontal axis). (Tenancy here includes sharecroppers, wage tenants, and all other forms of tenancy.) At every level of proportion slave in 1860, the average difference in tenant shares between blacks and whites is always above zero, meaning that, in the average Southern county, blacks are historically more likely to be under tenancy agreements than are whites. The figure also demonstrates that this gap grows as proportion slave increases. That is, the former strongholds of slavery are where we see the biggest gaps between black and white tenancy shares—where there is a large black tenant class, but a relatively small white tenant community.

The right panel of figure 6.6 shows the related story of farm ownership. Here the vertical axis represents the difference between the county-level share of the black population owning the farm surveyed versus the share of the white population owning the farm. Again, no matter the proportion slave, the average gap is negative; this shows that white farmers across the South were far more likely to own their farms relative to black farmers in 1925, a fact that put them on much more secure financial footing. In addition, the gap in ownership grows with the proportion of the population that was enslaved in 1860. That is, Black Belt counties were the ones in which blacks were even less likely to own their own farmers compared to whites; again, this is evidence that blacks in these areas were more economically vulnerable and susceptible to the economic repression strategies of the time period.[71]

BLACK VOTER DISENFRANCHISEMENT

Remarkably, even the strong threat of violence could not keep blacks (and white Republicans) from the polls during Reconstruction. Democrats did control much of the politics of the late nineteenth-century and early twentieth-century South, but opposition candidates were able to achieve fairly high support, especially in the border states and especially considering the widespread election fraud.[72] The limits of these extralegal tools to suppress the opposition vote in the last quarter of the nineteenth century eventually led to legal restrictions on the franchise. This included the passage of state constitutions throughout the South that sought to further curtail the ability of African Americans to vote. These state constitutions— many of which are on the books today—include South Carolina (1895), Louisiana (1898), North Carolina (1900), Alabama (1901), Virginia (1902), Georgia (1908), and Oklahoma (1910). All of them contained voter suppression devices. In addition, Arkansas, Florida, Tennessee, and Texas all adopted some form of a poll tax. Combined with systematic racial violence and other forms of intimidation, and with the waning support and enthusiasm from the federal government, the shares of African Americans voting plummeted.

This long-standing institutional persistence in black disenfranchisement stems from four general policies (or laws), which were designed specifically to limit black voting. The first were poll taxes, which set fees for voting; although modest by today's standards, these taxes were enormously burdensome for blacks struggling to make a living. Many of these laws were also cumulative: one could vote only if all previous years' taxes were fully paid, resulting in a backlog of taxes that were significant enough to permanently disenfranchise the working poor, men who had debt obligations, and those who had previously served jail time or were part of the convict leasing system. The second were literacy tests, which were difficult even for well-educated whites, but nearly impossible for blacks, who had been systematically denied educational opportunities and many of whom were simply illiterate.[73] The third basic form of "tests or devices" were designed to allow less well-educated whites to avoid these voting restrictions. Many of these included grandfather clauses, which originated in the Louisiana Constitution of 1898 and which effectively served to sort black and white potential voters. The fourth kind of disenfranchisement technique concerned the so-called white primary. Democratic primaries were restricted to members of the Democratic Party, technically a private membership organization. Local party officials were therefore legally able to limit who could participate in primaries; since the Democratic Party was effectively the dominant party in the South, this lead to massive underrepresentation of African Americans on electoral ballots and in elected office. The white primary was one of the quickest institutions to be dismantled, with the Supreme Court ruling its use unconstitutional in 1944 (see chapter 8).

We have statistics to demonstrate the effectiveness of these early twentieth-century disenfranchisement efforts. According to estimates from Morgan Kousser, two-thirds of adult black men voted in the 1880 presidential election in every Southern state except Mississippi and Georgia—illustrating the overwhelming desire of blacks to vote even in the face of fraud and intimidation. However, thanks to the disenfranchising state constitutions of the late nineteenth and early twentieth centuries, estimated black voter turnout experienced a massive decline in the early twentieth century. In 1890, the share dropped from a majority to just around half and dropped further after.[74] To give one example, in Louisiana, Richard Pildes reports that "there had been 130,334 black voters on the registration rolls and around the same number of white voters (the state's population was about fifty percent white and black); by 1900, two years after the new constitution, registered black voters numbered a mere 5,320. By 1910, 730 registered black voters were left (less than 0.05 percent of eligible black men)."[75] The disenfranchisement was felt more strongly in certain areas; for example, in twenty-seven out of sixty Louisiana parishes, not a single black voter remained by 1910.[76] These patterns were echoed by similar mass disenfranchisement in other parts of the South.[77] In total, from its peak in late Reconstruction, black voter turnout plummeted over ninety percent in Alabama, Louisiana, and Virginia before and after implementation of these restrictions.[78]

EXAMPLE OF A RESTRICTIVE STATE CONSTITUTION AND THE PREVALENCE OF SLAVERY: ALABAMA IN 1901

On their face, many voter suppression tactics were state-level decisions, often made at state constitutional conventions or in the state legislatures. But while laws may have been somewhat uniform across a given state, public support for these measures and subsequent enforcement of the laws were not. They tended to vary according to regional political interests and whether, and to what extent, counties had an interest to suppress black suffrage. For that reason, the Black Belt's whites—who had the most to lose from black enfranchisement—were some of the staunchest supporters of these measures. Thus, although many disenfranchisement policies were passed at the state level, local level variation in the enforcement and public support for these laws was substantial.

We lack public opinion and attitude measures to demonstrate this variation across the South, but we do have some reliable measures for a representative case—that of Alabama at the turn of the twentieth century— that illustrates this variation. By the end of the nineteenth century, white elites in Alabama were, like white elites in other Southern states, in a state of political crisis: the war and Reconstruction had divided them politically, leaving the former ruling class politically vulnerable. If blacks were allowed or encouraged to vote, although they might perhaps not have the votes to govern, they would certainly be pivotal—that is, in a position to decide which of the white factions would win. In other words, for Southern Democrats, the threat of the black vote came from its potential independence and its potential ability (as yet unrealized) of moving in a Republican direction. For Southern Republicans, those who otherwise would be black allies, the danger of the black vote lay in the fact that, ironically, it could be manipulated and the ballot stuffed.[79] The end result was that state constitutions across the South—including Alabama's—had to be rewritten to protect white dominance and to eliminate the dangerous and divisive black vote. This also had the benefit of uniting white interests from across the state, not just in Black Belt high-black cotton areas, but also within increasingly industrialized areas.

The 1901 Alabama constitutional convention—like many Southern constitutional conventions at the turn of the century—was convened in part with the purpose of disenfranchising African Americans and politically unifying whites. This was made clear by the opening statements from Calhoun County (twenty percent enslaved in 1860) businessman John Knox, who spoke about the urgent need for disenfranchisement and segregation. "There is a difference it is claimed with great force, between the uneducated white man and the ignorant negro," he declared. "There is in the white man an inherited capacity for government which is wholly wanting in the negro ... That the negro, on the other hand, is descended from a race lowest in intelligence and moral perception of all the races of men."[80] Accordingly, the constitutional debate culminated in a document that institutionalized heavy and cumulative poll taxes, literacy tests, and a large personal-property requirement. For example, the poll tax, set at $1.50 (equivalent to around $45 in 2014 purchasing power), represented a

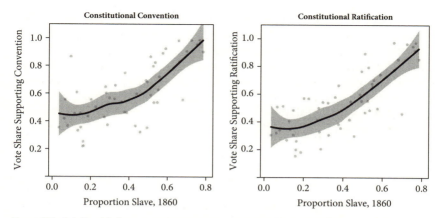

Figure 6.7. Relationship between proportion slave in 1860 and proportion of voters (1) supporting holding a constitutional convention (left) and (2) supporting the ratification of the Alabama Constitution of 1901 (right). Source: Alabama Official and Statistical Register, 1903; U.S. Census, 1860.

significant share of the average wage in the rural South at this time. (Many sharecropping families could expect to earn around $1 to $2 per week.) And these measures were very effective. According to the Alabama Official and Statistical Register, around forty-five thousand whites were registered to vote between 1906 and 1908, which were some of the first registration drives under the new constitution. In the same interval, fewer than one hundred African Americans were registered.

Historical accounts suggest that constitutions like the Alabama Constitution of 1901 engendered especially strong support in the Black Belt, garnering enough support to call into question the integrity of the process. For example, in a study of the 1901 convention, Malcolm Cook McMillan writes that Black Belt counties "gave such large majorities for the convention that it is safe to conclude that even on an issue so vital to the Negro as his franchise, the Black Belt leaders could still manipulate the Negro vote."[81] We investigate this general pattern with quantitative data: Were formerly high-slave areas those most likely to support these Jim Crow state constitutions? We are helped by the fact that Alabama's constitution was unique in (1) being called by popular referendum and (2) being ratified by popular referendum. We therefore have reliable data on which parts of Alabama most supported the drafting of a new constitution and which parts of Alabama most supported the oppressive constitution once it was presented to the public.

This analysis is presented in figure 6.7, which presents the share of the population enslaved in 1860 on the horizontal axis and the share of the population that voted (1) in support of holding the convention (left) or

(2) in favor of ratification on the vertical access (right). The two figures show clear positive relationships: a higher share of the population enslaved in 1860 is predictive both of supporting the constitutional convention and also of the ratification of the 1901 constitution.[82] These relationships are statistically significant at conventional levels, meaning that we are fairly certain that chance alone is not explaining these patterns. Thus, we see the political geography of slavery rearing its head in the push to disenfranchise African Americans, driven by the economic and political incentives of whites in the Black Belt.

INFORMAL INSTITUTIONS AND SOCIAL NORMS

The sorts of local-government-backed institutions discussed above were just one part of the new post-emancipation, post-Reconstruction political environment. In the face of the radical changes brought about by the abolition of slavery, social practices—both legally sanctioned and also those informally nurtured and propagated—limited blacks' freedoms and created significant physical and social barriers separating blacks and whites. A key function of these informal institutions was to support the continuation of the racial hierarchy, including violence toward blacks and antiblack institutions. In addition, from the perspective of the white elite, these social norms were instrumentally useful, since they also undercut any possibility of a political alliance between blacks and nonelite whites.

What did these norms entail? In addition to de facto segregation and racial violence, sociologists studying whites' social responses have noted the development of a certain kind of "racial etiquette" (to use the term from historian Jennifer Ritterhouse). This "code," Ritterhouse writes, meant that "whites withheld from blacks all forms of civility that might imply they were equals. At the same time, whites demanded that blacks display not only civil but often servile behavior, to be manifested in a wide array of verbal and physical cues."[83] Thus, whites were to be referred to using formal titles, including "Mr.," "Ma'am," or "Miss," while blacks were to be referred to by their first name or generic appellations ("boy") or racial slurs.[84] More broadly, this racial code governed all interactions between blacks and whites, including business transactions and sexual relationships; roughly, any behavior by blacks that could indicate an unwelcome familiarity or coequal status with whites could be punished, thus establishing that any digression from the established racial order could incur racial violence. In addition, children were an important part of the racial order, with white children being taught this "racial etiquette" from an early age.[85] This point speaks to a broader pattern, which concerns how the oppressive and violent treatment of blacks, as well as segregation, could in turn have affected or spurred on antiblack attitudes, even among other local whites who had little to gain personally from black labor subordinancy.[86]

The white supremacy of Jim Crow appealed to whites beyond the planter class and the political elite. To see why, note that, in the antebellum South, slaves were black and, by and large, blacks were slaves. Thus, slavery, by its racial nature, represented a strong legal basis for white supremacy. However poor a white person was, at least he or she was not a slave and could not become one. Emancipation and Reconstruction changed this calculus by putting blacks and whites on the same legal footing, at least in theory, which would represent a relative decrease in status for whites. While the above political and economic threats mainly applied to the white elite, this social threat of equality affected all classes of whites. If freedmen were able to address whites as coequals, poor whites might lose perhaps the only source of social deference they had. In this way, poor whites had good reason to support a system of racial hierarchy that placed blacks in the lowest position, since that would mean at least they themselves were not on the bottom.[87] Indeed, distinctions between blacks and poorer whites were also important and strictly enforced.[88] As James Baldwin noted about whites in the South, "They've been raised to believe, and by now they helplessly believe, that no matter how terrible their lives may be... and no matter how far they fall, no matter what disaster overtakes them, they have one enormous knowledge in consolation, which is like a heavenly revelation: at least, they are not Black."[89]

Thus, in the Black Belt, the elite whites and poorer whites had aligned incentives to create and support Jim Crow. And, indeed, both classes participated in perpetuating white supremacy. It is difficult, if not impossible, to determine whether the elites or the broader white community drove these developments, but the historical record gives us some hints. Woodward observed that the most significant antiblack sentiment appeared to be independently prevalent among the lower white class, with the former patrician class providing "the most commanding and effective voice raised in defense of the submerged race."[90] However, this is a view challenged by others—for example, Eric Foner's work on Reconstruction, in which he writes,"[m]ost of all, blacks identified the old political leaders with slavery."[91] Key repeatedly cited the Black Belt elites as the ones to defend white supremacy when "the political chips are down."[92] They were also among the most culturally influential citizens within their areas, not just wielding influence in terms of business and politics but also helping shape local public opinion, attitudes, and customs. In this sense, the role of the elite class may have been a hugely important one in shaping the attitudes and racial sentiments of poorer whites—whites who in the absence of racial cleavages would have been natural allies with blacks.[93]

However, regardless of which group was more antiblack, there is no question that both factions united together against African Americans. Du Bois, writing on Reconstruction, discussed this psychological unification when he wrote that "a determined psychology of caste was built up. In every possible way it was impressed and advertised that the white was superior and the Negro an inferior race. The inferiority must be publicly acknowledged and submitted to."[94] The historian C. Vann Woodward, writing in the 1960s, echoed some of this when he noted that the ultimate "determination of the Negro's 'place' took shape gradually under the influence of economic and political conflicts among divided white people—conflicts that were eventually reserved in part at the expense of the Negro."[95]

Finally, we note that, while it is straightforward to explain Jim Crow in terms of the incentives for Southern whites, its creation was not a forgone conclusion after the Civil War. Scholars of the South have noted the uncertainty and uneasiness of this transition period—again suggesting a point of transition consistent with a critical juncture. For example, Woodward developed an argument centered around "forgotten alternatives," in reference to the time between the Civil War and the turn of the century.[96] During this time period, as Southern society experimented—with varying success and interest—on how to approach race relations between whites and newly freed blacks, whites and blacks mingled more freely than they did later. For example, as Woodward notes, in Mississippi in the 1870s, there were reports of blacks and whites being served at the same bar and attending dance halls and events together.[97] In another instance, at the International Exposition in New Orleans in 1885, blacks and whites paraded together and "the races mingled in the grounds in unconscious equality of privileges."[98] From these examples, Woodward concludes that before the "triumph" of the "fanatical advocates of racism" was complete, subordination "was not yet an accepted corollary that the subordinated had to be totally segregated and needlessly humiliated by a thousand daily reminders of their subordination."[99] Likewise, from his review of post-Reconstruction day-to-day life, the historian Edward Ayers notes that the movement toward segregation moved in fits and starts, although it did move rapidly postemancipation and post-Reconstruction. "The segregation begun in the decade following the end of the Civil War did not spread inexorably and evenly across the face of the South," he writes. Instead, the "1880s saw much uncertainty and much bargaining, many forays and retreats."[100]

Ultimately, however, the path that Southern society set down was the path that prioritized racial segregation and the maintenance of the racial hierarchy, codified by the sweeping set of state constitutions enacted around the turn of the century—that is, the path that was taken was the one that led to Jim Crow. Woodward observed, "[u]nder slavery, control was best maintained by a large degree of physical contact and association. Under the strange new world the old methods were not always available or applicable." Indeed, "[t]o the dominant whites it began to appear that the new order required a certain amount of compulsory separation of the races."[101] With much to lose, and with an internal justification firmly in place, whites turned away from the "old" familiarity between blacks and whites and moved instead toward socially sanctioned (and legally sanctioned, where possible) segregation.[102]

Economic historians have also noted how the end of Reconstruction ushered differing justifications for the suppression of blacks' educational and social opportunities. Economic historian Stanley Engerman observed that "ending slavery actually exacerbated racism, or at least led to racism taking a different form, and racism was still able to outweigh other forms of differences between groups."[103] For Ransom and Sutch, the justifications were internalized and tautological. The former white ruling class took "the absence of educated, skilled, and independent Negroes as proof that his belief in Negro inferiority was well founded," which in turn provided justification for segregation.[104] Thus, an important point from this literature is that this was not the only path, and that Southern society had made choices about how to deal with the new landscape.

6.3 CONCLUSION

We conclude by outlining the reasons why the time period after emancipation was likely a critical juncture in the trajectory of Southern whites' racial attitudes. Recall our definition of a critical juncture from chapter 2, which is that it is a historically important moment in time in which society (loosely defined) is faced with several alternative paths. Ultimately, the choices made at that time set society moving down a particular path, eventually closing off alternative options. We see this in the broader pattern of behavioral path dependence, in which regions diverge after the moment of the critical juncture; this in turn leads to the regional patterns in behavioral outcomes that we see today.

As this chapter has shown, the time period around emancipation appears to fit this description. First, slavery had carried with it the institutional backing of an enforced racial hierarchy, but its collapse ushered in significant economic, political, and social uncertainty. While the postwar Southern economy was in shambles and badly in need of rebuilding, the white elite had lost their most valuable source of capital: slaves. Meanwhile, aided by federal government oversight, many blacks started to vote and others enjoyed some limited movement and commingling with whites. An initial number of blacks were elected to state offices as Republicans, further threatening Black Belt Southern Democrats. This uncertainty, Woodward notes, meant that Southern whites, particularly those of the Black Belt, had several alternatives. They could explore the possibility of increased equality in its various forms, or they could retreat and recreate a racial hierarchy based on racist social and legal norms—one that hewed close to slavery but was supported by different means.

In thinking about this "choice," we consider the arguments made by economic historians. The Black Belt agricultural and business elite throughout had the objective of maintaining an inexpensive, readily available (and rapidly replaceable) labor class. Newly freed blacks served this role. And black labor provided not just the labor necessary both to rebuild the South and the Southern economy, but also to supply much of the raw materials needed to drive the emerging industrial revolution of the late nineteenth century. This, we believe, incentivized white agricultural and business elite to foment a more racially hostile environment. The end result was labor-restrictive legislation that targeted black laborers; these were further supported by attempts at voter disenfranchisement, Black Codes (and early Jim Crow laws), and norms. In sum: the way that society ultimately moved in the period after emancipation and in the early twentieth century centered around the maintenance of the existing racial order in the face of new political and economic developments.

Second, the choices made during this period set society down a certain path in terms of attitudes and behaviors and closed off other alternatives.[105] The antebellum period and the institution of slavery offered whites no need to maintain such excruciatingly tight controls over their labor supply; after all, slavery had the strong sanction of both state-level governments and the federal government. In the postbellum period, the institutional "protections" to whites of slavery vanished, incentivizing agricultural and business elites to redevelop a racial hierarchy, one that hinged more on localized racial codes of conduct. Importantly, as this "racial etiquette" entered into everyday relationships—specifically institutionalized via segregation and separation of the races—whites' attitudes about blacks only hardened.[106] Blacks could no longer be trusted in the homes, in the fields, and in public spaces; their activities instead had to be closely monitored, while at the same time keeping white women and white children "safe" from the "dangerous" influence and unlawfulness of black men. Importantly, this was the case not just among the white upper class—who probably stood the most to lose from black economic mobility—but also among working-class whites. This was also the case for white and black children, who were reared in this racial code of conduct. This set the stage for the further propagation of antiblack attitudes among whites.

As a final point, these patterns were highly dependent on the strength of the economic and political incentives and the degree to which slavery had been prevalent in the antebellum period. The Southern Black Belt was in the antebellum period the most economically dependent on the inexpensive labor provided by African Americans. This need was maintained even after emancipation, but was also coupled with the growing pressures of black economic mobility, black enfranchisement, and the industrial revolution. The end result was devastating for the newly freed black men and women and served to harden whites' racial attitudes. Our argument is that these historical forces began a path-dependent process, one that was felt via more racially hostile attitudes in places where black labor was the most urgently needed and where black votes needed to be the most suppressed: the Black Belt. We now turn to tracing the local patterns of behavioral path dependence from this tumultuous time period to today.

PART III

Mechanisms of Persistence and Decay

CHAPTER SEVEN

PERSISTENCE AND THE MECHANISMS OF REPRODUCTION

"You've got to be taught before it's too late,
Before you are six or seven or eight,
To hate all the people your relatives hate,
You've got to be carefully taught!"
          Lyrics from *"You've Got to Be Carefully Taught,"* South Pacific

In the decades leading up to the Civil War, Georgia's cotton belt—clustered mainly in the northeast part of the state—grew more and more reliant on slavery. One example of this is Oglethorpe County (sixty-five percent enslaved in 1860). In Oglethorpe County, plantation owners switched from tobacco to cotton in the first half of the nineteenth century and increased the number of slaves, to the point where blacks outnumbered whites roughly two to one. After the war, with whites making up only around thirty-five percent of the county, and with concern about the newly enfranchised freedmen reaching panic levels, the Ku Klux Klan became an active participant in unleashing racial violence and political intimidation on the newly freed slaves. For instance, in the 1868 gubernatorial election, the more racially progressive Republican candidate for governor received 1,144 votes (presumably from newly freed slaves) and the Democratic candidate 557; in the 1868 presidential election, after a series of Klan rides and intimidation, 116 votes were cast for the Republican candidate and 849 for the Democrat—a remarkable drop in Republican vote shares that speaks to the efficacy of the Klan and its racial intimidation.[1]

The Klan and its rides left an indelible shadow across the Southern psyche. One example of this, and of the extremely long-term impact of the Klan's activities in Oglethorpe County, comes from the well-known memoirs of Katharine Du Pre Lumpkin. Lumpkin was born in 1897 in Macon, Georgia (Bibb County, 42.6 percent enslaved in 1860), but her father, William Lumpkin, was born in Oglethorpe County to a planter who owned several dozen slaves. William, a former Confederate soldier in the Civil War, joined Oglethorpe County's extremely active Ku Klux Klan as a young man after the war, and he would regale his daughter with stories of his time. He would speak of "insolent" or "uppity" blacks who required white admonishment, lessons that the younger Lumpkin would devour without critical thought.[2] As a child, one of her favorite stories was of a Klansman who pretended to be a Confederate ghost in order to scare a newly freed black man. So strong was this tradition that Lumpkin's parents signed her up in a children's Ku Klux Klan club, which she and her siblings and friends knew little about.[3]

This oral tradition of sharing stories with children about white suppression and blacks' appropriate role was not atypical, and Lumpkin's upbringing showcased the deeply embedded nature of the Southern racial structure and the importance of "racial etiquette."[4] But these stories frequently transcended simple narrative, with white children often being exposed directly to racial violence and, in many instances, actually participating in the violence itself. For example, Lumpkin tells the story of how one day she found her father whipping the cook, a black woman, with a stick; the father later explained that the cook was being punished for "impudence."[5] At this moment, Lumpkin later wrote in her memoir, she learned about what behavior whites should expect from blacks and how blacks should be punished, much like her father learned how to treat blacks from his rides with Oglethorpe County's Ku Klux Klan after the Civil War.

Katharine Lumpkin's account of her upbringing—as well as her father's experience as a young man riding with the Klan—is reflective of how millions of white children across several generations were reared in the racial ideology of the postbellum and Jim Crow South. White adults—mothers, fathers, grandparents, aunts, uncles, and schoolteachers—taught white youth about white supremacy and how it should influence race relations in their lives. In turn, white children experienced first-hand the racial violence that terrorized blacks; many of them were active participants, taking part in the infliction of pain and damage without having much (if any) understanding of the underlying context of their actions. Throughout these narratives, a recurring theme is that, from an early age, white children were exposed to, and absorbed, the respective roles of blacks and whites in Southern society.[6]

Stories like Lumpkin's and her father's help us address a key component of behavioral path dependence, which is how attitudes have been passed down over time—in our context, from the time of slavery's collapse in the 1860s through to today. We believe that intergenerational socialization—such as Lumpkin's—is a key way that behavioral path dependence operates, both in the South and beyond. Furthermore, as we show in this chapter, the contextual features of places (such as Oglethorpe County and Bibb County) help to enhance this transmission of beliefs.

To clarify this, we focus this chapter on exploring what we believe to be the two primary mechanisms that reproduce slavery's effects. The first is intergenerational socialization: children in the South tended to inherit the political and racial attitudes of their parents, providing a plausible chain across generations. To further bolster the case for intergenerational socialization in political attitudes, we show that there is no effect of slavery for whites who were raised outside of the states with the highest rates of slavery. Second, we turn to institutional and contextual mechanisms of reproduction and reinforcement, including those that have caused decay in these attitudes. These include the changing incentives for labor coercion as the Southern economy moved away from labor-intensive cotton farming to more mechanized agriculture, as well as the role of violence, the size of local black populations, and public school desegregation as possible moderators of slavery's effects. These institutional changes provide evidence of how attitudes were carried forward across generations, providing a key link between the historical period and today.

This chapter is organized as follows. We begin by exploring the evidence for the persistence of attitudes, tracing the effects of slavery on whites' political attitudes over time. Finding this evidence sets the stage for the second investigation, which involves the more specific mechanisms of reproduction, or how these attitudes have actually been passed down. We present evidence on two fronts. The first is intergenerational transmission. For this we examine evidence from parent-child surveys, showing a strong correlation between parents' racial preferences and those of their children, consistent with qualitative works focusing on the American South and also with political science scholarship documenting the intergenerational consistency of partisan and ideological beliefs.[7] The second is institutional reinforcement. For this, we present evidence showing that those places where labor incentives relaxed earlier—i.e., those areas that had mechanized earlier—are those where attitudes attenuated more quickly. We then buttress this by looking at contextual institutional factors, such as racial violence (lynchings) and segregated schooling. We conclude by addressing how these factors help explain the behavioral path dependence in political attitudes over a time span of 150 years.

7.1 TRACING THE PERSISTENT EFFECTS OF SLAVERY

Before we explore explanations of why slavery's effects have persisted over time, understanding the empirical contours of this persistence is important. Is the divergence in white attitudes today between formerly high-slave and low-slave areas lesser (or greater) now than it was in the early parts of the twentieth century? Given the discussion in the last chapter about the causes of the divergence in the period between emancipation and the turn of the century, we might expect these differences to have dissipated. After all, as of the early twenty-first century, the political and economic features of the postbellum South have diminished. Agricultural production is largely mechanized, making the Southern economy considerably less dependent on labor-intensive crops (such as cotton) or extractive industries that require significant labor. The middle of the twentieth century brought striking changes to the political landscape of the South and a dramatic increase in the political participation of African Americans (a topic we discuss at greater length in the next chapter), and the Voting Rights Act created majority-minority districts, thereby changing the nature of political competition between blacks and whites. Furthermore, there have been great strides in the norms of racial equality in the United States, with many of the more blatant forms of "old-fashioned" racism becoming socially unacceptable.

If the effects of slavery were due solely to contemporaneous political and economic incentives, we would expect massive convergence between the Black Belt and the rest of the South—that is, significant *attenuation*, or a lessening of differences in attitudes between the former high-slave areas and former low-slave areas. However, as we show in this section, the effect of slavery in predicting regional differences across partisan attitudes is largely the same now as it was around the middle of the twentieth century, despite substantial realignment in party support in the years following. The distinctiveness of the Black Belt appears to have survived this realignment.

PERSISTENCE IN HISTORICAL VOTE SHARES

As a first attempt to trace the effects of slavery over time, we revisit an earlier analysis, presented in figure 7.1. This depicts the relationship between the county-level proportion enslaved in 1860 and county-level presidential vote share (in a Democratic direction) from 1900 moving forward.[8] To put the figure in substantive context, each point represents the effect of a twenty-five-percentage-point increase in the share of the county population enslaved in 1860 on the vote share for the Democratic Party candidate in that particular presidential election. (Note that, for the pre-Voting Rights Act elections, these are nearly exclusively *white* vote shares.) As we discussed in chapter 5, the differences between the Black Belt and the non-Black Belt parts of the South increased in magnitude in the early twentieth century, with the Black Belt whites leaning more strongly to the Democratic Party than whites living elsewhere in the South. However, the figure also shows a pattern of attenuation, which is what concerns us here. Specifically, as the twentieth century progressed, and as the issue of civil rights rose in

Presidential Elections

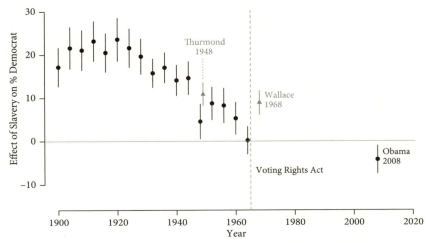

Figure 7.1. Effect of proportion slave on the vote for Democratic presidential candidate in the South over the 20th century. Each point is the effect of a twenty-five-percentage-point increase in proportion slave from separate IV models of county-level Democratic share of the presidential vote on proportion slave, using cotton suitability as an instrument.

political prominence in the 1940s and 1950s, the high-slave counties appear increasingly like low-slave counties.

However, is this pattern genuine evidence of attenuation in whites' political and racial attitudes over time? The problem with reaching such an inference is that, as a measure of attitudes, presidential votes are confounded by the changing nature of politics and partisan platforms over time. In particular, what appears as attenuation in attitudes (particularly on race) may actually be attributable to Southern realignment—i.e., the movement of Southern whites away from the Democratic Party and toward the Republican Party. We suspect that the "attenuation" visible in the figure is simply this realignment. By many accounts, the election of Democrat Franklin Roosevelt in 1944 was the last time that Southern whites united behind a single Democratic presidential candidate. By 1948, Harry Truman and the national Democratic Party had adopted increasingly progressive stances on civil rights, offending Southern Democrats and pushing them to form a separate States' Rights Democratic Party (more commonly referred to as the Dixiecrats). Over the next few decades, Southern whites increasingly voted for Republican candidates; some studies have identified the early 1960s (in particular 1963) as a point at which the South was definitively lost.[9] By the year 2000, Southern whites were mostly united in their support for the Republican presidential nominee, George W. Bush.

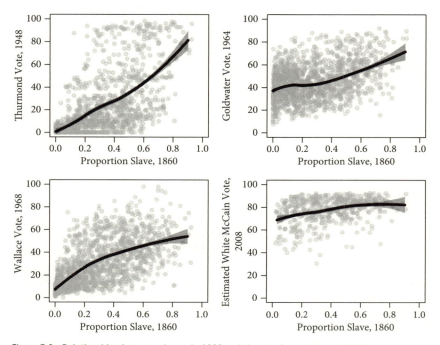

Figure 7.2.   Relationships between slavery in 1860 and the vote for various candidates in presidential elections. Clockwise from top left: States Rights candidate Strom Thurmond in 1948, Republican candidate Barry Goldwater in 1964, American Independent candidate George Wallace in 1968, and Republican candidate John McCain in 2008. Thurmond and Goldwater are vote shares out of the total vote, Wallace votes are out of the total white voting-age population, and McCain votes are the estimated white vote shares at the county-level (see chapter 3 for a description of this estimation). Source: Clubb, Flanigan, and Zingale, *Electoral Data for Counties in the United States: Presidential and Congressional Races, 1840–1972*, U.S. Census Bureau.

Realignment suggests to us that the patterns we see in figure 7.1 may not be due to underlying attenuation, but, rather, to the changing nature of the two main political parties. There are two pieces of evidence that suggest the changing effects of slavery are not due to attenuation in political attitudes. First, figure 7.2 examines voting for several key candidates who were extremely conservative on racial issues specifically and who had special resonance in the Black Belt: South Carolina's Strom Thurmond in 1948 (before realignment), Arizona's Barry Goldwater in 1964, and Mississippi's George Wallace in 1968 (both after realignment). The figure demonstrates that all three candidates carried more support in the formerly high-slave areas than in other parts of the South, even though Thurmond ran as a Dixiecrat, Goldwater a Republican, and Wallace an Independent.[10] Thus, during this time of partisan upheaval, racially conservative presidential candidates such as these men could, regardless of their actual party affiliation, rely on the votes of Southern whites from the former slave counties.

Second, examining survey data (as opposed to elections data) suggests that differential voting between Southern whites living in the former high-slave South and whites living elsewhere actually continues up until the present day. For example, we look at vote shares won by Republican John McCain, who ran against Democratic candidate Barack Obama in 2008. (As scholarship exploring racial resentment has shown, the most racially resentful whites were more likely to oppose Obama's candidacy.[11]) The bottom-right panel of figure 7.2 shows, using survey data limited to self-identified whites, that McCain secured the highest share of the white vote in formerly high-slave counties and Obama the smallest. Further statistical modeling reveals that the strength of the relationship between the prevalence of slavery in 1860 and conservative voting is roughly similar in magnitude in 1968 and 2008—further evidence of robust persistence in political ideology over time.

PERSISTENCE IN BELIEFS ABOUT RACE

Although the above analysis shows persistence in political behavior, there are two remaining concerns. First, perhaps it is the direct experiences and attitudes of older individuals, rather than intergenerational transmission, that explains our results. For example, we could simply be detecting an effect among older whites of the South, whose exposure to the tail end of Jim Crow could have had a lasting impact until today.[12] However, behavioral path dependence is about more than the persistence of attitudes within a person over the course of his or her life: more broadly, the concept is about subsequent generations inheriting the views of their elders. A second lingering concern is that our arguments about the political legacy of slavery concern racial attitudes more broadly, not just voting behavior or partisan affiliation. That is, perhaps we would not see similar patterns for racial attitudes.

To further assess both points, we estimate the effect among a group less likely to be directly affected by Jim Crow: whites born after the Civil Rights Act of 1964 and the Voting Rights Act of 1965. While segregation and race-related oppression extended well past this time, both pieces of legislation have been acknowledged as influential in strongly reducing segregation in the South and increasing black enfranchisement.[13] Thus, the people born after these two monumental pieces of legislation would not themselves have been exposed to the height of Jim Crow as their parents and grandparents likely were. This allows us to more closely examine the exposure of intergenerational influence (as opposed to their

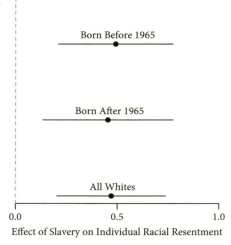

Figure 7.3. Effects of slavery for all Southern whites, those born before 1965, and those born after 1965. Effects calculated from OLS with cluster-robust standard errors. Source: Acharya, Blackwell, and Sen, "The Political Legacy of American Slavery."

contemporary context). To assess an outcome besides partisanship, we examine these individuals' levels of racial resentment—that is, how they respond on questions designed to assess how cooly or warmly they view African Americans.

Figure 7.3 displays these results. These show that the effect of slavery on racial resentment for these younger whites is just as strong and statistically significant as it is for older whites. Thus, there appears to be at least some intergenerational transmission of racial beliefs at work here.

7.2 INTERGENERATIONAL TRANSMISSION OF BELIEFS

If the political geography of slavery has persisted in terms of attitudes, what are the mechanisms that cause behavioral path dependence to continue? There are two broad classes of mechanisms for this effect. One is a purely social mechanism, that of intergenerational transmission, which is that attitudes—both political and social—are passed down across generations, from parents, grandparents, uncles, and aunts onto children. The other mechanism involves the reinforcement of this transmission through local institutions such as churches and schools.

This is an argument well supported by a literature documenting that children's political attitudes (including attitudes on race-related issues) tend to correlate closely with that of their parents.[14] There is also a large body of scholarship in sociology and history that provides a rich portrait of how racial attitudes in the South were reinforced within families. Much of this work is based on autobiographies of those Southerners, like Katharine Du Pre Lumpkin, who grew up to regret the white supremacy of their youth. These accounts paint a portrayal of white children navigating the Southern racial hierarchy learning "lessons" on what type of behavior they should expect from African Americans. For example, Jennifer Ritterhouse documents how white children learned that blacks should yield at sidewalks, tip their hats to older whites, and address whites by formal titles (such as "Sir" or "Ma'am"). White children also learned that the Southern racial order required them to participate in policing black behavior. Many of these accounts thus include stories of white youth feeling shame or guilt for failing to reprimand a black person after an encounter that violated the racial order of the South. One example is the autobiography of Lillian Smith, born in 1897 to a prosperous businessman in Jasper, Florida (Hamilton County, 33.6 percent enslaved in 1860), who wrote about the feelings she had encountering black children on the sidewalk. "Each lesson was linked to the other, drawing strength from it," she wrote. While she herself did not "mind" black children walking on the sidewalk, "other parents seem to think pushing little Negroes into sandspurs funny, like tying tin cans to a dog's tail, and they who make the rules seem not to mind at all."[15] This is just one example of local society—including parents of other children—working in tandem with families to ensure the survival of white supremacist ideology.

Beyond families, these lessons were reinforced by other local institutions such as clubs (especially race-based organizations, including the children's Ku Klux Klan or Confederacy Club) and schools. Thus, even if parents failed to enforce the racial hierarchy, there was a system of other whites that would encourage children to partake in it. We discuss schooling in more detail below, when we consider evidence for institutional reinforcement of behavioral path dependence.

EVIDENCE FROM PARENT-CHILD SURVEYS

Can we detect the passing of beliefs from parents to children empirically? To explore such inheritance of racial attitudes, we rely on the Youth-Parent Socialization Panel Survey, which measured the racial attitudes of a national probability sample of high school seniors in 1965 along with their parents. This study followed up with the students and interviewed them again in 1973, 1982, and 1997, with response rates over eighty percent in each of the subsequent waves. We focus on the subset of this sample who are identified as white and who lived in the South in 1965 ($n = 120$), the overwhelming majority of whom were also raised

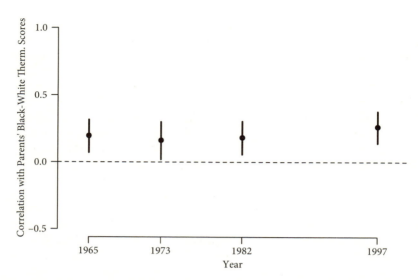

Figure 7.4. Correlation coefficients between parents' white racial preference in 1965 and their children's white racial preference measured at four time periods: 1965, 1973, 1982, and 1997. White racial preference here is measured as the difference between the respondent's thermometer scores for white and black people. This figure reproduced from Avidit Acharya, Matthew Blackwell, and Maya Sen, "The Political Legacy of American Slavery."

in the South. Each wave asked respondents numerous questions, but we focus on the "feeling thermometer" scores for whites and the feeling thermometer scores for blacks. As we did in chapter 3, we use these to construct a measure of racial preference by taking the difference between a respondent's thermometer scores for whites versus blacks. For most high school seniors in 1965, we have at least one of their parents' responses to this question as well, which allows us to track the correlation between parents' and children's attitudes over time. If behavioral path dependence is at work through intergenerational transmission, we should expect to see a positive correlation that persists from a student's youth until well into his or her adulthood.

Figure 7.4 shows the correlation between parents' white racial preference in 1965 and their children's white racial preference, separately analyzed, in 1965, 1973, 1982, and 1997. For example, the first point represents the correlation between parents' racial views in 1965 and their children's racial views in 1965; the second point is the correlation between parents' racial views in 1965 and their children's racial views in 1973, and so on. Positive values mean that parents and children tend to have similar racial views.[16] What is clear from these results is that there is a statistically significant intergenerational correlation in racial attitudes, one previously documented by the original investigators of this survey.[17] Interestingly, this relationship persists even when we control for the 1860 proportion slave in the student's county of residence in 1965, indicating that at least part of the persistent effect of slavery could be explained by parent-to-child transmission of beliefs. Even more striking is the persistence of these relationships over time—the correlation is as high in 1997 as it is at any point in the panel. These results, while limited in terms of the sample size and geographic dispersion, thus suggest that direct parent-to-child influence could be a mechanism by which these beliefs could have been passed down from generation to generation.[18]

Of course, parent-to-child transmission of beliefs is one among many ways that attitudes can persist locally over time. Schools, in some cases churches, and other social and civic institutions provide opportunities for local beliefs to be shared both within and between generations. It is difficult to know how much of the persistence we see across generations is due to social connections in these places and how much is due to parental socialization. What is important about these correlations is, however, that they give us evidence for the microfoundations of persistence and behavioral path dependence. The aggregate persistence that we see, with high-slave counties being more conservative today, makes sense if we know that beliefs tend to persist locally within families—an argument supported by the evidence here.

EVIDENCE FROM CHILDHOOD PLACES OF RESIDENCE

To further bolster the case for behavioral path dependence, we now test an implication of the theory. If the contemporary differences in white attitudes between formerly high- and low-slave areas really are attributable to intergenerational socialization, as behavioral path dependence would suggest, then we would expect those who grew up *outside* the South to be relatively immune to slavery's persistent effects. After all, these are individuals who grew up with different political cultures, with their own folkways, and who did not have older relatives steeped in the kinds of attitudes native to the South. Comparing this group to those who grew up *inside* the South would then give us insight into how and when behavioral path dependence operates. If we see large effects among those from the South as well as from those outside of the South, then we might think that people adjust to the political culture of their residence at any age. If, on the other hand, we see no effects among those who grew up outside the South (but who now live in the South), then we would conclude that behavioral path dependence is a process tied to one's youth and which may be a persuasive mechanism of persistence.

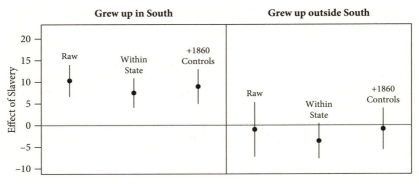

Figure 7.5. Effect of 1860 slavery on the difference in respondents' thermometer scores for white and black people, disaggregating between those who grew up in the former Confederacy (left plot) and those who did not (right plot). Source: ANES.

Fortunately, the American National Election Survey (ANES) asks respondents where they were raised in addition to where they currently reside. This allows us to address whether those relatively new to the South differ from those who grew up there and were exposed to intergenerational socialization. Specifically, we break our ANES sample into two groups: (1) those who reported that they "grew up" in the states of the former Confederacy and (2) those who grew up outside that region.[19] We then estimated the effect of 1860 slavery in the respondent's contemporary county of residence under the various models of chapter 3. The outcome that we examine is the difference in the "feeling thermometer" scores for whites and blacks (for white respondents).

Figure 7.5 shows theses analyses. Substantively, the figure demonstrates that slavery appears to influence those whites who grew up in the South, but not those whites who grew up *outside* of the South. The differences between the effect sizes for each group within each model are statistically significant, meaning it is unlikely for the difference between the groups to be due to chance alone. (Although we do not have access to the respondent's genealogical profile in order to investigate how their full lineages impact our effects, we would expect that the deeper the connections to the South, the stronger the transmission of beliefs and the stronger the impact of slavery.) Thus, it appears that the lessons taught to Southerners as children are an important component of the overall impact of slavery on subsequent attitudes—a finding entirely consistent with the literature on childhood socialization among white Southerners, particularly during the times of Jim Crow.[20]

This result also speaks to how population sorting (or migration) may, in the long run, wash away the effects of institutions such as slavery. In chapter 4, we showed that migration is unlikely to be the primary driver of our effects, but it is possible that population sorting could indeed play a role in attenuating slavery's effects at the margins. For example, our analysis suggests that those from outside the South are somewhat more "immune" to slavery's lasting effects than those who grew up in these areas. This suggests that local political culture—such as that exhibited by formerly high-slave areas—can dissipate into the flows of migration. However, the levels of in-migration would have to be quite high to overwhelm the effects of slavery, and our earlier analyses, which still show a detectable effect of slavery despite such possible migration, suggest that the overall levels of in-migration into formerly high-slave areas have not been sufficiently high. One possible exception to this might be the counties surrounding Washington, D.C., in Maryland, where slavery was very prevalent but which today are home to thousands who have moved to the area to work in and around metropolitan D.C. in government-related industries. We would expect the effects of slavery in these counties to be substantially attenuated.

7.3 REINFORCEMENT MECHANISMS AND DECAY

Attitudes passed down within families and from elders to young people are only part of the story, and intergenerational socialization is only one of the mechanisms of reproduction of behavioral path dependence. As we discussed in chapter 2, there could be institutional and contextual factors that also serve as institutional reinforcement of behavioral outcomes, including beliefs, opinions, and attitudes. These could operate alongside intergenerational forces as well, both working to promote the transmission of attitudes across generations. Schools, community organizations, private clubs, and businesses all worked to reinforce attitudes during Jim Crow and after.

In this section, we investigate how different features of the local environment in the postbellum period enhanced the effect of slavery. These reinforcement mechanisms give us insight into how behavioral path dependence works and when we might expect it to occur in other settings. We focus on four mechanisms here: (1) the mechanization of agricultural production that occurred roughly from 1920 to 1940; (2) racial violence; (3) local white exposure to black populations; and (4) educational segregation.

AGRICULTURAL MECHANIZATION AND EASING OF ECONOMIC INCENTIVES

Our discussion in chapter 6 explored the critical juncture of emancipation and how the economic and political fabric of the American South was severely threatened by emancipation and by developments during Reconstruction. African Americans, who under slavery had been captured labor, were freed within the scope of several years and could in theory move, switch jobs, and begin to demand wages and nonpecuniary benefits.

This was particularly threatening to whites in the Black Belt, where blacks both outnumbered whites and where blacks were the core bedrock of the labor supply. Thus, the Black Belt white elite had every incentive to suppress black labor; doing so maintained wages low, kept laborers from departing to other regions (or other parts of the South), and helped keep the local economy moving forward. These incentives were a crucial part of the critical juncture arising out of the abolition of slavery. But these incentives could also be a reinforcing mechanism for the behavioral path dependence we document above. So long as the white elite had incentives to reduce the costs of black labor, they also had an incentive to maintain the racial hierarchy of the South via racial violence, antiblack economic laws (such as vagrancy laws), and social and educational segregation.

This raises a key question, however. As the nature of demand for farm labor changed, so too did the incentives to suppress black labor. As economic historians have noted, the mechanization of cotton and tobacco in the South lagged compared to agricultural production elsewhere in the United States; however, starting around 1920, with a movement away from mules and toward general tractor use, the mechanization of Southern agriculture accelerated rapidly. By one account, "[t]he number of tractors in the South rose from a mere 36,500 in 1920 to more than 271,000 in 1940, and during the next two decades, they increased by a factor of more than 5 to more than 1.4 million."[21] Subsequent incorporation of the more expensive (but more specialized) cotton picker in the 1940s and 1950s again increased production and further accelerated the reduction in demand for manual agricultural labor.[22] This change in the means of production meant that labor costs for agricultural production drastically declined over this era. Writing in 1933, two specialists with the Department of Agriculture described the potential gains to early mechanization (before the advent of the cotton picker) to be an approximate fifty percent reduction in labor costs in some areas of the South. Once the mechanical cotton picker became widely available after 1944, these reductions in labor costs became even greater.[23]

From our perspective, this changing economic environment had the possibility of changing whites' economic incentives. If white elites and landowners required less black labor (because of increased mechanization), then they would also lose a key incentive for the racial violence, policing, and oppression that suppressed black wages and mobility. Thus, we would expect that local mechanization would undermine a key institutional

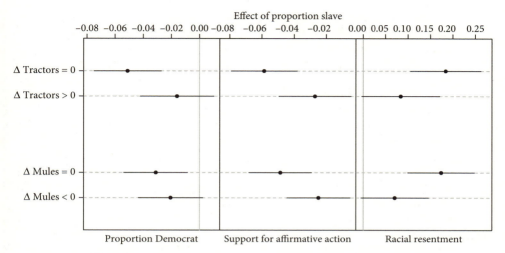

Figure 7.6. Effect of slavery on white attitudes by mechanization of farms between 1930 and 1940. Counties that mechanized had increases in the number of tractors and decreases in the number of mules. Each point reflects the effect of a 25-percentage-point increase in proportion slave. Source: U.S. Agricultural Censuses, 1930 and 1940.

reinforcing mechanism of the Southern racial hierarchy. Without reinforcement, furthermore, the divergence between the high-slave and low-slave areas might start to attenuate. Accordingly, we should see differences in the contemporary period between areas that mechanized earlier versus later.

To test this account, we look at two proxies for the mechanization of cotton: (1) the growth in the number of farming tractors, and (2) the decline in the number of mules, both between 1930 and 1940, collected by the 1930 and 1940 U.S. Agricultural Censuses.[24] The average county in 1930 had 0.0285 tractors per 100,000 acres, but by 1940 this figure had almost doubled to 0.049 tractors per 100,000 acres. Both of these are indications of a move away from manual labor and toward mechanization in the production of cotton. We use our baseline models from chapter 3 and examine how the effect of the proportion enslaved in 1860 varies according to the change in the number of tractors per 100,000 acres of agricultural land in the county between 1930 and 1940. We then estimate the effect of this interaction on our three contemporary outcome measures, which are the share of whites in the county who today (1) identify as Democrats, (2) indicate opposition to affirmative action, and (3) agree with statements that many scholars believe may indicate racial resentment.[25]

The results are presented in figure 7.6 with tractors (top) and mules (bottom) within each panel separately; the point represents an estimate of the effect of slavery on the three outcomes, while the horizontal lines represent ninety-five percent confidence intervals. For each set, we present two results, one for the effect where there was no change in the number of tractors or mules (represented as Δ Tractors = 0 or Δ Mules = 0) and then again when there was a change (Δ Tractors > 0 or Δ Mules < 0). Substantively, figure 7.6 shows that the effects of slavery on the three contemporary outcomes are *lower for counties where mechanization grew between 1930 and 1940, measured either by tractor growth or decline in mules.*[26] To put this into more concrete terms, where tractors did not grow between 1930 and 1940 (Δ Tractors = 0 or Δ Mules = 0), a twenty-five-percentage-point increase in proportion slave leads to a 4.7-percentage-point drop in the percent of whites who identify as a Democrat today. Where mechanization grew rapidly, with 0.05 more tractors per 100,000 acres (ninetieth percentile), the same change in proportion slave leads to only a 1.4 percentage-point decrease in the percent Democrat, though this decrease is not statistically significant at typical levels.[27]

Thus, this analysis strongly suggests that the dissipation of economic incentives—via the increased mechanization and attendant move away from African American labor—served to attenuate slavery's effects on behavioral outcomes. In turn, we believe that this presents strong evidence of the effectiveness of a certain kind of institutional reinforcement mechanism (i.e., the incentive to depress black wages) as a pathway for behavioral path dependence.

LYNCHINGS AND REINFORCEMENT OF RACIAL ATTITUDES

As we have discussed in previous chapters, both the threat and execution of racial violence was a pervasive feature of the postbellum and Jim Crow South that had the potential to reinforce and sustain the intergenerational transmission of racial attitudes. There is strong historical evidence that lynchings were often communal events, ones in which white children played an important role as spectators and, occasionally, as participants. Indeed, narratives from this time period are full of instances where white children were "witnesses" (real or contrived) to the purported instigating crime or to the actual racial violence, scavengers for horrific "souvenirs" in the aftermath, and, sometimes, participants in the violence itself. For example, historian Kristina DuRocher tells of a public lynching that took place in 1893 in Paris, Texas, in which a black man was accused of killing a four-year-old white girl: "In celebration of his arrival [into town], the mayor granted the town's children a holiday from school and they joined their families in waving handkerchiefs at [the man] as he was paraded through town on a carnival float drawn by four white horses. [During the lynching] the crowd, including the white schoolchildren, shouted their approval."[28] In another particularly grisly example, Jennifer Ritterhouse details the lynchings of two black men in Statesboro, Georgia. After the lynching, "a couple of boys scavenged fragments of bone, which they wrapped in a handkerchief and presented to the judge who heard the case prior to the lynching."[29] In addition, children would see how lynchers would be welcomed back to society with no public condemnation. In her memoirs, Lillian Smith describes how a "nice white girl" like her would be allowed to accept a gift of a soda from a murderer who participated in one of these lynchings, but "would have been run out of town or perhaps killed had she drunk a Coke with the young Negro doctor who was devoting his life in service to his people."[30]

While we don't have detailed data on the psychological mechanisms, it is not hard to imagine how these children would over time internalize the underlying implication of these actions. As DuRocher concludes, "[e]xamining children's experiences and reactions to racial cruelty reveals that many white children accepted their socialization and viewed violence as a necessity of daily life in the Jim Crow South." Indeed, "older whites, fearing that these youth would fail to control African Americans, took steps to disseminate their own racial beliefs," and they would "[encourage] white children to participate in the lynchings of blacks in order to maintain white domination."[31] This had the effect of buttressing the established social order, as Ritterhouse notes: "Whenever blacks rejected the command performance of deference—whenever whites lost the zero-sum game of racial etiquette—violence could and often did result."[32] Thus, violence served to reinforce the teachings of older whites about the racial system of Jim Crow.

On the other hand, it could be that racial violence played no role in the transmission of attitudes or that, if anything, it pushed children away from the Southern social hierarchy. Indeed, DuRocher notes that, for some white children, the witnessing of violence marked a turning point—an epiphany of sorts—in distancing themselves from the accepted Southern hierarchy and toward more egalitarian thinking. For example, she tells the story of Marion Wright who witnessed a violent altercation involving a well-dressed black customer entering a store in Trenton, South Carolina. After asking to use the washroom, the black customer was chased away by the store owner, who wielded a buggy whip. DuRocher explains, "[u]pon adult reflection, Wright realized that his reaction of sympathy for the black man being assaulted with a buggy whip represented a turning point in his life, triggering a lifelong activism for racial equality."[33] Another prominent example is the historian C. Vann Woodward, who "encountered a lynch mob in Morrilton, Alabama, an experience that affected him deeply."[34]

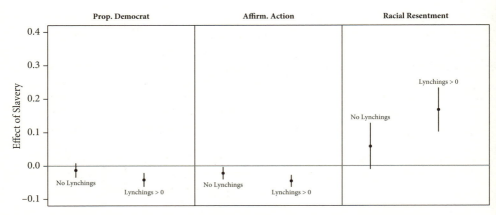

Figure 7.7. Effect of slavery by presence of lynchings in the county, 1877–1950. Each plot represents the effect of a 25-percentage-point change in proportion slave for counties that had no lynchings (left point) and that had at least one lynching (right point). Source: Beck and Tolnay.

To investigate this possibility that violence was (or perhaps was not) a means of transmitting attitudes to children, we leverage data on lynchings from the last chapter. We show there that the prevalence of slavery leads to an increased likelihood of lynchings in the postemancipation period, suggesting a lasting legacy of slavery and of antiblack attitudes via this kind of violence. But could it also be possible that these lynchings *enhanced* the effect of slavery? That is, was the impact of slavery in affecting attitudes in later generation amplified through the widespread use of racial violence? Was racial violence a vehicle for this transmission?

This question implies a simple test: Is the effect of slavery higher or lower in counties that had lynchings, compared to those that had none? Figure 7.7 shows this exact comparison across three outcomes: (1) the share of whites in a county who identify as Democrat, (2) the share who support affirmative action, and (3) the average level of racial resentment in the county.[35] Differentiating the analyses is whether a county had no lynchings at all in the time period ("No Lynchings") or whether they had at least one reported lynching ("Lynchings > 0"). Comparing the two side by side shows that the effect of slavery is much larger in magnitude in counties with lynchings than those that had no lynchings.

Substantively, this means that lynchings helped to preserve the differences between the high-slave and low-slave South.[36] This in turn lends credence to the idea, as argued by scholars of white socialization, that violence—and lynchings in particular—was an important tool for younger generations to learn about the South's racial order.

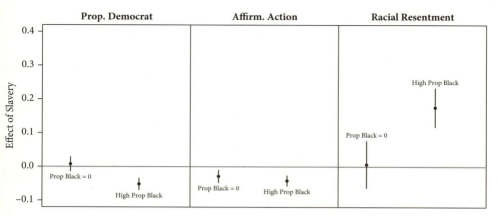

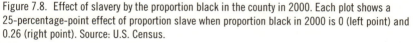

Figure 7.8. Effect of slavery by the proportion black in the county in 2000. Each plot shows a 25-percentage-point effect of proportion slave when proportion black in 2000 is 0 (left point) and 0.26 (right point). Source: U.S. Census.

LOCAL BLACK POPULATIONS

In chapter 4, we showed that racial threat and the black concentration hypothesis could not fully explain the effect of slavery, but this does not rule out the possibility that the presence of local black populations cannot affect the magnitude of slavery's effect. In fact, there is good reason to suspect that counties in the South without local black populations are likely to show less impact of slavery since these areas were less likely to deal with issues related to the social, economic, or political rights of black people. In high-black areas, on the other hand, white parents would have a sense of urgency to relay racial etiquette to their children, given the regular interracial contact that they would have. If slavery were to have an effect that was passed down, we would predict that it would be in these areas. Thus, we might expect that while proportion black does not directly cause racial conservatism, as predicted by racial threat, it provides the context for behavioral path dependence to play out.

To this end, we analyze the effect of slavery by the relative size of the black population in the year 2000.[37] Specifically, we estimate the effect of slavery for two levels of proportion black in 2000: zero and twenty-six percent (the seventy-fifth percentile). What we find in figure 7.8 is that areas with high black populations today have greater effects of slavery than those with small black populations. Here, we used proportion black in 2000, but one could replace this with a census year earlier in the twentieth century, such as 1940, and the results still hold. This tells us that the presence of a local black population appears to reinforce the effects of slavery. This could be because these are areas that were most likely to produce conflict along racial lines, or where the white elite had to work the hardest to maintain the norms of white supremacy.

PUBLIC SCHOOLING AND SEGREGATION AS INSTITUTIONAL REINFORCEMENT

The density of black populations is a coarse measure of black-white social interactions and so does not speak to how different types of interactions might reinforce or mitigate the effect of slavery. To help shed light on this latter question, we now look at one possible reinforcing mechanism: Southern schools in the twentieth century. The influence of Southern schools on white children runs deep and, apart from their immediate family, children were likely the most susceptible to influences and pressure from their peers and teachers. This influence extended not just to the classroom environment, but also to educational materials. For example, as DuRocher notes, textbooks throughout the South "presented white children with information about and images of African Americans that identified blacks as unquestionably racially inferior" while "applaud[ing] the history of white men."[38] Thus, schools provided an important venue for the education of white children into the Southern racial order.

In addition, public education was segregated by race throughout the South until the landmark ruling in *Brown v. Board of Education* (1954), in which the Supreme Court overturned the "separate but equal" standard of *Plessy v. Ferguson* (1896) and ruled that segregation in public education was unconstitutional. But because the Court failed to demand swift desegregation of public schools, many localities maintained segregation for years after the decision.[39] Some areas, however, did desegregate in years after *Brown*, and this variation in how quickly counties desegregated allows us to explore how the effect of slavery varies by the repealing of key Jim Crow-era policies. Specifically, what would a county's unwillingness to desegregate any of its schools say about the transmission of attitudes? Would white children be more effectively socialized into Jim Crow "racial etiquette" in an exclusively segregated setting? Much of the literature, including the literature on the psychological effects of segregation, would suggest that areas in which schools were slower to desegregate would be places where slavery's "lessons" were most effectively taught to younger generations.[40]

We examine this by comparing counties in 1960 (six years after the Supreme Court decision in *Brown v. Board of Education*) that had no desegregated schools to counties that had at least one desegregated school. Figure 7.9 shows how the effect of slavery varies by whether or not there was at least one desegregated school in the county in 1960. What we find is that the effect of slavery from chapter 3 only appears for those counties with no desegregated schools and there is limited evidence of the

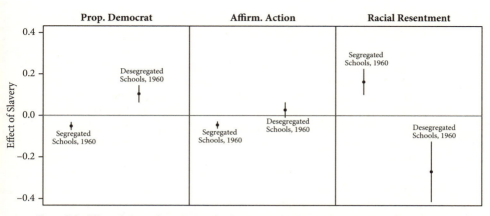

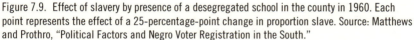

Figure 7.9. Effect of slavery by presence of a desegregated school in the county in 1960. Each point represents the effect of a 25-percentage-point change in proportion slave. Source: Matthews and Prothro, "Political Factors and Negro Voter Registration in the South."

reverse effect for those counties with at least one desegregated school. In other words, slavery's effects appear the strongest in places where schools were exclusively segregated. The differences in effects here are themselves statistically significant and remain so even if we control for proportion black in the county in 1960. These results give us some indication that interracial contact on a more equal basis can lead to a dampening of the effect of slavery, but that desegregation also helped maintain the effect.

Ultimately, early integration of schools led to an early decline in slavery's effects. We interpret this as evidence for segregated schools as reinforcing institutions, but we note that there could be alternative explanations. First, it could be the case that partial desegregation occurred in places where the effect of slavery was the weakest to begin with. In this case, segregation would not be an instance of institutional reinforcement, but, rather, simply a consequence of slavery and its heterogeneous effects. Second, desegregation might have led to increased levels of white flight, pushing more racially conservative whites out of the threat of integrated schools. While we do find that desegregated counties lose white population over the course of the 1960s relative to segregated counties, this loss is very small (estimated to be less than one percentage point).

Third, white backlash to desegregation attempts might have reinforced the effects of slavery and staved off integration past the 1960 date at which we measure it. In this case, it would be the racial backlash, not the social environment of the schools themselves, that reinforced the effects of slavery. Mickey, for example, describes the striking white backlash to attempts at school desegregation and their ties to white supremacy.[41] One way to assess this account is to investigate the role of white and black racial organizations, which were often the vehicles of the racial conflict in this era. If backlash drives our results, we would expect areas with these groups to have more conservative whites today. However, we find no significant differences between counties that had white racial organizations compared with those that did not.[42] And those counties with black racial organizations have white residents today that are more liberal. Furthermore, the effects of slavery were not significantly different in counties with black or white racial organizations compared to those without them. Thus, while we cannot rule out this explanation entirely, the evidence points to these organizations not being reinforcing mechanisms.

Ultimately, we believe the differential effects of slavery by speed of desegregation are due to the impact that segregation or desegregation had on white children. Among counties with exclusively segregated schools, it appears that maintaining complete segregation had the effect of promoting more racially conservative attitudes. This would also be consistent with existing work in social psychology documenting that people develop more racially hostile attitudes along with increased segregation.[43] Another way to consider this is that, among counties with at least one desegregated school, having black and white children attending school together may have broken down racial norms in more high-slave areas thereby diminishing the effect of slavery. On this point, Sokol gives some historical evidence that exposure to integrated schools did alter some whites' views toward African Americans in a positive direction. These are, moreover, findings consistent with the contact theory of, for example, Allport, which is that increased contact between people of different backgrounds will serve to lessen racial or ethnic animosity.[44]

7.4 CONCLUSION

Our goal in this chapter has been to trace with more precision the contours of behavioral path dependence in explaining the long-term relationship between slavery—which collapsed 150 years ago—and contemporary political attitudes in the South. More broadly, this chapter considers how behavioral outcomes—including attitudes and opinions—can be passed down over time over several generations.

Indeed, we started this discussion by noting that there exists a degree of persistence in the relationship between slavery and contemporary outcomes that requires explanation. Although we see what appears to be attenuation (a reduction in differences between regions) over time in the effects of slavery, this attenuation appears to be mainly driven by the changing orientation of political parties in the United States rather than by a softening of slavery's effect. Thus, the analysis points us to the fact that slavery's effects persist, lasting across several generations and nearly 150 years. This raises the question of how these effects have persisted and how attitudes have been carried across generations over time.

In explaining this persistence, we consider two mechanisms of reproduction. The first of these mechanisms is intergenerational transmission of beliefs, or that parents, grandparents, and older relatives often pass on their attitudes and behaviors to their children. To demonstrate that intergenerational transmission could be at play here, we used data from the Youth-Parent Socialization Panel Survey to show that the racial attitudes of children are correlated with the racial attitudes of their parents in data starting from passage of the Civil Rights Act to the end of the twentieth century. As further evidence for local community socialization across generations, we also show that the effects of slavery on adult attitudes are weakest for Southerners who did not grow up in the South. If community socialization is an important factor in explaining the effects of slavery, then people who moved into large slaveholding areas but who were not socialized in these areas should be influenced by slavery less, even though they have, in their adult life, become exposed to an external environment shaped by slavery.

The second mechanism of reproduction is institutional reinforcement. This mechanism suggests that, in addition to factors internal to an individual or to his or her family, one's environment also matters in perpetuating attitudes and behaviors across generations. Looking at the American South, various features of the South's economic, social, and political environment served to reinforce or moderate the effect of slavery over the course of the twentieth century. Economic incentives matter, as our evidence on the mechanization of Southern agriculture reveals. So too does the visibility of violence shape the way individuals perceive the victim group. The extent of contemporaneous contact with the victim group also matters in influencing the political legacy of slavery, as both our interaction results with contemporaneous percent black and the degree of public school segregation, show. In particular, in places that had desegregated schools, the effect of slavery is weaker.

Taken together, these analyses paint a portrait of how behavioral path dependence creates a political culture at the local level. From families to schools to violent mobs, it took the whole community to instill the attitudes of the previous generation in the next.

CHAPTER EIGHT

INTERVENTIONS AND ATTENUATION

"The law may not make a man love me, but it may keep him
from lynching me."

Martin Luther King Jr.

When Americans think of the movement for civil rights, many think of
Selma, Alabama. Incorporated in the 1820s, Selma is a city that has always
had deep roots within the Black Belt—so much so that it is sometimes
called the "Queen City of the Black Belt." Since the Civil War, Selma has
been the county seat of Dallas County (76.8 percent enslaved in 1860),
which had the distinction of producing the most cotton of any county in
Alabama through the war, Reconstruction, and post-Reconstruction. But
Selma was not just a locus of agricultural production and trade; through
the Civil War, the city was an important manufacturing hub, making it
a strategic center for the Confederacy. By the 1920s, however, the area's
cotton economy was undergoing collapse and, like many other Black Belt
towns, Selma's economy receded, bringing down many city residents—
particularly African Americans—in a cycle of poverty, inequality, and
racial strife.

Just as Selma's fortunes have reflected the broader economic rise and
fall of the Black Belt, so too have its politics. For most of the twentieth
century, Selma's politics were dominated by the Democratic Party. This
one-party system operated during the 1950s and 1960s in tandem with
segregation and racial hostility, supported by not just Jim Crow but also
racial violence. At the political level, Sheriff Jim Clark openly worked
with the Ku Klux Klan to terrorize potential black voters and liberal
white volunteers, and Selma was the first city in Alabama to have a White
Citizens' Council, a social organization created in response to attempts at
desegregation. These tactics were remarkably effective at suppressing the
rights of black residents. In 1964, for example, only two percent of Dallas

County's eligible black voters were registered to vote in spite of prolonged effort to change this.[1]

Today, the picture that many Americans have of Selma is a singular one. This is the image of the confrontation that took place on Sunday, March 7, 1965, when John Lewis and Hosea Williams assembled civil rights activists at Selma to march to Montgomery to protest black disenfranchisement. Ordered to stop at the Edmund Pettus Bridge by Sheriff Clark and a slew of Alabama state troopers and white citizens, the protesters refused.[2] What followed was one of the most significant events of the civil rights movement. The nonviolent protesters were attacked and teargassed by Clark and his men, with cameras transmitting the disturbing images across the country. Close to sixty people were seriously injured and taken to hospitals, and over fifty were arrested. The events of that day—known today as "Bloody Sunday"—marked a nadir in terms of public perceptions of race relations in the South and served to spur nationwide public support for minority voting rights. Some six months later, President Lyndon Johnson signed into law the Voting Rights Act of 1965.

The middle decades of the twentieth century would leave an indelible mark on Southern society. The combination of the civil rights movement, the Civil Rights Act of 1964, and the Voting Rights Act of 1965 dismantled a large portion of the institutional infrastructure of white domination in the South. Jim Crow segregation in public accommodations quickly fell by the wayside. Black citizens registered to vote and turned out in record numbers. The one-party domination of the South by Democrats fell apart as state parties navigated a treacherous divide between the white backlash to the progress on civil rights and remaining loyal to a national party pushing for that progress. Public opinion about blacks and civil rights underwent marked shifts, both in the South and in the rest of the United States.[3] These massive changes to the South were often driven by active interventions by the federal government and black activist groups.

In this chapter we explore the role of active interventions during the mid-twentieth century—including events like the Selma to Montgomery marches, the Civil Rights Act of 1964, and the Voting Rights Act of 1965—and how these factors could have served to attenuate differences in social, economic, and political outcomes within the South. What do these changes mean for the idea of behavioral path dependence in politics? Are all legacies of slavery equally static, as the persistence of political attitudes would imply? Or did the civil rights movement and the legal mandates of *Brown v. Board of Education*, the Civil Rights Act, and the Voting Rights Act attenuate the potential lasting impact of slavery on Southern society?[4]

As we show in this chapter, there has been a strong and sometimes quite rapid attenuation in the relationship between slavery and a host of sociological outcomes: black-white education gaps, black-white income inequality, and black voter mobilization. This attenuation, we believe, is evidence of the effectiveness of midcentury forces, both within and outside the control of Southerners. This is not to say that the issues associated with these outcomes have been permanently resolved; what we show instead is that the variation in these factors is less aligned with the density of slavery in the antebellum period. In other words, legal and cultural changes—including greater vigilance by the federal government in tandem with increased activism by black leaders—has moderately improved various black-white inequalities and led to extant inequalities being more constant across regions in the South. The results of this chapter highlight how slavery has produced a variety of legacies beyond its influence on white attitudes and that not all of these legacies persist to the present day. Thus, path dependence in the South is not a fixed concept that applies uniformly across all domains of Southern life.

The attenuation of the legacy of slavery in these policy arenas expands our understanding of where persistence does occur—in white attitudes—in two ways. First, the massive changes to Southern society in the middle of the twentieth century and their attenuating effects make the persistent effect of slavery on attitudes appear even more resilient. The intergenerational transmission of beliefs described in the previous chapter appears to survive massive changes to Southern society when attenuation occurs in other arenas. Second, these effects help to cast doubt on the idea that statistical discrimination, or that whites are discriminating not on the basis of race but on factors that may correlate with race (such as income or education), is a key driver of our results. A reasonable hypothesis would be that the persistence of the effect of slavery on white attitudes is about the long-term consequences of Jim Crow segregation on differences in the local black and white populations. These might lead to systematic differences in the types of local black populations that whites interact with today, which in turn could lead to different beliefs and attitudes about black populations. These outgroup-driven attitudes would be less about the transmission of beliefs within the white community and more about contemporaneous income and educational inequalities. The results of this chapter show that this type of statistical discrimination is unlikely to be driving our results, since we see large attenuation in these types of black-white differences over the course of the twentieth century.

We organize this chapter as follows. First, we begin with a brief discussion of how events that took place in the early-to-mid-twentieth century affected the paths of development of political attitudes in the South. These include (1) the wave of constitutional challenges to Jim Crow in the courts, (2) black mobilization and the Civil Rights Movement, and (3) legislative interventions, such as the Civil Rights Act and the Voting Rights Act. Next, we document how these intervening forces served to attenuate slavery's intergenerational effects within the Black Belt across several important issue areas: educational outcomes, income and economic inequality, voter suppression and voter registration.

8.1 KILLING JIM CROW

As the U.S. South transitioned into the middle of the twentieth century, the Black Belt and its allies had come to dominate the politics of the South. This iron grip included domination of state politics and imposition of a coarse system of apartheid and black suppression. In assessing the politics of this time period, Key noted that an "underlying liberal drive permeates southern politics," but that its expression was always kept in check by the conservative wing of the Southern Democrats, which centered in the plantation counties.[5] For reasons that we described in chapter 6, this wing, full of the planter and business elite, had strong incentives to keep the system of racial hierarchy in place for as long as possible, whereas whites in the upcountry, with few slaves in the antebellum period and few blacks in the early twentieth century, were "indifferent about the whole business".[6] Regardless of any liberal drive in the white population or indifference to the question of race, conservative whites in the Black Belt ruled much of the region as separate enclaves of authoritarian rule.[7]

In the North, views of race were beginning to evolve, though not always in a steady manner. Some white elites in the North greatly admired the artistic contributions of the Harlem Renaissance, and white supremacy as an ideology was tainted in the Northern mind by the Nazis and Hitler's "master race" ideology. As the 1940s unfolded, non-Southern Democrats began to embrace racial equality, much to the dismay of their copartisans in the South. Unfortunately, racial liberals in the North were often ineffective or slow when pursuing these goals, especially considering the urgency of Jim Crow to Southern blacks. A divide was developing, but its promise had not quite been realized.[8]

Against this background, we isolate four particularly important developments that would form the deathbed for Jim Crow and one-party rule in the South. These are (1) the legal challenges against Jim Crow, (2) the civil rights movement, and (3) legislative interventions, usually spearheaded by the federal government. Although these operated within the context of (and no doubt helped furthered by) sweeping cultural change, and there were obviously other important forces and interventions, these three factors probably had the greatest potential to alter the relationship between whites and African Americans in the South, particularly those living in the Black Belt. They also had the greatest potential to attenuate differences between the former slaveholding and nonslaveholding South in terms of whites' political and racial attitudes.

LEGAL CHALLENGES TO JIM CROW

The first of these "interventions" was a number of impactful legal challenges to Jim Crow. Much of these were spearheaded by Howard Law School Dean Charles Hamilton Houston and his former student (and future Supreme Court Justice) Thurgood Marshall, who together crafted the legal strategy for the Legal Defense Fund of the National Association for the Advancement of Colored People (NAACP). The strategy was simple but brilliant: choose sympathetic plaintiffs and build legal challenges incrementally, eventually making a compelling, morally grounded case for major change. These challenges were eventually aided by a Supreme Court that, under the leadership of Chief Justice Earl Warren, was sympathetic to the rights of racial, ethnic, and religious minorities.

Although legal challenges to Jim Crow took a variety of tacks, we focus here on two substantive areas where they were particularly successful. The first concerned the white primary, which barred black citizens from voting in Democratic primary elections. State and local branches of the Democratic Party enacted this policy, claiming that parties were private organizations and could accordingly control membership. As we noted in previous chapters, the South was solidly Democratic until well into the 1940s; thus, Democratic primaries represented the only meaningful venue for voters to express political preferences. The white primary was therefore not only a powerful tool to undermine black enfranchisement but also a fairly absolute bar to black representation.[9] By the 1940s, for example, Southern black officeholding at the state or national level was largely a distant memory and, by some estimates, black voter registration hovered around two percent in several Black Belt states.[10] More symbolically, the white primary served to reinforce and encourage white attitudes about the unsuitability of blacks to engage in political participation.

The challenges to the white primary extended from the 1930s to the 1940s, culminating in *Smith v. Allwright* (1944)[11] which originated out of Harris County (twenty-three percent enslaved in 1860), and was one of the first Supreme Court cases argued by Thurgood Marshall himself. In that case, the Supreme Court declared the white primary unconstitutional, affirming that it violated the protections of the Fourteenth and Fifteenth Amendments. Importantly, as has been noted by V. O. Key and others, *Smith*'s greatest impact, and the greatest resistance to it, was in the Black Belt areas of the South. "The decision," Key wrote, "had the most agitated reception in the states containing the largest proportions of counties with Negro majorities. The pattern recurs thematically from act to act in the history of the adjustment of racial relations."[12]

To give some context on *Smith*'s impact, table 8.1 shows the number of black registered voters before and immediately after *Smith* was decided,

Table 8.1. Estimated number of African Americans registered to vote in the South. *Smith v. Allwright* was decided in 1944.

	1940	1947	1950	1952	1954	1956
Alabama	2,000	6,000		25,596	49,377	53,366
Arkansas	21,888	37,155		61,413	67,851	75,431
Florida	18,000	49,000	116,145	120,919	128,329	137,535
Georgia	20,000	125,000		144,835		163,389
Louisiana	2,000	10,000		120,000	118,183	152,378
Mississippi	2,000	5,000		20,000	19,367	20,000
North Carolina	35,000	75,000		100,000		135,000
South Carolina	3,000	50,000		80,000		99,890
Tennessee	20,000	80,000		85,000		90,000
Texas	30,000	100,000		181,916		214,000
Virginia	15,000	48,000	65,286	69,326	71,632	82,603

Source: Lawson, *Black Ballots: Voting Rights in the South, 1944–1969*, p. 134.

showing a marked jump. As we investigate in further detail later in this chapter, however, the share of blacks registered to vote continued to remain far below their share of the voting-age population even after *Smith*. For example, South Carolina attempted to circumvent *Smith* by deregulating the state Democratic Party, though the party's reestablishment of the white primary was overturned in a 1947 lower court decision.[13] On the other hand, as noted by scholars such as Manfred Berg, *Smith* had the effect of providing "a tremendous boost to black political awareness."[14] Indeed, the decision galvanized the NAACP toward voter registration, and it began a decades-long effort to register Southern Blacks, one of the most successful voter registration campaigns in American history.[15] We return below to additional evidence about the long-term impact of *Smith* and, perhaps more importantly, the Voting Rights Act of 1965, in possibly attenuating long-term differences in suppressed African American participation across the South.

The second substantive area in which the NAACP Legal Defense Fund had greatest legal success was in its challenges to Jim Crow racial segregation, in particular in the realm of public education. The legal strategy began by attacking the doctrine of "separate but equal" within graduate education, including challenges to segregation policies at the University of Texas Law School (in *Sweatt v. Painter*[16]) and at the University of Oklahoma graduate school of education (in *McLaurin v. Oklahoma State Regents*[17]). By 1951, however, the NAACP Legal Defense Fund was ready to mount a head-on challenge to "separate but equal." The result of this challenge was the landmark 1954 Supreme Court ruling of *Brown v. Board of Education of Topeka*, which struck down "separate but equal" and overturned *Plessy v. Ferguson* (1896).[18]

Brown was striking for several reasons that speak to its possible impact on the path dependence of political and racial attitudes. First, by calling for an end to segregation in primary schools in the South, *Brown* significantly undermined a pillar of Jim Crow. As many scholars of the South have argued, maintaining segregation in schools was a key institutional mechanism by which attitudes were transmitted and taught to children. Textbooks, instruction, and resources were frequently directed toward teaching children from a very young age the importance of the Southern racial hierarchy.[19] In addition, the soft impact of maintaining segregated schools—and the message this conveyed about whites' supremacy—was indubitable. Second and relatedly, Chief Justice Earl Warren's unanimous opinion was sensitive to these deep and morally significant attitudinal issues. The opinion was not only written in straightforward, nonlegal language that the ordinary American could understand, but it explicitly called attention to the behavioral effects that segregation could have on the population.[20]

Although the first *Brown* decision (*Brown I*) overturned "separate but equal," the opinion stopped short of calling explicitly for swift desegregation. Instead, the follow-up opinion issued by the Court in 1955, *Brown v. Board of Education II*,[21] called for Southern school districts to desegregate with "all deliberate speed," an ambiguous phrase that racial progressives claimed would simply frustrate progress. For their part, Southern white elites responded forcefully, rapidly seizing on the ambiguous language to slow down or actively resist forced desegregation of public schools throughout the South. We discuss these responses in further depth below, but for now note the compelling argument made by the political scientist Gerald Rosenberg: that *Brown* and other desegregation cases were highly ineffective at changing on-the-ground culture within the Black Belt and in lessening educational inequalities between blacks and whites.[22]

THE CIVIL RIGHTS MOVEMENT

The ferocious response by Black Belt political elites in pushing back against *Brown*'s desegregation mandate provides some evidence that *Brown* by itself did little to improve the welfare of black communities in the South. These failures meant that the broad mantle of trying to promulgate broader equality eventually was borne by the civil rights movement—a systematic wave of political activity organized by national and regional-level advocacy groups, grassroots volunteers, and civic leaders.[23] This included many prominent African American figures such as Martin Luther King Jr., John Lewis, Rosa Parks, Hosea Williams, James Farmer, and others. Black churches and black religious leaders, moreover, were key figures in the civil rights movement, with religious beliefs providing a grounding conviction for ordinary African Americans' activism.[24]

The civil rights movement also attempted to confront, among other things, Jim Crow segregation and disparities in voter registration by race—and it did so with highly visible nonviolent confrontations and peaceful boycotts. The decisions on where to mount these efforts often depended on local conditions, prospects for success, and the possibility of dramatizing the harshness of white backlash.[25] For the latter goal, the aim was often not to influence local white populations, but rather to exploit the racial attitudes of Southern whites to gain the sympathy and support of whites outside the Black Belt.[26] Kenneth Andrews offers a detailed look at the legacy of the civil rights movement in Mississippi, noting that it developed dynamically in response to both allies and adversaries— shifts that in turn had differential effects on key outcomes.[27] This strategy suggests that the civil rights movement may have decided to deploy more strongly in the Southern Black Belt, where white racial attitudes were the most ingrained. In fact, moving chronologically from the 1955 murder of fourteen-year-old Emmett Till in Money, Mississippi (in Leflore County, 71.5 percent enslaved in 1860), the list of events that happened in the Black Belt includes *nearly every single major event of the civil rights movement*:

- **Montgomery Bus Boycott**, 1955–56, in Montgomery, Alabama (Montgomery County, sixty-six percent enslaved in 1860). The boycott originated when Rosa Parks, seamstress and secretary for the Montgomery chapter of the NAACP, refused to yield her seat on a segregated bus.
- **Little Rock Nine**, 1957, in Little Rock, Arkansas (Pulaski County, thirty-three percent enslaved). Nine African American students attempted to enroll at Little Rock Central High School, which was at that point open only to white students, generating threats and harassment from local whites. In a rare instance of federal intervention, Dwight Eisenhower federalized Arkansas national guard troops to ensure that the "Little Rock Nine" could attend the high school.
- **Greensboro Counter Sit-Ins**, 1960 (Guilford County, 18.1 percent enslaved), staged over the course of several months by four African American college students to protest the refusal of the local Woolworth's to serve African American customers.
- **Freedom Riders**, 1961, in parts of Louisiana, Mississippi, and Alabama. Composed of staggered groups of civil rights activists, both black and white, the Freedom Riders used interstate buses to

challenge segregation. Riders were harassed, beaten, or detained in Montgomery and Birmingham, Alabama, and Jackson, Mississippi (Hinds County, 71.4 percent enslaved). A number of Freedom Riders were eventually arrested; some were held in Jackson and Hinds County jails.

- **Birmingham Campaign**, 1963, in Birmingham Alabama (Jefferson County, 22.6 percent enslaved). The campaign involved several months of coordinated nonviolent action, including protests, sit-ins, peaceful boycotts, and other kinds of demonstrations. The protesters were met with violent responses from the city's police chief, Bull Connor, leading to provocative media images of peaceful protesters (including children) pelted with water cannons. Martin Luther King Jr., one of the campaign's organizers, was jailed during the course of the protests and, while in jail, penned his famous "Letter from a Birmingham Jail."
- **Murder of Medgar Evers**, 1963, in Jackson, Mississippi (Hinds County, 71.4 percent enslaved). The long-time activist and civil rights leader was assassinated outside of his home in Jackson by a white supremacist from nearby Greenwood, Mississippi (Leflore County, 71.5 percent enslaved). His killer was released by an all-white jury, although he was subsequently convicted in 1994.
- **16th Street Baptist Church Bombing**, 1963, in Birmingham, Alabama (Jefferson County, 22.6 percent enslaved), which was the bombing by the Ku Klux Klan of an African American church on a Sunday morning. Four girls were killed by the blast.
- **The Freedom Summer and the Killings of CORE Activists**, 1964, through parts of Mississippi. Volunteers—many of them white and from elite colleges outside the South—arrived in large numbers to register as many African Americans as possible. Three Freedom Summer CORE volunteers—James Chaney, Andrew Goodman, and Michael Schwener—were abducted by members of the Ku Klux Klan in Neshoba County (26.5 percent enslaved) and killed.
- **Marches from Selma to Montgomery and Bloody Sunday**, 1965. The marches were a series of protests from Selma (Dallas County, 76.6 percent enslaved) to Montgomery (Jefferson County, 22.6 percent enslaved) to push for the passage of a voting rights act. The best-known altercation involved Bloody Sunday in Selma.

The possible long-term effects of the civil rights movement are tremendous. Not only did the images of protesters and their harassment by local officials fuel the indignation of whites living outside the South, but they also had the effect of shocking international observers. And nearly all of the major events—particularly those earlier on—took place in the heart of the Southern Black Belt and in areas that were focal points for antebellum Southern slavery.[28]

As scholars, commentators, and especially black political leaders at the time were well aware, elites outside the South remained hesitant to intervene. The early parts of the civil rights movement were thus met with little assistance from white liberal elites outside of the South and downright hostility from many white conservatives within the South.[29] The exasperation of black leadership was evident from Martin Luther King Jr.'s "Letter from a Birmingham Jail," in which he wrote that "the Negro's great stumbling block in his stride toward freedom is not the White Citizen's Councilor or the Ku Klux Klanner, but the white moderate, who is more devoted to 'order' than to justice." He went on to write, "Shallow understanding from people of good will is more frustrating than absolute misunderstanding from people of ill will."[30]

FEDERAL CIVIL RIGHTS AND VOTING RIGHTS LEGISLATION

For many historians, legal scholars, and political scientists, the key step in Jim Crow's collapse was the twin intervention of the Civil Rights Act of 1964 and the Voting Rights Act of 1965.[31] The Civil Rights Act, signed into law by Lyndon Johnson on July 2, 1964, despite overwhelming opposition from Southern Democrats,[32] was different from earlier, less successful civil rights measures in key ways. First, the act was enacted under Congress's power under the Commerce Clause, as opposed to the federal government's more restricted enforcement power under Section 5 of the Fourteenth Amendment. Second, in part because of the different constitutional origins of the act, it was more expansive than other efforts, speaking to racial discrimination in (1) segregated schools; (2) businesses; (3) places of public accommodation such as hotels, theaters, and restaurants; and (4) public facilities and establishments, such as public libraries, swimming pools, and community centers. Third, the act gave the Department of Justice the authority to pursue legal action against those in violation, lessening the pressure on individual African Americans to initiate costly legal action. Importantly, however, although the Civil Rights Act spoke to economic and business concerns and discrimination occurring in public spaces, it did not speak to (1) the use of discriminatory tests or devices at the polling place, and (2) discrimination happening between individuals, or *de facto* segregation or discrimination.[33] As Republican Arizona Senator Barry Goldwater said in opposing the bill, "You can't legislate morality."[34]

After segregation, many saw voting rights as the next target, and the Freedom Summer of 1964 and the marches from Selma to Montgomery in 1965 represented a direct push toward greater voter registration for African Americans. These also followed a coordinated NAACP strategy, which for a decade prior had attempted to increase black voter registration.[35] From the perspective of federal intervention, these events culminated in the passage of the Voting Rights Act of 1965, passed and signed into law by Lyndon Johnson on August 6, 1965, with relatively little support from the Southern Democrats.[36] We discuss the impact of the Voting Rights Act extensively in the next section, but for now we note that the act had three important purposes. The first was to reaffirm the Fifteenth Amendment rights of racial minorities to vote, which had long been cast aside in the era of Jim Crow. The second explicitly outlawed voter repression instruments, such as literacy tests, which were extensively in use throughout the South at the time of its passage. Third, the Voting Rights Act set up a system under which certain jurisdictions ("covered jurisdictions") had to submit any proposed changes to voting laws to the federal government for review, a system known as "preclearance."[37] Because, as we argue, those elites holding power in former slaveholding areas had strong incentives to hold onto that power, many of those jurisdictions that were "covered" under the Voting Rights Act were former slaveholding areas.[38]

8.2 ATTENUATION OF THE LEGACY OF SLAVERY IN THE SOUTH

What do we make of this historical progression? Although the literature is mixed on whether the legal strategy of the NAACP Legal Defense Fund or the events of the civil rights movement by themselves spurred on greater racial equality, or whether it was primarily the effects of federal involvement via the Civil Rights Act or the Voting Rights Act, no one can doubt that all of these events taken together were significant in securing greater equality and protections for Southern blacks.[39]

In this section, we examine the possible attenuating effects of these interventions by looking at how they affected regional differences within the South. In doing so, we focus on *attenuation* as a central concept in path dependence, and specifically the idea that *certain differences between the Black Belt and other parts of the South lessened during this time period, possibly in response to these interventions*. To emphasize this point, these interventions, we believe, may have been effective in ameliorating or lessening slavery's impact on modern-day outcomes, reducing potential differences between the Black Belt and other parts of the American South. This stands in relatively stark contrast to the stubbornly persistent effects of slavery on attitudinal measures that we saw in the last chapter. We investigate the potential attenuating effect of these forces across three types of outcomes related to differences between local black and white populations: (1) educational inequalities, (2) income inequalities, and (3) inequalities in voter registration. These were, after all, the intended targets of the legal challenges leading up to *Brown*, the Civil Rights Act, and the Voting Rights Act. For each issue area, we note how the Black Belt differed before and after these interventions and whether differences between the Black Belt and other regions within the South in fact attenuated.

Examining the potential attenuating effect of these interventions is important for our argument for several reasons. First, our argument has turned on the idea of historical persistence of attitudes and outcomes, which stem directly from the earlier institution of slavery, including the incentives created after its collapse. Finding attenuation among these patterns would suggest that interventions can actually be effective in addressing systemic historical inequalities. Second, finding differences across certain outcomes would perhaps suggest that different kinds of interventions might be more or less effective, depending on the circumstances. This has significant policy importance as we think about the kinds of interventions that might be effective moving forward.

BROWN, THE CIVIL RIGHTS ACT, AND EDUCATION IN THE BLACK BELT

The civil rights movement, and in particular the legal challenges brought by the NAACP Legal Defense Fund against segregation, transformed African American education throughout the South, ending "separate but equal." However, as has been noted by scholarly commentators, Southern elites strongly resisted the Supreme Court's mandate, and it was not until the passage of the Civil Rights Act in 1964 that blacks started attending the same schools as whites.[40] Table 8.2 documents this transition, using data from Rosenberg. In 1952, for example, close to zero black children were attending integrated schools in the South. The figures barely moved upward after both *Brown I* in 1954 and *Brown II* in 1956. It was only after the Civil Rights Act was enacted in July of 1964 that the numbers started to move aggressively. For example, the percentage of black students attending integrated schools went from just 2.3 percent in 1962 to 16.9 in 1964 and to 32 percent in 1968. This is strong evidence of the powerful effects of the Civil Rights Act and its call for federal enforcement of the educational provisions.[41]

Did these patterns vary regionally within the South? Were former slaveholding strongholds in the Black Belt less inclined to operate fully segregated schools? Since so few black children attended desegregated schools due to laws at the state level (as table 8.2 shows), there is little localized variation to exploit before the Civil Rights Act. Instead, we

Table 8.2. Percent of African American children attending integrated schools (schools with white children) in the South.

1952	1954	1956	1958	1960	1962	1964	1966	1968	1970	1972
0	0.001	0.14	0.13	0.16	0.45	2.3	16.9	32	85.9	91.3

Source: Rosenberg, *The Hollow Hope: Can Courts Bring About Social Change?*

look at a different, perhaps more meaningful measure: the educational attainment gaps between blacks and whites, pre- and post-1964. After all, the primary objective of desegregation was to attack the widely understood purpose of "separate but equal," which was to systematically deny black children the same educational opportunities afforded to white children. Thus, comparing the eventual educational outcomes of whites and blacks, and how they vary geographically, is a meaningful measure of educational inequality. Seeing strong geographical differences would suggest a lasting institutional legacy of slavery and regional resistance to the Civil Rights Act; seeing little or no regional variation would suggest attenuation.

We conduct two analyses on this question, one before the passage of the Civil Rights Act in 1964 and one after. For the first analysis, we examine data from the 1960 U.S. Census. Note that this analysis, because it uses data from 1960, captures educational differences after *Brown I* and *Brown II*, but before the enactment and subsequent enforcement of the Civil Rights Act, which many scholars believe to have been the impetus for effective desegregation.[42] To operationalize the level of education, we simply look at the median white attainment (in years) and compare it to the median black attainment (also in years). Seeing a positive gap would suggest that whites are typically securing higher levels of education than are blacks. As we have done previously, we examine whether this varies according to the share of the county that was enslaved in 1860 from the 1860 U.S. Census. If this varies according to the share enslaved, then we also have good evidence that the Black Belt areas of the South were areas in which blacks were particularly disadvantaged before the Civil Rights Act in terms of this important educational outcome.

This analysis is presented in the left panel of figure 8.1. The figure shows both that (1) a sizable white-black education gap exists in the years before the Civil Rights Act was enacted in 1964 (and after *Brown I* and *Brown II*, consistent with the arguments of Rosenberg), and that (2) the size of the gap is indeed correlated with the share that was enslaved in 1860. That is, the gap in the median years of education between whites and blacks in a given county is much larger in formerly high-slave counties, ranging from a white-black gap of around five or even six years in the high-slave areas of the Black Belt to around two or three years for areas that were

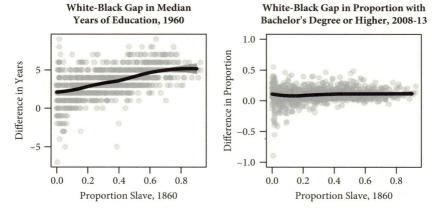

Figure 8.1. Relationships between slavery in 1860 and (left) difference in median years of education between white and black adults, 1960, and (right) difference between proportion of whites and proportion of blacks with a bachelor's degree or higher, 2008–13. Source: Matthews and Prothro, "Political Factors and Negro Voter Registration in the South"; American Communities Survey, 5-year average, 2008–13.

formerly low-slave. Numerous structural and attitudinal factors could be explaining this pattern, including increased discrimination by local whites, diminished returns to educational achievement, and pressure within family structures to enter the labor market instead of pursuing education. The data are, however, clear as to the result: educational inequalities at the midcentury mark were the largest in formerly high-slave areas of the South. The data are also clear that these inequalities lasted well beyond *Brown I* (1954) and *Brown II* (1956), although we note the caveat that these data include white and black adults, and so include individuals educated substantially earlier than either *Brown* decision.

Does the difference in educational outcomes between high-slave and low-slave areas persist over time, after the enactment of the Civil Rights Act in 1964 and to the present day? To explore this, we look to contemporary data on educational outcomes. These data come from the 2013 American Community Survey, conducted by the U.S. Census. Unfortunately, these data do not have the exact same educational measures as the 1960 U.S. Census; however, they do include measures on the share of the population that obtained a bachelor's degree (or higher), and thus capture educational inequalities to a substantial extent. As before, we look at the attainment gap between whites and blacks and whether any such gap varies by geography. Seeing persistent predictive patterns associated with the proportion enslaved would suggest a very long impact of slavery, one that would have survived *Brown*, *Brown II*, the civil rights movement, and the Civil Rights Act. Seeing no pattern would suggest a strong impact of these interventions and movements.

The right panel of figure 8.1 presents these results. Looking at the relationship between slavery and the white-black gap in the share who have bachelor's degrees, we see no pattern. Unlike many of our previous analyses, the line is close to horizontal, suggesting no change in the size of the white-black college gap as the share of people enslaved in an area rises. Although there is a gap that suggests poorer outcomes for blacks compared to whites, we detect no variation across different regions of the South. Although this is only one kind of educational outcome, this suggests to us that the difference between former slaveholding and nonslaveholding counties *has attenuated, perhaps significantly, when it comes to certain kinds of educational outcomes*. This is evidence that the Civil Rights Act, perhaps combined with *Brown*, *Brown II*, and the legal dismantling of Jim Crow, had an effect in evening out educational opportunities between blacks and whites and, for the purposes of our argument on slavery's lasting effects, lessening the previously existing differences between areas of the Black Belt and other parts of the South in terms of educational outcomes.[43]

POVERTY AND INCOME INEQUALITY IN THE BLACK BELT

In addition to educational outcomes, both the civil rights movement and also the Civil Rights Act may have had effects on the economic and living conditions of blacks throughout the South. Part of blacks' socioeconomic status was intimately tied to discrimination: so long as many businesses could legally discriminate against African Americans, black workers and customers (not to mention entrepreneurs) would be at a systematic disadvantage compared to whites. Thus, it is no surprise that, according to the 1970 U.S. Census, over ninety-five percent of Southern counties had black poverty rates of over twenty-five percent, with nearly half of black families in the Deep South living below the poverty line. By penalizing discrimination, it is possible that the Civil Rights Act may have also served to attenuate regional differences in income inequality.[44]

To investigate the possibility that (1) the former slaveholding areas of the U.S. South were the ones with highest levels of black-white income inequality before the civil rights movement, and whether (2) the differences between the Black Belt and the rest of the South attenuated after the Civil Rights Act, we look to two sources of data. The first is the 1940 U.S. Census, which was the first to ask respondents about wages. The second is the more contemporary 2006–10 American Community Survey, which also asked respondents about earnings (in the form of income). Using both of these data sources, we then calculate a measure of white-black income inequality, which we take as the ratio of median white wages (or in 2010, income) to

Figure 8.2. Relationships between slavery in 1860 and the log of the white-black median wage ratio in 1940 (left) and the log of the white-black median income ratio, 2009–14 (right). Source: 1940 U.S. Census, American Community Survey, 2009–14.

black median wages (or income). Because ratios can be highly nonlinear, we take the log of these values.

Is there a relationship between a county being in the Black Belt and black-white income inequality in the midcentury? The data suggests as much. The left panel of figure 8.2 shows the relationship between county-level proportion slave in 1860 and the natural log of the white-black wage ratio in 1940. This strong, positive trend is robust to both controlling for 1860 covariates and to using the cotton-suitability instrumental variables approach for estimating the effect. (Note that because we rely on median incomes in this analysis, the results are unlikely to be driven by a few very rich whites.) This is perhaps not surprising: as we discussed in chapter 6, the sharecropping system that had replaced plantation agriculture in the Black Belt had left blacks with little opportunity for economic mobility, and black farmers were in a much more tenuous position economically in the Black Belt than elsewhere. Given the economic and political environment of these areas, our finding that black median incomes are lower is hardly surprising and is consistent with our theory of the economic and political incentives of this time period and of their persistence into the mid-twentieth century.

Does the persistent Black Belt effect on white-black wage gap extend to the present day? It appears only weakly so. The modern-day relationship between racial income inequality and slavery is shown in the right panel of figure 8.2, and it is far more muted. Overall, the relationship between slavery and income inequality is lower today than it was in 1940, even as the variance of inequality between counties has decreased. This attenuation has been the most dramatic for the highest-slave counties: those with more than sixty percent enslaved in 1860 have seen their white-black income inequality ratio fall in half, from 3.40 to 1.72. More broadly, a comparison of the two time periods suggests that the baseline level of income inequality between whites and blacks in the South has gone down: in 1940, the average county had a white-to-black wage income ratio of 2.45, while in 2010, the average county only had a white-to-black income gap of 1.56. Regression analyses controlling for state fixed effects, geography, and 1860 demographic and economic factors indicate that this attenuation is statistically significant. Our conclusion is that, while these income gaps clearly still exist and they do have some residual correlation with slavery in 1860, the sharp economic variation *within* the South appears to have diminished over time.[45]

POLITICAL SUPPRESSION AND VOTING

Perhaps the most important strides following the civil rights movement and the twin federal interventions of the Civil Rights Act and the Voting Rights Act came with regard to voting rights and relief from voter suppression. The consensus among many scholars has been that the Voting Rights Act was highly effective in terms of increasing the share of African Americans registered to vote. As Supreme Court Chief Justice John Roberts wrote in the 2013 Supreme Court case of *Shelby County v. Holder*, "[s]hortly before enactment of the Voting Rights Act, only 19.4 percent of African-Americans of voting age were registered to vote in Alabama, only 31.8 percent in Louisiana, and only 6.4 percent in Mississippi. Those figures were roughly 50 percentage points or more below the figures for whites."[46]

The early 1960s witnessed civil rights organizations making major attempts to register Southern blacks, usually in the face of strong white resistance.[47] However, the effectiveness of these initiatives within the Black Belt, where blacks were most likely to be disenfranchised, were only modestly successful. To put some context to this, in the left panel of figure 8.3 we show the relationship between the prevalence of slavery in 1860 and the black voter registration in 1964, a year before the implementation of the Voting Rights Act. As might be expected given the local political oppression in the former slaveholding areas discussed in previous chapters, there is a strong *negative* relationship between the extent of slavery in 1860 and the extent of black voter registration before the passage of the Voting Rights Act. Thus, the more prevalent slavery was in 1860, the more disenfranchised blacks were before the Voting Rights Act.[48] This result remains when looking at the relationship between slavery and black voter registration within states. Given that most of the voter disenfranchisement laws were constant within a state, this provides strong evidence that local organizations and customs were important in the disenfranchisement of African Americans.

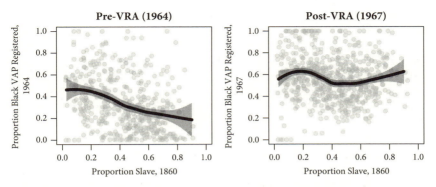

Figure 8.3. Relationships between slavery in 1860 and proportion of the black voting-age population (VAP) registered in 1964 (*left*) and the proportion of the black VAP registered in 1967, after implementation of the Voting Rights Act (VRA) (*right*). Source: Matthews and Prothro, *Negroes and the New Southern Politics*; Alt, "Race and Voter Registration in the South Before and After the Voting Rights Act."

Does the relationship between slavery and black voter registration persist after the passage of the Voting Rights Act in 1965? The data suggest that it does not: the Voting Rights Act had an almost immediate impact on the relationship between slavery and voting rights in the South. We show this in the right panel of figure 8.3, which shows the same relationship between slavery and black voter registration, now in 1967, *two years after the implementation of the Voting Rights Act*. The data show, quite clearly, that there exists little to no relationship between slavery and black registration rates, a very dramatic shift in just a three-year span. Substantively, this means that black registration rates between 1964 and 1967 were the highest in the areas of the South that had the strongest legacy of slavery, even when looking within states and controlling for 1860 covariates.[49]

There are two caveats here. The first is that this is an analysis of voter *registration*, not voter *turnout*. The second is that this analysis does not intend to estimate the causal effect of the Voting Rights Act on voter registration, since the act was intended to apply more forcefully to specific regions of the South. However, what is clear from this analysis is that persistent inequalities in black registration significantly attenuated in the years after the Voting Rights Act's passage. This analysis thus highlights how some lasting effects of historical institutions can be undone at a very rapid rate with the appropriate policy interventions.

WHY ATTENUATION?

In the previous chapters, we have shown that the legacy of slavery for political attitudes continues until today. Why do we see attenuation on the above measures of local populations, but not for persistence? We first note that there have been large changes to how Southerners view black people and civil rights. In 1965, Southern whites in the Youth-Parent Socialization Survey rated whites on average thirty points higher on the thermometer scores than blacks. By contrast, in 1998, this gap had dropped to just two points. Thus, there has been substantial decay in white anti-black attitudes over the second half of the twentieth century.[50] What is important for attenuation, however, is *differential decay* across the South. For attenuation in attitudes to occur, white racial attitudes in high-slave areas would have to decay faster than in low-slave areas. We find this to not be the case. In the ANES data, from 1984 until 1998, there is significant decay in Southern whites' thermometer score differences between whites and blacks, but this decay is statistically indistinguishable across levels of slavery.[51] Thus, while there has been a large mean shift in white Southern attitudes, the relationship with slavery has largely been preserved.

Why, then, do we see differential decay in these measures related to the federal interventions? Answers to this question could fill an entire volume, but we can offer suggestive evidence that the federal government targeted their interventions to areas with a legacy of slavery. One piece of evidence on this point comes from the Voting Rights Act, which authorized the Department of Justice to send examiners to oversee voter registration efforts in counties. While the administration of Lyndon Johnson was hesitant to dispatch these examiners for fear of white backlash, they did send examiners to forty-six counties in the South by 1966. All but one of these examiners were sent to counties with over twenty percent enslaved. Using the statistical modeling approaches of chapter 3, we find a consistent, positive effect of slavery on the presence of federal examiners in 1966 and 1969–71.[52] These results point to a reason for the differential decay in the above institutional outcomes—the federal government appears to have focused their energy in areas that had a legacy of slavery, leading to attenuation in the relationships with slavery.[53]

As argued above, black protest organizations also focused their efforts on areas where local conditions were bad for blacks and where they might generate white backlash. We find that thirty-seven percent of high-slave counties had black protest organizations in 1960 compared to only sixteen percent of low-slave counties. Furthermore, there appear to be higher levels of white countermobilization in the Black Belt: six percent of low-slave counties had white racial organizations (such as White Citizens' Councils), compared to twenty-seven percent of high-slave counties.[54] There are two reasons why these factors might not have attenuated attitudes in spite of differential activity across high- and low-slave areas. First, the increased activity of white and black organizations in Black Belt areas might have offset each other, leading to no net change in attitudes.

Second, the organized activity of these groups, especially the black protest organizations, might have had effects that spilled over into other areas, including the low-slave South and the North. Indeed, as we discussed above, these types of spillovers were a major goal of these organizations.[55]

8.3 CONCLUSION

In this chapter, we have reviewed some of the more prominent intervening factors of the late twentieth century as pertains to civil rights—specifically the great strides of the civil rights movement, the Civil Rights Act, and the Voting Rights Act. In many ways, the focus of these movements was the former slaveholding regions, where local discrimination and inequality were at their highest. These were the places where whites sought to restrict the economic and political rights of blacks and so it is no surprise that these were also the places of the strongest black resistance in the middle of the twentieth century. The resulting court rulings and legislation of this era sought to partially fulfill the promises of equality that Reconstruction was supposed to bring.

The federal interventions of this era had a massive impact on the South and had a strong impact on the relationship between slavery and inequality. We have shown how in the middle of the twentieth century there were strong relationships between slavery and inequality on a host of measures, including voting, income, and education. This is not surprising given the legacy of Jim Crow we detailed in the chapter 6. What is perhaps surprising is how these relationships have attenuated over time. In voting rights, the Voting Rights Act destroyed the relationship between slavery and black voter registration in a matter of years. In education, we see almost no relationship between slavery and the educational attainment gap today. In income, we have seen a massive decay in the relationship between slavery and the household income gap between whites and blacks. Overall, it appears that the federal interventions of the 1960s and beyond were effective at not only improving the political and economic rights of African Americans but also attenuating the political geography of slavery for these same outcomes.

Another lesson we can draw from these analyses is on the role of statistical discrimination in driving our results. If whites are responding to their localized environment (not just via racial threat, which we consider in chapter 4), then perhaps whites are simply responding in a contemporaneous way to increased poverty, lack of education, and other sorts of inequalities. Thus, a possibility is that whites' attitudes are explained by this concept of statistical discrimination; that is, they are not responding in an explicitly racially motivated way, but they are responding to those characteristics that appear to vary jointly with race—for example, income, education, poverty, etc.[56] Put simply: maybe whites in high-slave areas have different attitudes about black people and politics because they interact with different *types* of black people than those in the low-slave South.

We argue that the attenuation of the effect of slavery weakens the case for statistical discrimination as a plausible mechanism for explaining the findings of this book. This is because, by and large, the black populations look very similar across the high- and low-slave South. To see this, we divided up all counties in our data and split them into two roughly equal-sized groups of high-slave and low-slave. In the low-slave group, the black arrest rate in the median county was about 67 per 1000 black citizens, whereas in the high-slave group it was 66.2 per 1000 black citizens. In the low-slave group, the percentage of black adults with bachelors' degrees in the median county was 7.2 percent, whereas in the high-slave group it was 9.4 percent. In the low-slave group, the median black income in the median county in 2014 was $28,848, whereas in the high-slave group, it was $27,460. Thus, from a demographic point of view, white people in high-slave areas live among very similar black populations as do white people in low-slave areas.[57] This leads us to believe that statistical discrimination plays a less important role in the legacy of slavery than one might hypothesize.

We conclude this chapter by noting a key takeaway, which is that we can still detect differences in political and racial attitudes across the South, despite the effectiveness of social changes and legislative interventions in changing educational and economic indicators. To us, these findings are actually powerful evidence of behavioral path dependence in political attitudes and show how remarkably persistent differences in beliefs are over time. Institutional interventions (such as the changes in institutional practices and in the legal environment engendered by the Civil Rights Act) can and do play a role in the reproduction of behaviors and attitudes, but the evidence here suggests that their effects on differences in beliefs may be modest, particularly so in terms of their impact on the intergenerational transmission of attitudes. Interventions, in other words, can perhaps change people's *behaviors*, but they are unlikely to go very far in changing people's *beliefs*.

CHAPTER NINE

CONCLUSION: WHAT LESSONS CAN WE DRAW FROM SOUTHERN SLAVERY?

We return to the example that we set out at the beginning of this book, in considering the differences between places like Greenwood, Mississippi, and Asheville, North Carolina. Greenwood, in the Mississippi Delta, was founded specifically to take advantage of the city's fertile location. Over the years, the "Cotton Capital of America" thrived as a focal point for the growth and export of cotton, propelled by slavery in the years leading up to the war and, in the years after, by the provision of inexpensive black labor. Today, the city is still majority African American, with the traditionally black neighborhood of Baptist Town providing a reminder of how black workers lived in the early part of the twentieth century. Nonetheless, the city is racially divided and politically polarized. Black residents overwhelmingly side with the Democratic Party and Democratic candidates; on the other hand, Greenwood's white residents are among the most politically conservative in the state. They have voted consistently for Republicans and support conservative policies. Many white children attend segregated schools.

Asheville, North Carolina, and places like it are different. These areas—many in the upland parts of the South—had their origins in more mountainous regions, where the climate or terrain was less hospitable to the large-scale agriculture that was the hallmark of the Black Belt. As a result, they were by far less dependent on the institution of slavery. Asheville also benefited from its cool weather, drawing visitors and students. Today, the city is more liberal than other parts of the state and the rest of the South.

As these two examples show, and as we have developed in this book, the South is hardly monolithic in terms of its political attitudes and preferences. Looking at whites living in the South, just like whites living elsewhere in the United States, some areas are quite conservative and others are comparably more liberal. These patterns illustrate the key puzzle behind this book: What explains differences in contemporary politics between places like Greenwood, Mississippi, and places like Asheville, North Carolina? Why are whites who live in areas of the Black Belt more conservative than whites who live elsewhere in the South? And, perhaps equally importantly, why are whites living in these parts of the South more conservative than whites living elsewhere in the country?

These have been long-standing, important questions that have puzzled scholars, political strategists, and even casual observers of American politics. Of course, political observers have known for at least a century and a half that the South is more conservative than the rest of the country. They've also known that the deep Southern Black Belt—including parts of Louisiana, Mississippi, South Carolina, and Alabama—has been one of the most conservative parts of the South. For example, V. O. Key, writing in the 1940s, noted the conservative nature of Black Belt whites and how this, combined with their state- and national-level prominence in politics, led the South to skew in a more conservative direction overall.

This is an important pattern. When it comes to race, although the South as a whole has made immeasurable strides, there is significant evidence that the whites of the Black Belt have been the most racially conservative and the most likely to oppose policies that could favor African Americans. And, due to their historical political power, Black Belt whites have been hugely important in influencing the tenor of Southern politics, and, as a result, national politics (as scholars such as Ira Berlin and others have noted). Key, for example, observed that the "fundamental explanation of southern politics is that the black-belt whites succeeded in imposing their will on their states and thereby presented a solid regional front in national politics on the race issue."[1] For many years, observers of American politics have simply chalked this up to a kind of "Southern exceptionalism," simply concluding that the South is, and always has been, more conservative, with certain parts being more conservative than others. This, for many, is just an immutable fact.

Scholars have also come up with some fairly unsatisfying answers to this question. On some level, many observers have long known that the answer lay in the complicated racial power dynamic within the South and with the relative status of blacks. For example, Key homed in directly on this pattern in a quote discussed above: "[i]t is the whites of the Black Belts who have the deepest and most immediate concern about the maintenance of white supremacy."[2]

However, since V. O. Key, social scientists following in his tradition have focused too much on politics within a time period rather than on the historical context of racial relations within the South. They focused their energies on documenting the fact that Southern white conservatism appeared to fluctuate according to the population in the 1940s that was black. As Key wrote, "the hard core of the political South—and the backbone of southern political unity—is made up of those counties and sections of the southern states in which Negroes constitute a substantial proportion of the population."[3]

This observation, and others like it, led many scholars to look not at historical factors, but at contemporaneous factors explaining race relationships—including explorations of income inequality, incarceration, religion, voter mobilization, and the like. Furthermore, the effect of these factors are often interpreted in terms of contemporaneous forces, rather than being a result of their historical context. The effect of proportion black is thus understood to be "racial threat," not the cumulative effect of slavery, segregation, and inequality. More contemporary inquiries have leveraged sophisticated experiments (both natural and researcher-driven) to try to understand what kinds of mobilization techniques, redistricting schemes, and voter suppression tactics might exacerbate racial differences. But these studies, although they find some modest effects, fail in capturing the whole picture and providing a comprehensive picture of why the South—and in particular the Black Belt—is more conservative.

As we have argued in this book, we believe that the core reason why the Black Belt is more conservative than other parts of the South lies more in long-standing political forces and in factors that predate a person's income, religion, or mobilization. We believe and we have sought to argue that at least part of the answer lies in the *behavioral path dependence of political attitudes*. Specifically, we look to the Black Belt's distinctive history of chattel slavery, which formed the basis for its settlement and which allowed the region to thrive economically and politically. The collapse of this institution was a tremendous shift in economic, political, and social life in the South and, over the uncertain course of Reconstruction, the South readjusted.

The end result, we believe, is that Southern society responded with whites becoming more resolute in antiblack attitudes, behaviors, and norms. This extended not only to institutional constraints on black mobility, but also to the establishment of a strongly held racial hierarchy.[4] This was particularly the case among the population that had been the most reliant on slavery and on the labor provided by African Americans— the whites of the Black Belt. This would explain why, among all of the areas in the South, the former bastions of slavery are among the most conservative and the most opposed to racially progressive policies. And, because the white voices of the Black Belt have historically dominated Southern politics, we believe that the issue of slavery and its abolition came at some point to dominate Southern politics.

How did these patterns persist over time, even after the shocks of emancipation and Reconstruction came to a close? We believe that behavioral path dependence provides a powerful explanation. This is an extension of work in political science and economics regarding institutional path dependence, but applied to outcomes that are specifically behavioral in nature. This sort of dependence can operate through intergenerational socialization, such as the nurturing that happens between older and younger generations. But it can also happen via institutional reinforcement, or when institutions reinforce the behavioral outcomes in each successive generation. Often, these two forces operate together, as they did in the American South. For example, scholars such as Jennifer Ritterhouse and Kristina DuRocher have documented how white children were educated from an early age in the racial order (or "racial etiquette," to use the phrase from Ritterhouse) of the South. Similarly, some institutions—such as schools—reinforced these attitudes.[5]

An important point here, as we have tried to demonstrate, is that current political patterns, and specifically the relationship between slavery and conservatism, cannot be explained by contemporary factors alone. Indeed, even documenting the fact that many millions of people of African descent continue to live in rural parts of the South, Southern whites are still more conservative. This counters the explanation provided by the literature on racial threat, that the contemporary concentration of blacks drive these patterns. For this reason, we believe that slavery and its collapse continues to have an independent effect on whites' attitudes, one that operates independently of any demographic persistence. What our analysis shows, then, is that slavery and its aftermath predicts contemporary attitudes independent of Southern demographics.

We think there are three broad lessons to be learned from these findings.

9.1 BEHAVIORAL PATH DEPENDENCE HELPS EXPLAIN CONTEMPORARY POLITICAL CULTURE

We have argued in this book, and the empirical evidence shows, that whites who live *today* in areas of the South where slavery was prevalent in the antebellum period are more likely to be racially conservative and more in opposition to policies that many believe could favor African Americans (such as affirmative action). These whites are also more likely to say that they believe that structural factors—such as a history of slavery or discrimination—are less consequential in dictating blacks' station in life than are other factors. Lastly, these whites are also more likely to express cooler feelings toward African Americans as a whole, as measured by public opinion surveys and other techniques. These are all people who are living in these areas today, 150 years after the collapse of slavery. Even so, slavery's prevalence is predictive of these attitudes.

As we have discussed, our analysis give us good reasons to think that these patterns are a direct and persistent remnant of an earlier time period. Indeed, as we have shown in this book, these patterns, although contemporary, appear to go back in time. The Black Belt is not only more conservative today, but it has consistently been more conservative over the last 150 years. Our analysis shows that, in each election dating back to approximately 1880, the whites of former slaveholding areas were more likely to support racially conservative candidates. We also find that the whites of the Black Belt were the most likely to support state constitutions that created the legal framework for Jim Crow. These parts of the South were also more likely to subject African Americans to racial violence, including lynchings. In the twentieth century, these were places with the greatest inequality between blacks and whites in terms of schooling and other outcomes; literature from sociology and history suggests that the formerly high-slave Black Belt was where segregation was the strongest and most enduring. In sum: these patterns are long-standing, suggesting the long-term persistence of antiblack attitudes that are stronger in the former slaveholding South.[6]

We believe that a broader, more generalizable lesson to draw from this is that political attitudes can persist over time, across generations and within geographical areas. To explain this, we have developed an inclusive, widely applicable theory of the origins and persistence of political attitudes, which we call *behavioral path dependence*. We take behavioral path dependence to be *path dependence in behavioral outcomes, including in individuals' attitudes, norms, and beliefs*. In general, the origins of a divergence in behavioral path dependence—which is what we see in our example across the American South—stem from a critical juncture. These critical junctures tend to be historically significant events that set societies down a certain path. Looking at the American South, we believe that one such critical juncture was the abolition of slavery and the subsequent regional strife that ensued. Emancipation was a tremendous shock to the Southern economy and to Southern politics, which we discuss again below. After emancipation, as historians of the era have noted, Southern society was mired in uncertainty. It could move forward from the collapse of slavery as a more egalitarian society. Or it could respond more sensitively to the economic and political incentives engendered by slavery's collapse—particularly the incentives for the maintenance of inexpensive black labor—and the instrumental alliance of whites across social strata. As our analyses show, we believe that the South—in particular the formerly high-slave South—took the latter path toward Jim Crow and stronger antiblack attitudes.[6]

A critical juncture by itself is not enough to see long-term divergences in behavioral path dependence, as we do in the U.S. South. For attitudes to last historically, we must also have *mechanisms of reproduction*. Here, we think there are at least two. The first is intergenerational socialization, or the way that parents and older relatives (grandparents, uncles, aunts, cousins) pass onto the younger generation their attitudes, norms, and behaviors. We have ample evidence of this across the American South and in particular in the Southern Black Belt, with scholars such as Ritterhouse and DuRocher documenting the important socialization of white children into antiblack norms. The second mechanism of reproduction is institutional reinforcement, or the idea that institutions can serve to reinforce (in any given generation) those attitudes, norms, and other behavioral outcomes backed by the community. In the South, Black Codes and Jim Crow policies of segregation, formalized voter suppression, and encroaching criminalization and policing of black lives further marked evidence of the institutional path dependence of antiblack legal suppression and of the institutional reinforcement of antiblack attitudes.

All of these factors point to a unifying theme, which is that political attitudes can persist locally over time—a phenomenon explained via behavioral path dependence. However, our setting of the American South and the effects of slavery is not the only one documenting this phenomenon. Many previous studies have explored similar patterns across the world. Local anti-Semitism has persisted in Germany for hundreds of years. Africans whose ancestors were targeted by the Atlantic slave trade in the fifteenth and sixteenth centuries are still more distrustful of strangers today. Other persistent local cultures with historical roots have been discovered in India, Germany, and Ukraine.[7]

These findings, combined with ours, lead us to believe that behavioral path dependence is a general phenomenon. Political attitudes, behaviors, and opinions—like wealth, religion, or language—are handed down over time and across generations. Looking across other contexts, we might think that behavioral path dependence can help explain other kinds of divergences in political attitudes and behaviors, including differences between immigrants and nonimmigrants, people whose lives have been impacted by exogenous shocks (natural or man-made), or even those who have been affected by war or disease. So long as we have a critical juncture and mechanisms of persistence, we might see evidence also of behavioral path dependence decades, even centuries later.

9.2 SLAVERY AND ITS COLLAPSE HAVE SHAPED CONTEMPORARY POLITICAL ATTITUDES

Our conclusions have broader lessons for the United States as well. Our analysis indicates that the origins of variation in political beliefs across the South have at their root slavery and its subsequent collapse. This is an answer to V. O. Key's observation about the Southern Black Belt and why it is more conservative. Indeed, enslaved labor formed the backbone of the antebellum Deep South economy and society. The collapse of antebellum chattel slavery substantially disrupted the Southern business economy and political culture. In response to these forces, Southern Black Belt whites emerged from Reconstruction and retrenched, unleashing a litany of antiblack ordinances, laws, and social practices—which created the bedrock of twentieth-century Jim Crow. Because of the influence that politicians from these areas had in shaping state- and national-level policy, we believe that our second lesson is the following: slavery was very important in shaping political attitudes across the South and, because of that, had a role to play in making state- and national-level policy more conservative.

Slavery in many respects was a fluid and expanding institution, one that gravitated westward from the eastern seaboard and into the territories of the Louisiana Purchase (1803). Without tension over the issue of slavery, or its expansion, both high-slave and low-slave areas in the South were mixed politically, with Whigs and Southern Democrats drawing support from both. But the Civil War and Reconstruction brought an end to this. Within a period of twenty years, former slaves became free and were granted basic rights by the federal government, including the right to be free from bondage (and thus free to take their labor elsewhere), the right to vote, and the right to enjoy equal protection under the law. Although the Reconstruction-era Thirteenth, Fourteenth, and Fifteenth Amendments were repeatedly thwarted in their implementation by unfavorable court rulings, there was no question that emancipation forced Southern whites to consider aspects of political and economic public life that they had never considered before. Among these issues included the radical notion that blacks—who in some Black Belt areas outnumbered whites by nine to one—could walk away from farms and fields, vote, and freely comingle with whites. All of these components were enormously threatening to Southern whites and particularly those whites in the Black Belt who were the most outnumbered and had the most to lose.

Propelling these anxieties were two broader concerns. The first was an elite-driven concern about labor. The agricultural and extractive economy demanded access to cheap, replaceable labor. Cotton, tobacco, sugar, indigo, and rice were all labor-intensive crops, requiring (in some cases) the steady work of the land under inhospitable conditions. And after Reconstruction, new industries like lumbering, mining, and road and railroad construction also demanded cheap, inexpensive, and replaceable labor. The previous regime in which labor was coerced and maintained relatively easily within the rubric of "slavery," was now replaced with a network of laws, Black Codes, and Jim Crow—all of which were now necessary to maintain white supremacy. For example, writing in his influential work on Reconstruction, W.E.B. Du Bois made the comment about the planter class of the Reconstruction-era South that it "sought to reestablish slavery by force, because it had no comprehension of the means by which modern industry could secure the advantages of slave labor without its responsibilities." Without these incentives for white agricultural and business elites, it is unlikely that the push for Jim Crow would have been so successful and the antiblack norms and behaviors so unifying for both lower-class and upper-class whites. On this point, Du Bois noted that "the resulting color caste founded and retained by capitalism was adopted ... and approved by white labor."[8]

The second source of concern was political. With some twenty percent of all Southern counties being majority black, a real concern for the white elite was not only that blacks could vote in high numbers, but that they could politically unite with upcountry whites to significantly change the nature of Southern politics. Initially restrained by Reconstruction, conservative whites in the South later sought to protect their political hegemony both by disenfranchising blacks and by preventing any kind of biracial alliance between blacks and upcountry whites or poorer whites.[9] The results of these legal efforts—which included poll taxes, literacy tests, and grandfather clauses—were highly effective at disenfranchising blacks. These also operated along with racial violence and Jim Crow, which further helped the Black Belt white elite maintain political control of Southern politics.[10] Again, such laws and norms were not necessary in the antebellum period; it was only after emancipation that Jim Crow was necessary to ensure white supremacy.

As we have argued in this book, these forces—after an important period of uncertainty—contributed to a reinforcing of the racial hierarchy in the South, especially in places where slavery was most dense. This political divergence between Black Belt whites and whites living elsewhere has lasted through the early twentieth century, through Jim Crow and even past the interventions of the civil rights movement and federal government. Over the last 150 years, the high-slave South followed its own, decidedly more conservative path. This is an example of how an institution can lead to a political geography that remains long after the demise of the institution.

We note a deeper lesson here regarding the broader fabric of Southern politics. As a number of political scientists—including V. O. Key—have noted, the Black Belt elite played an outsized, politically influential role for decades. Key himself said as much when he commented that "if the politics of the South revolves around any single theme, it is that of the role of the Black Belts." And he further noted that "[a]lthough the whites of the Black Belts are far and few in number, their unity and their political skill have enabled them to run a shoestring into decisive power at critical junctures in southern political history."[11] Our analysis bears this out: with whites voting in a consistent, unified fashion, and with a shared interest in what Key referred to as "the maintenance of white supremacy," Black Belt elected officials were able to effectuate their antiblack preferences across much of the South at the state level. Consider, for example, our analysis of the Alabama Constitution of 1901, which was motivated by antiblack animus and which contained many provisions making it more difficult for blacks to vote and move. As we show, that document was ratified with Black Belt counties leading the way. And it is still the governing document of the state. This dovetails squarely with the points made by Key.

More broadly, we consider the larger impact that slavery and its collapse has had on *national* (not just Southern) politics and on American discourse. Although our focus has been on the Southern Black Belt, the institution of slavery left an imprimatur on the entire South—for example, via Black Belt elected officials at the state and national level. For that reason, the importance of the Southern Black Belt more broadly in terms of national politics cannot be overstated. This has particularly been the case in the U.S. Congress, in which Southern delegations have historically wielded tremendous influence.

To give a concrete example, Southern politicians sat on the most important congressional committees during the 1930s and 1940s.[12] So influential were these Southern representatives that, as Ira Katznelson writes, "[they] frequently were the pivotal members of winning coalitions in the House and Senate" and "thus in a position to choose which solutions should form the basis of public policy."[13] Although "[m]ost of the region's political leaders almost giddily propelled the New Deal's radical economic policies," Southern political actors placed the maintenance of the existing Southern racial order at the forefront of their agenda. On this front, Southern Democrats were able to garner several victories, including an informal (yet effective) embargo on the taking up of racial issues after the Democratic Party landslide win in 1932, the strengthening of Jim Crow provisions via the decentralization of administrative discretion over funds and decision-making, and, most concretely, the effective roadblocking of a 1934 federal anti-lynching bill.[14]

In the more modern era, although their veto position has perhaps weakened, Black Belt politicians have led opposition movements against national legislation on civil rights, immigration, and voting rights. Now affiliated with the Republican Party, these considerations have joined a broader partisan platform that includes support for gun rights and law and order issues, hawkish military positions, and a more limited government in terms of redistribution.[15] The Republican Party and the whites of the Black Belt have been aligned regarding the importance of states' rights—which historically has been used to defend Southern states against the involvement of the federal government on civil rights issues. This is in addition to their shared concern for limiting the government's role in redistributive politics, including welfare and government-provided health care. As political scientist Marty Gilens notes, opposition to policies such as wealth redistribution (e.g., welfare) is itself predicted by attitudes on race.[16] Thus, it is not surprising to see white Black Belt politicians—and therefore influential Southern congressional delegations—assume conservative positions on these topics.

Although our analysis was not a comparative one, we do note that our study has implications for how the United States is viewed compared to other Western democracies. Of these peers, the United States is not only alone in its historical prevalence of slavery, but it is also distinguished by taking the longest to abolish the institution. In the United States around the time of the Civil War, approximately twelve percent of the entire population was enslaved, with that number rising to nearly thirty-two percent when just looking at the American South. Moreover, the United States has been among the most conservative of the Western democracies. It has historically been conservative on issues of taxes and redistribution, civil rights and civil rights enforcement, and gun and law and order issues.[17] Ten percent of Americans were completely disenfranchised before 1965, and the United States federal and state prisons currently incarcerate 1.4 percent of its population and 4.3 percent of its black population.[18] Again, opposition to more progressive approaches on these issues has come from conservative Southern delegations—which include large numbers of Black Belt politicians.

For these reasons, it seems to us that the second lesson is that a logical connection exists between America's slave history, behavioral path dependence, and a more conservative leaning regional-level politics. Furthermore, this slave history has substantially influenced the tenor of politics within the American South. And, because of the important political influence of this part of the country, we believe, slavery has also influenced the tenor of American politics overall.

9.3 INTERVENTIONS CAN HELP PROMOTE ATTENUATION AND DECAY IN POLITICAL ATTITUDES

An important takeaway from our argument and our review of the empirical evidence is that historical progress is not necessarily linear, nor without decay or attenuation of regional differences. This could result from important interventions—both from external actors (such as the federal government) and internal forces (such as the civil rights movement, African American leaders, and other actors within Southern politics). Many interventions—particularly at the federal level and also via the civil rights movement—served to attenuate (or lessen) regional divergence in politically important outcomes (if not necessarily behavioral ones). Other events have led to an overall decay in attitudes over time. Thus, we have our third lesson: decay and intervening factors, both externally imposed or homegrown, matter and, in some instances, can lead to attenuation of politically important outcomes, but not necessarily in attitudes.

To consider the lessons here, the twentieth century was one of remarkable interventions: the civil rights movement, federal legislation such as the Civil Rights Act and the Voting Rights Act, and individual resistance by African Americans against Jim Crow are all examples. Taken together with accomplishments of black leaders across many fields, this has led to remarkable decline in overt racism across the country, as has been noted by many scholars.[19] The South has been no exception. Here, in line with this scholarship, we see remarkable evidence for decay—specifically, big changes in white attitudes over the last half of the twentieth century, with a movement away from "old-fashioned" racism. However, and importantly, these changes have not been specific to the Black Belt; to the contrary, all areas of the South (and, as other research shows, across the entire country) have experienced this kind of decay in racially conservative attitudes. We believe that this is part of the natural process of behavioral path dependence: over time and across generations, the transmission of attitudes will be imperfect.

We also consider possible attenuation in slavery's many other legacies—including its legacies for African Americans in terms of education, income inequality, and voting. Here, the decay is more significant, and we also see evidence of attenuation (i.e., reduced differences between the former slaveholding and nonslaveholding South). The Civil Rights Act of 1964 outlawed the practice of segregation in businesses, places of accommodation, schools, and libraries—an immensely effective piece of legislation. Likewise, the Voting Rights Act of 1965 reaffirmed the Fifteenth Amendment (granting the right to vote regardless of race) and gave authority to the Department of Justice to oversee any changes in election laws in any jurisdiction that had used a "test or device" (such as poll taxes, literacy tests, or grandfather clauses) to suppress minority voting. Both laws were hugely effective. And both laws were targeted at the Southern Black Belt; as a result, we see significant attenuation in differences across the American South when it comes to black-white gaps in education, voter turnout, and income inequality.

However, although we see much evidence for overall decay, and although the interventions we just mentioned were effective at attenuating regional differences across some of slavery's other legacies, the events of the twentieth century *have been less effective at serving to attenuate differences in behavioral outcomes*—including political attitudes, opinions on race, and support or opposition for race-related policies. For example, we still find that Southern whites who live today in areas of the Black Belt express cooler feelings toward blacks. There is good reason to think that these differences would be even more striking in the absence of federal interventions and the civil rights movement; however, the fact that we can still detect this kind of divergence between whites living in these areas and whites living in other parts of the South is a testament to slavery's lasting political and cultural legacy.

In this sense, one takeaway from our empirical analyses is that, while interventions might be effective in reducing inequalities in contexts such as workplace or education discrimination, economic outcomes, and educational spending, it proves difficult for interventions to specifically target behaviors, attitudes, or opinions. The Civil Rights Act provided significant impetus for businesses, restaurants, and other public accommodations to allow blacks equal treatment at shops, restaurants, and other public establishments throughout the South; but the Civil Rights Act could not, by itself, compel Black Belt whites—or whites anywhere, for that matter—to accept blacks as social or economic equals. Likewise, the Voting Rights Act was hugely effective at addressing the significant gaps in black-white voter turnout across targeted jurisdictions through vigilant federal oversight and the outlawing of certain voter test or devices; but the Voting Rights Act by itself could not attenuate political polarization associated with race and racial attitudes in the South and, in particular, the Black Belt.

Our conclusion from this is that institutional interventions may be highly effective, but their efficacy in addressing public opinion is less straightforward. For this reason, we are unsurprised to see interventions across policies that are ineffective at changing opinions, have small effects, or have effects that tend to fade over time.

9.4 CONCLUSION

Given these lessons, what do our findings mean for America's future? How can we reconcile a forward-thinking American polity with the fact that, when we look at contemporary political attitudes and beliefs, we can still detect the footprint of an institution that collapsed 150 years ago?

We acknowledge that some of the lessons here are difficult. Many believe strongly that America is a nation where each generation not only has the potential to achieve the promises of the American dream, but it is also a country where each individual has the ability to formulate his or her own opinions. Our findings suggest, however, that political attitudes and policy positions are strongly persistent across generations and that behavioral path dependence in attitudes strongly predicts attitudes today.

Here, the country's history of slavery has strongly shaped, and consequently predicts, the politics of the American South, even over 150 years after the end of the Civil War. By extension, we believe that this means that slavery's legacy has been to shift American politics and policies in a more racially conservative direction over time. How people think about politics, race, and race-related issues can be a product of historical forces.

Although ours is a story of path dependence in behavioral outcomes, it is also a story about effective interventions on slavery's other legacies. The Voting Rights Act, the Civil Rights Act, and the civil rights movement were enormously effective at reducing inequalities between blacks and whites across the South—another of slavery's legacies. Moving forward, these are examples of the kinds of interventions that are both proven effective and can have a lasting impact, particularly on important, nonattitudinal outcomes—such as voter turnout, political participation, education, and discrimination in public accommodations.

But even these sorts of powerful interventions by themselves do little to attenuate differences in attitudes and opinions. Here, we can still detect more conservative beliefs on racial issues in places deeply impacted by slavery. This suggests vigilance. To give some context, at the time of this writing, several states have moved forward in enacting several requirements to voting that, although legal, have raised criticisms that they impair minority voting. For example, North Carolina imposed a voter identification law, restricted the amount of time potential voters have to register, and reduced the amount of time for early voting—often used by African Americans. Alabama and Mississippi both returned to their voter (photo) identification laws, which were on the books but never implemented until key portions of the Voting Rights Act were struck down by the Supreme Court in 2013. As of the 2016 election, all of the former states of the Confederacy had implemented some voter identification law and five of the ten strictest laws in the country have been enacted in these states. This is not a surprising fact, given our argument.[20] In fact, we would expect that, without involvement from the national government or from advocacy groups (or minority voters), path dependence in political attitudes would lead Black Belt areas—and perhaps also Southern states more generally—to adopt more racially conservative policies.

Ours is ultimately a story of behavioral persistence in political attitudes and opinions, triggered by historical forces and pushed forward via behavioral path dependence. Going back to where we started, with places like Greenwood, Mississippi, and Asheville, North Carolina, and the differences in their political attitudes, we believe that the most compelling explanations for these differences are precisely the social and historical forces that shaped their past. As we have argued here, slavery, and the downstream consequences of that institution and its collapse, led to differences in political attitudes and opinions, and these have been sustained across generations. This is the case even though the forces that led to this divergence have subsided. As a result, today, the opinions of whites in places like Greenwood, Asheville, Elaine, and Eufaula are still shaped and influenced by the events of the last 150 years.

We conclude by going back to V. O. Key, whose work was among the first to explore the contours of Black Belt political conservatism. Key once noted that social and historical forces have "an impact on political habit whose influence has not worn away even yet."[21] In this observation, he was completely correct. This might be the case for the development of political attitudes not just in the South but also in other contexts within American politics and elsewhere in the world. The challenge for scholars and for other observers of political attitudes and public opinion will be to understand, analyze, and predict where these forces will again occur and where they will take us.

APPENDIX A

DATA NOTES

A.1 SURVEY QUESTIONS

PARTISANSHIP

The partisanship question asked the following:

> Generally speaking, do you think of yourself as a ... [Democrat, Republican, Independent, Other]

and then for "leaners"[1]:

> Do you think of yourself as closer to the Democratic or Republican Party?

We aggregated these questions together to create a single measure for when the respondent indicated any inclination whatsoever toward the Democratic Party. That is, either the respondents indicated in the first question that they were Democrats, or they indicated political independence but "leaned" toward the Democratic Party.

JOBS VS. ENVIRONMENT

This question read as follows, with a five-point response scale:

> Some people think it is important to protect the environment even if it costs some jobs or otherwise reduces our standard of living. Other people think that protecting the environment is not as important as maintaining jobs and our standard of living. Which is closer to the way you feel, or haven't you thought much about this?

We coded responses of the economy being more important than the environment as a one, all other responses as a zero.

PRO-CHOICE

We coded respondents as pro-choice if they agreed with the first of the following options about abortion:

- By law, a woman should always be able to obtain an abortion as a matter of personal choice.

- The law should permit abortion for reasons other than rape, incest, or danger to the woman's life, but only after the need for the abortion has been clearly established.
- The law should permit abortion only in case of rape, incest, or when the woman's life is in danger.
- By law, abortion should never be permitted.

GAY MARRIAGE BAN

This variable is coded as a one if respondents supported a constitutional ban on gay marriage.

THERMOMETER SCORES

The question begins with a broad inquiry about certain individuals (for example, the president or other leaders, both domestic and international), but then transitions to ask about respondents' attitudes toward specific groups:

> I'd like to get your feelings toward some of our political leaders and other people who have been in the news. I'll read the name of a person and I'd like you to rate that person using something called the feeling thermometer. You can choose any number between 0 and 100. The higher the number, the warmer or more favorable you feel toward that person; the lower the number, the colder or less favorable. You would rate the person at the 50 degree mark if you feel neither warm nor cold toward them. If we come to a person whose name you don't recognize, you don't need to rate that person. Just tell me and we'll move on to the next one.
>
> And still using the thermometer, how would you rate the following (groups): Blacks.

A.2 ADJUSTING COUNTY BOUNDARIES

One obstacle to using historical data is that county borders have shifted over time. Such shifts represent a methodological problem: political attitudes today are measured using contemporary county borders, but data on the prevalence of slavery, such as those from the 1860 U.S. Census, are measured using historical borders. An example of the size of this problem is shown in figure A.1, which compares the counties in Alabama at both the time of the Civil War (1860) and today (as of the 2000 census). As the map shows, many more counties exist today than in the historical period. How can we reconcile the two?

To overcome this issue, we use areal weighting to interpolate data from the 1860 U.S. Census onto modern county boundaries.[2] While

■ 1860 Counties   ⋯⋯ 2000 Counties

Figure A.1. Changes in the county boundaries between 1860 and 2000 in Alabama. Source: Atlas of Historical County Boundaries.

population-weighted interpolation generally produces better estimates of the underlying rates of various subpopulations, we use areal weighting because we are interested in interpolating both proportions (enslaved, free, etc.) and levels (total population, improved farming acreage, etc.), and areal interpolation allows us to use a consistent set of interpolation weights across these disparate measures. Reece and O'Connell use a population-weighting approach to estimate proportion slave in modern county boundaries and our measure correlates with their measure at $r = 0.986$.[3] We use the Newberry Atlas of Historical County Boundaries for historical county boundaries.[4]

The areal weighting scheme works as follows. For a given census year, we create a $n_s \times n_t$ matrix A, where n_s is the number of source (1860) counties and n_t is the number of target (2000) counties. A is a row-normalized matrix, where each entry a_{ij} is the proportion of the area of source county i that is contained in target county j. Let y_t be the vector of target values that we are trying to estimate and y_s be the observed source vector of values. Then, we construct areal weighted estimates by $y_t = A'y_s$. Essentially, this distributes the population in each 1860 county to 2000 counties according to how much of the 1860 county is contained in the 2000 county. Areal weighting assumes that distributions are evenly spread throughout the source counties, which may be false, and many methods exist to incorporate additional information, such as roads, to correct for these issues. Unfortunately, there is little information about the distribution of individuals or farms within counties in the antebellum period that we could reliably use across the entire country.

NOTES

Chapter 1: Introduction

1. These figures are based on data from Haines, *Historical, Demographic, Economic, and Social Data: The United States, 1790–2002.*
2. Demographics data from the 2010 U.S. Census; income and poverty data from the 2015 American Community Survey; Greenwood High enrollments data from U.S. Department of Education, National Center for Education Statistics, Common Core of Data (CCD); Pillow Academy enrollments data from the U.S. Department of Education, National Center for Education Statistics, "Private School Universe Survey (PSS)," 2011–12.
3. The estimate of the white vote for Obama comes from our estimation strategy in chapter 3.
4. See, e.g., Klinkner and Smith, *The Unsteady March: The Rise and Decline of Racial Equality in America.*
5. Schuman, Steeh, and Bobo, *Racial Attitudes in America: Trends and Interpretations.*
6. "America's Oldest Citizen Dies in Mississippi at 130," *Jet,* November 4, 1971.
7. Valelly, *The Two Reconstructions: The Struggle for Black Enfranchisement.*
8. Woodward, *The Strange Career of Jim Crow,* is a canonical account of the development of the Jim Crow system, with a discussion of the segregation aspects of the laws. Kousser, *The Shaping of Southern Politics: Suffrage Restriction and the Establishment of the One-Party South, 1880–1910,* provides a robust account of disenfranchisement over this period. Also see Wright, *Sharing the Prize: The Economics of the Civil Rights Revolution in the American South* (especially chapter 2), for a discussion of the economic and educational aspects of Jim Crow.
9. Yglesias, "Charleston Shooting Suspect Dylann Roof's Apparent Manifesto Surfaces."
10. Tocqueville, *Democracy in America.*
11. See Pierson, *Politics in Time: History, Institutions, and Social Analysis,* and our discussion in chapter 2.
12. This is not to say that people don't change; they do. Children change, they grow up, and they marry, but—similar to religion—politics is a culturally ingrained quality that extends across multiple generations and changes only slowly and in response to significant life events. See, e.g., Green, Palmquist, and Schickler, *Partisan Hearts and Minds: Political Parties and the Social Identities of Voters.*
13. Gerber and Green, "The Effects of Canvassing, Telephone Calls, and Direct Mail on Voter Turnout: A Field Experiment"; Gerber, Green, and Larimer, "Social Pressure and Voter Turnout: Evidence from a Large-Scale Field Experiment"; Broockman and Kalla, "Durably Reducing Transphobia: A Field Experiment on Door-to-Door Canvassing."
14. Du Bois, *Black Reconstruction in America, 1860–1880,* p. 671.

15. We use the term "South" to mean the states with legal slavery at the time of the Civil War: Alabama, Arkansas, Florida, Georgia, Kentucky, Louisiana, Maryland, Mississippi, Missouri, North Carolina, South Carolina, Tennessee, Texas, Virginia, and West Virginia. This represents the 11 confederate states plus Kentucky, Maryland, Missouri, and West Virginia, though the inclusion or omission of these states is not important to the broad conclusions of the book. We omit Delware from our analyses because of the low numbers of slaves and its limited number of counties (just three).

16. To divide the formerly low- and high-slave parts of the South, the figure uses 25% population enslaved as the cut-off point; this represents roughly the median. That is, approximately half of counties in the South had fewer than 25% of the population enslaved in 1860 and roughly half had more.

17. Huckfeldt and Sprague, "Networks in Context: The Social Flow of Political Information"; Huckfeldt and Sprague, *Citizens, Politics, and Social Communication: Information and Influence in an Election Campaign*.

Chapter 2: A Theory of Behavioral Path Dependence

1. Republican candidates won some of these elections by significant margins. In 2016, Donald J. Trump won 61% of the vote in McLennan County; in 2012 Mitt Romney won 64.3%; and in 2008 John McCain won 62%.

2. DuRocher, *Raising Racists: The Socialization of White Children in the Jim Crow South*, p. 114.

3. Ritterhouse, *Growing Up Jim Crow: How Black and White Southern Children Learned Race*.

4. Collier and Collier, *Shaping the Political Arena: Critical Junctures, the Labor Movement, and Regime Dynamics in Latin America*.

5. Sewell, "Three Temporalities: Toward an Eventful Sociology," p. 263.

6. Levi, *Consent, Dissent, and Patriotism*, p. 28.

7. Pierson, "Increasing Returns, Path Dependence, and the Study of Politics," p. 252. However, for a critique of this argument, see Page, "Path Dependence," who argues that increasing returns are neither necessary nor sufficient for path dependence.

8. The early contributions, for example, include Polanyi, *The Great Transformation: The Political and Economic Origins of Our Time*, on the political development of the capitalist state in England; Bendix, *Nation-building and Citizenship: Studies of Our Changing Social Order*, on the developing structure of civil society-state relations; and Lipset and Rokkan, "Cleavage Structures, Party Systems, and Voter Alignments: An Introduction," on the development of party systems in Europe. More recent contributions include Skocpol, *States and Social Revolutions: A Comparative Analysis of France, Russia, and China*; Ertman, *Birth of the Leviathan: Building States and Regimes in Medieval and Early Modern Europe*; and Thelen, *How Institutions Evolve: The Political Economy of Skills in Germany, Britain, the United States, and Japan*. Even within American politics, the focus has been almost entirely on institutional evolution. Examples include Skowronek, *The Politics Presidents Make: Leadership from John Adams to Bill Clinton*, on the development

of the American presidency; Orren, *Belated Feudalism: Labor, the Law, and Liberal Development in the United States*, on the political impact of evolving structure of labor-capital relations in United States; Hacker, *The Divided Welfare State: The Battle over Public and Private Social Benefits in the United States*, on the development of the American welfare state in a comparative perspective; and Smith, *Civic Ideals: Conflicting Visions of Citizenship in U.S. History*, on the development of American citizenship laws.

9. North, *Institutions, Institutional Change and Economic Performance*, p. 97.
10. Ritterhouse, *Growing Up Jim Crow: How Black and White Southern Children Learned Race*, p. 123.
11. Sokol, *There Goes My Everything: White Southerners in the Age of Civil Rights, 1945–1975*, p. 24.
12. Bednar and Page, "When Order Affects Performance: Institutional Sequencing, Cultural Sway, and Behavioral Path Dependence," use the term in the context of studying the impact of individual behavior on incremental institutional change, but their use of the term is different from ours because we focus on behavior (not institutions) as the outcome of interest.
13. Key and Munger, "Social Determinism and Electoral Decision: the Case of Indiana."
14. Ibid., p. 287.
15. Dogan, "Political Cleavage and Social Stratification in France and Italy," p. 183.
16. Voigtländer and Voth, "Persecution Perpetuated: The Medieval Origins of Anti-Semitic Violence in Nazi Germany."
17. Charnysh, "Historical Legacies of Interethnic Competition: Anti-Semitism and the EU Referendum in Poland."
18. Wittenberg, *Crucibles of Political Loyalty: Church Institutions and Electoral Continuity in Hungary*.
19. Peisakhin, "Living Historical Legacies: The 'Why' and 'How' of Institutional Persistence–The Case of Ukraine."
20. Fontana, Nannicini, and Tabellini, "Historical Roots of Political Extremism: The Effects of Nazi Occupation of Italy."
21. Nunn and Wantchekon, "The Slave Trade and the Origins of Mistrust in Africa."
22. Guiso, Sapienza, and Zingales, "Long-Term Persistence."
23. See, for example, Fischer, *Albion's Seed: Four British Folkways in America*.
24. See Acemoglu et al., "The Consequences of Radical Reform: The French Revolution."
25. The concept of critical junctures is central to work on institutional development. See, for example, Collier and Collier, *Shaping the Political Arena: Critical Junctures, the Labor Movement, and Regime Dynamics in Latin America*, which is a detailed comparative study of labor incorporation in Latin America. Critical junctures have also featured prominently in scholarship such as Polanyi, *The Great Transformation: The Political and Economic Origins of Our Time*; Krasner, "Sovereignty : An Institutional Perspective"; and, more recently, Acemoglu and Robinson, *Why Nations Fail: Origins of Power, Poverty and Prosperity*.

26. Pierson and Skocpol, "Historical Institutionalism in Contemporary Political Science," p. 700.

27. North and Weingast, "Constitutions and Commitment: The Evolution of Institutions Governing Public Choice in Seventeenth-Century England"; Wantchekon and García-Ponce, "Critical Junctures: Independence Movements and Democracy in Africa"; Lee and Schultz, "Comparing British and French Colonial Legacies: A Discontinuity Analysis of Cameroon."

28. Valelly, *The Two Reconstructions: The Struggle for Black Enfranchisement*, p. 52.

29. For example, one possible feedback loop was in terms of education. Segregation meant that blacks were not educated at comparable rates to whites, which in turn led to some whites to think that blacks were inherently less intelligent than whites.

30. Collier and Collier, *Shaping the Political Arena: Critical Junctures, the Labor Movement, and Regime Dynamics in Latin America*.

31. Nunn and Wantchekon, "The Slave Trade and the Origins of Mistrust in Africa," p. 3224.

32. Green, Palmquist, and Schickler, *Partisan Hearts and Minds: Political Parties and the Social Identities of Voters*.

33. Jennings, Stoker, and Bowers, "Politics across Generations: Family Transmission Reexamined," p. 786. See also works such as Glass, Bengtson, and Dunham, "Attitude Similarity in Three-Generation Families: Socialization, Status Inheritance, or Reciprocal Influence?"; Jennings and Niemi, "The Transmission of Political Values from Parent to Child"; Jennings and Niemi, *Generations and Politics: A Panel Study of Young Adults and Their Parents*.

34. Boyd and Richerson, *Culture and the Evolutionary Process*; Bisin and Verdier, "The Economics of Cultural Transmission and the Dynamics of Preferences."

35. On Bangladeshi families, see Dhar, Jain, and Jayachandran, "The Intergenerational Transmission of Gender Attitudes: Evidence from India"; on American servicemen and their sons, see Campante and Yanagizawa-Drott, "The Intergenerational Transmission of War."

36. Alesina, Giuliano, and Nunn, "On the Origins of Gender Roles: Women and the Plough."

37. The literature here is significant, but works that are particularly on point include Ritterhouse's and DuRocher's accounts of how white and black children were socialized into the racial hierarchy in the early to mid-twentieth century and Sokol's account of how the civil rights movement upended deep-rooted white norms. Ritterhouse, *Growing Up Jim Crow: How Black and White Southern Children Learned Race*; DuRocher, *Raising Racists: The Socialization of White Children in the Jim Crow South*; Sokol, *There Goes My Everything: White Southerners in the Age of Civil Rights, 1945–1975*.

38. Ritterhouse, *Growing Up Jim Crow: How Black and White Southern Children Learned Race*, pp. 55–56, observes that

> lessons in racial etiquette were the most common *direct* means that white adults used to teach their children to be white—the closest thing to a "core curriculum" white southerners had. And, given women's primary role in child rearing, teaching such lessons was one of white women's chief

forms of collusion in the maintenance of white supremacy. Children who learned to treat blacks as inferiors at an interpersonal level were unlikely, as adults, to question laws and institutions that discriminated against blacks at a societal, structural level. Rather, they became all the more receptive to racist imagery and other cultural narratives that assured them that blacks were unworthy of whites' civility because they were themselves uncivilized: dirty, uneducated, immoral, bestial, less than human.

39. The lynching of Rubin Stacy is especially infamous. One particularly shocking picture shows a young girl smiling at the feet of Stacy's dangling, lynched corpse. Of this picture, Ritterhouse, *Growing Up Jim Crow: How Black and White Southern Children Learned Race*, p. 72, writes, "While the two younger girls' expressions are hard to read (and the face of a uniformed black maid in the background is, almost symbolically, hidden), the older girls' satisfied look suggests, in a way that only photographic evidence can, her appreciation for the lesson about white men's readiness to 'protect white womanhood' that she has just seen acted out." Of the same picture, DuRocher, *Raising Racists: The Socialization of White Children in the Jim Crow South*, p. 1, writes that "[s]uch images attest to the normalcy of white children attending events of racial violence during Jim Crow segregation."

40. See also Tabellini, "Culture and Institutions: Economic Development in the Regions of Europe."

41. Jennings and Niemi, *The Political Character of Adolescents*. More generally, Jennings, Stoker, and Bowers, ("Politics across Generations: Family Transmission Reexamined") explain that

[t]ransmission rates tended to vary in a systematic fashion according to type of political trait. The more concrete, affect-laden, and central the object in question, the more successful was the transmission. More abstract, ephemeral, and historically conditioned attributes were much less successfully passed on (p. 782).

A possible contemporary example is changing attitudes in Western countries about lesbian, gay, bisexual, and transgender (LGBT) groups, which cleave along generational lines. Whereas a higher share of older people are likely to oppose same-sex marriage and LGBT rights, younger people are much more likely to support same-sex marriage and LGBT rights. We discuss another explicit example—the generational shift around the time of the civil rights movement in the 1960s—in greater detail in chapter 8.

42. See, for example, Gintis, "The Hitchhiker's Guide to Altruism: Gene-Culture Co-evolution and the Internalization of Norms"; Bowles and Gintis, "The Evolutionary Origins of Collective Action"; Bowles, *Microeconomics: Behavior, Institutions, and Evolution*.

43. Jha, "Trade, Institutions, and Ethnic Tolerance: Evidence from South Asia."

44. Alesina and Fuchs-Schündeln, "Goodbye Lenin (or Not?): The Effect of Communism on People's Preferenes."

45. This is the case for nearly all studies of behavioral path dependence, which focus on regions (counties, states, discrete geographic areas) as the units of analysis.

46. O'Connell, "The Impact of Slavery on Racial Inequality in Poverty in the Contemporary U.S. South"; Nunn, "Slavery, Inequality, and Economic Development in the Americas"; Mitchener and McLean, "The Productivity of U.S. States Since 1880"; Alexander, *The New Jim Crow: Mass Incarceration in the Age of Colorblindness*; Reece O'Connell, "How the Legacy of Slavery and Racial Composition Shape Public School Enrollment in the American South."

47. Key, *Southern Politics in State and Nation*, p. 5.

Chapter 3: How Slavery Predicts White Political Attitudes Today

1. Alabama governors from Barbour County include William Jelks (1901–07), Braxton Comer (1907–11), Charles McDowell (1923–27), Chauncey Sparks (1943–47), George Wallace (1963–67, 1971–79, and 1983–87), and Lurleen Wallace (1967–68). Another Barbour County resident, Jere Beasley, briefly assumed the governorship in 1972 when George Wallace was recovering from an assassination attempt.

2. Quoted in Alsobrook, "William D. Jelks, December 1900, June 1901–1907," p. 164.

3. Quoted in Holloway, *Getting Away with Murder: The Twentieth-Century Struggle for Civil Rights in the U.S. Senate*, p. 49.

4. Wallace, who was born in Clio in Barbour County, had a reputation earlier in his career of being more egalitarian on racial issues. However, many believe that Wallace was a shrewd political opportunist who saw that speaking to whites' racial anxieties in the 1960s represented his best chance of achieving success in state-level politics. See Carter, *The Politics of Rage: George Wallace, the Origins of the New Conservatism, and the Transformation of American Politics*.

5. For more on the history of this area, see Byrd, "Wiregrass: The Transformation of Southeast Alabama, 1880–1930."

6. Folsom, Speeches of Governor James E. Folsom, 1947–1950, p. 184.

7. Several other studies have relied on the 1860 U.S. Census to examine the long-term impact on slavery on other outcomes, including O'Connell, "The Impact of Slavery on Racial Inequality in Poverty in the Contemporary U.S. South," and Nunn, "Slavery, Inequality, and Economic Development in the Americas." Note that many of the analyses that we present here can actually be replicated using the 1850 U.S. Census. Slavery in 1850 and slavery in 1860 are highly correlated, although there were more slaves (and a higher share of the population was enslaved) in 1860.

8. We measure the density of slavery by looking at the proportion of the county that was enslaved. However, this is not the only way to measure the density or prevalence of slavery. Other strategies include the number of slaves per white family or the number of slaves per slaveholder. The results that we present in this chapter are not substantively changed when replacing the measure of proportion slave with these measures.

9. Carney, *Black Rice: The African Origins of Rice Cultivation in the Americas*; Foner, *Nothing But Freedom: Emancipation and Its Legacy*.

10. See, e.g., Berlin, *Many Thousands Gone: The First Two Centuries of Slavery in North America*, ch. 7.

11. Kolchin, *American Slavery: 1619–1877*, pp. 78–79.
12. Kentucky, Maryland, and West Virginia are not always considered part of the South, but we include them since they had sizable enslaved populations. The results of this book are substantively similar if we restrict our attention to just the former Confederacy. We do omit from our analysis Washington, D.C., and the counties in Maryland and Virginia that have territory inside the I-495 Beltway. These include Prince George's County and Montgomery County in Maryland, and Arlington County, Fairfax County, and the independent city of Alexandria in Virginia.
13. King, *A Solution to the Ecological Inference Problem: Reconstructing Individual Behavior from Aggregate Data*, p. xv.
14. Black and Black, *Politics and Society in the South*, pp. 269–71.
15. The sampling methodology for the CCES is called sample matching and is not based on a simple or even stratified random sample of the U.S. population. Rather, respondents are drawn from a set of opt-in respondents such that they match a random sample from the target population on a host of covariates. This approach is as accurate as more traditional methods like random digit dialing; for more details, see Ansolabehere and Schaffner, "Does Survey Mode Still Matter? Findings from a 2010 Multi-Mode Comparison."
16. A technical note is that the number of respondents per county varied in this particular survey. For example, there are 284 respondents from Fulton County, Georgia, but only 5 from Jefferson Davis County, Mississippi. These sorts of fluctuations are natural and do not call into question the validity of what we report here. Relying on survey samples that vary in size does, however, mean that some estimates will be more precise than others. In other words, we will have more precise information about Fulton County than about Jefferson Davis County, due to the size of the two samples. (More technically, using a standard ordinarily least squares specification (OLS) would mean that we would violate the constant variance assumption, and our variance estimates would be biased.) Thus, for many of the analyses, we weight by the different county-level sample sizes to account for this. Furthermore, we also incorporate survey weights into this weighting to account for survey non-response and the sampling frame.
17. Bullock, Hoffman, and Gaddie, "The Consolidation of the White Southern Congressional Vote."
18. Key, *Southern Politics in State and Nation*, p. 277.
19. Key, *Southern Politics in State and Nation*.
20. Katznelson, *Fear Itself: The New Deal and the Origins of Our Time*.
21. Alston and Ferrie, *Southern Paternalism and the American Welfare State: Economics, Politics, and Institutions in the South, 1865–1965*.
22. There are many studies that link attitudes on race to substantive attitudes on policy and partisan stances. For example, Gilens finds a strong association between how whites view African Americans and their attitudes on welfare policy. Gilens, *Why Americans Hate Welfare: Race, Media, and the Politics of Antipoverty Policy*. More broadly, Sears and Henry, "The Origins of Symbolic Racism," make the connection between attitudes on race and a host of related policy positions.

23. Berinsky, "The Two Faces of Public Opinion"; Mendelberg, *The Race Card: Campaign Strategy, Implicit Messages, and the Norm of Equality.*

24. Sears and Kinder, *Racial Tension and Voting in Los Angeles*; Kinder and Sears, "Prejudice and Politics: Symbolic Racism Versus Racial Threats to the Good Life."

25. Tesler and Sears, *Obama's Race: The 2008 Election and the Dream of a Post-Racial America*, p. 18.

26. Ibid.

27. Kinder and Sears, "Prejudice and Politics: Symbolic Racism Versus Racial Threats to the Good Life"; Gilens, *Why Americans Hate Welfare: Race, Media, and the Politics of Antipoverty Policy*; Kinder and Sanders, *Divided by Color: Racial Politics and Democratic Ideals.*

28. Sniderman and Carmines, *Reaching Beyond Race.*

29. Feldman and Huddy, "Racial Resentment and White Opposition to Race-Conscious Programs: Principles or Prejudice?"

30. Jones, "In U.S., Most Reject Considering Race in College Admissions."

31. Only certain (Southern) states collect data on the race of registrants. Historically, some of these states collected this data to carry out white only primaries; others collected this data as part of their compliance with the Voting Rights Act of 1965. For more, see Hersh, *Hacking the Electorate: How Campaigns Perceive Voters*, ch. 6. We omit two states from this analysis, Mississippi and Tennessee, because the response rates for the race question in these states is quite low (ibid., p. 124). Finally, we cannot project further back in time because Catalist's historical voter file data is not comprehensive.

32. An interaction term between 2006 and proportion slave in an individual-level analysis of Democratic identification and support for affirmative action is insignificant for both. This analysis isn't possible for racial resentment because it was only measured in the CCES starting in 2010.

33. For a more technical description of these covariates, see Acharya, Blackwell, and Sen, "The Political Legacy of American Slavery."

34. Fogel and Engerman, *Time on the Cross: The Economics of American Negro Slavery*; Key, *Southern Politics in State and Nation.*

35. Nunn, "Slavery, Inequality, and Economic Development in the Americas."

36. Kolchin, *American Slavery: 1619–1877*, p. 84.

37. This difference was suggested by Kousser, "The Immutability of Categories and the Reshaping of Southern Politics."

38. For a similar strategy, see Banerjee and Iyer, "History, Institutions, and Economic Performance: The Legacy of Colonial Land Tenure Systems in India."

39. We omit a technical discussion here; interested readers may refer to Angrist and Pischke, *Mostly Harmless Econometrics: An Empiricist's Companion*, for an introduction to the applied use of instrumental variables in the social sciences.

40. We use suitability for growing cotton—and not suitability for growing other labor-intensive crops in the South (such as rice, indigo, or tobacco)—because cotton suitability is a far better predictor of the prevalence of slavery in 1860 than suitability for rice, indigo, or tobacco.

41. We use contemporary measures of cotton suitability, but argue that cotton suitability now is approximately the same as in 1860. Although the contours of the land have changed, and climate change is a global concern, characteristics like the number of days without frost, the richness of the soil in terms of sand and clay, and approximate hours of sunlight have only changed at the margins. If anything, increased global warming would mean that more parts of the United States are suitable for growing cotton than they were in 1860, which would mean that we are including more areas in our analysis than we would otherwise. That is, what we present here is a conservative estimate of our findings.

42. The purpose of these crop suitability measures—available for all parts of the world—is to promote the "rational" use of agricultural planning in developing areas. But the measure is useful in determining which areas of the United States are more or less amenable for growing cotton and other crops such as tobacco, rice, indigo, corn, wheat, and so on, because it adequately captures the various growing conditions across the county. There are actually three measures, depending on assumptions about how hard the land is worked (for example, subsistence farming versus commercial farming). Our measure of cotton suitability is the average of two of these measures (the ones more associated with commercial farming), which creates an instrument that is strongly associated with slavery in 1860.

43. To be specific, we run a two-stage least squares analysis including the state fixed effects and the geographic controls as exogenous covariates in both stages of the model. For the county-level analyses on the CCES data, we include the same weights from the ordinary least squares (OLS) approach to account for the varying sample sizes of the CCES across counties. For individual-level analyses, we weight this model by the sampling weights. Because suitability is determined by nature and not by human intervention, we believe this approach provides more plausible causal estimates. Of course, IV analyses rely on many assumptions. A more technical discussion, including on the strength of the exclusion restriction assumption, is provided by Acharya, Blackwell, and Sen, "The Political Legacy of American Slavery."

44. In these analyses, slavery is measured at the county level, but the surveys are conducted at the individual level. To make these correspond to each other, we aggregate the survey data to the county level to create a county-wide measure. However, because the CCES has more respondents in some counties than others, we cannot treat the observations as equal in size or as having the same variance; this would be a clear violation of the ordinary least squares (OLS) assumption of constant variance. We therefore weight each county-observation by the sum of the sample weights for each respondent within a county.

45. Many social scientists prefer to examine individual—not county-(aggregated) level—results. The advantage of doing so is that it allows researchers to assess whether things like one's education, income, age, gender, or religion could affect individual attitudes. Here, however, the historical prevalence of slavery has downstream consequences on all of these things, affecting how people in an area were educated, whether they had opportunities to attend university, and the religion with which they were raised. Including these as controls in a

statistical analysis would therefore bias the estimated overall effect of slavery. However, as we have shown elsewhere, these results do not change even if we account for differences in individual income, education, age, or gender. See Acharya, Blackwell, and Sen, "The Political Legacy of American Slavery."

46. These are linear regression models (or two-stage least squares models) of respondent thermometer scores regressed on proportion slave and whatever covariates are specified. Confidence intervals in this individual-level analysis are clustered at the county-level. We include state-year fixed effects in these models due to the long time period (1984–98).

47. Due to low geographic coverage of the ANES, conducting a neighbors analysis for this data set is impossible.

Chapter 4: An Alternative Account

1. The 2010 U.S. Census reported the per capita income in Richland County as $26,026 and the share of the population with a bachelor's degree or higher as 36.4%, compared with state averages of $24,604 and 25.8%.

2. See, for example, Broom, *So. Ca. College to W. B. Broom*.

3. Beam, "Racist Graffiti Causes Furor."

4. Kennedy, "GOP Activist DePass Apologizes After Joking on Facebook That Gorilla Is Related to Michelle Obama."

5. Borden, "KKK Met With Skirmishes at Rally to Protest Confederate Flag Removal."

6. Fausset and Southall, "Video Shows Officer Flipping Student in South Carolina, Prompting Inquiry."

7. Our discussion in this book about the early history of slavery is brief and oriented toward the arguments we make about contemporary politics. For a broad historical survey of American slavery, see Kolchin, *American Slavery: 1619–1877*. Morgan, *American Slavery, American Freedom: The Ordeal of Colonial Virginia*, and Berlin, *Many Thousands Gone: The First Two Centuries of Slavery in North America*, which provide accounts of the early development of slavery in colonial and early United States. Jordan, *White Over Black: American Attitudes Toward the Negro, 1550–1812*, traces the evolution of slavery and white views on race. Degler, *Neither Black nor White: Slavery and Race Relations in Brazil and the United States*, compares slavery in the U.S. and Brazil.

8. This database can be accessed at http://www.slavevoyages.org.

9. Fogel and Engerman, *Time on the Cross: The Economics of American Negro Slavery*, pp. 24–26.

10. Ibid., pp. 20–29.

11. The formal prohibition the importation of enslaved people into the United States did not, however, stop kidnappings, smuggling, and abduction of northern blacks or other free blacks into slavery.

12. Wright, *Old South, New South: Revolutions in the Southern Economy Since the Civil War*.

13. This westward expansion in the early nineteenth century is one of the reasons why we use the 1860 U.S. Census, which captures slavery at its peak dispersion (and, thus, influence) before the Civil War.

14. Fogel and Engerman, *Time on the Cross: The Economics of American Negro Slavery*, p. 42, also note, however, that not all of the labor was spent in actual cultivation and that the "single most important crop on large cotton plantations" required only around 34% of the labor time of slaves.

15. Foner, *Reconstruction: America's Unfinished Revolution, 1863–1877*, pp. 198–205.

16. Wright, *Old South, New South: Revolutions in the Southern Economy Since the Civil War*.

17. Du Bois, *Black Reconstruction in America, 1860–1880*, p. 28.

18. Ibid.

19. See Gregory, *The Southern Diaspora: How the Great Migration of Black and White Southerners Transformed America*, for an overview of the migration of both white and black Southerners.

20. Key, *Southern Politics in State and Nation*, p. 5.

21. Ibid., p. 9.

22. Key devotes significant attention to detailing the relationship between black concentrations and the white vote (e.g., pp. 318–329) or voter turnout (pp. 513–517), but often mentions the mechanisms for these relationships only in passing (e.g., p. 329 or p. 517).

23. Key, *Southern Politics in State and Nation*; Wright Jr., "Contextual Models of Electoral Behavior: The Southern Wallace Vote"; Knoke and Kyriazis, "The Persistence of the Black-Belt Vote: A Test of Key's Hypothesis"; Black and Black, "The Wallace Vote in Alabama: A Multiple Regression Analysis"; Wrinkle and Polinard, "Populism and Dissent: The Wallace Vote in Texas"; Schoenberger and Segal, "The Ecology of Dissent: The Southern Wallace Vote in 1968"; Rogin, "Politics, Emotion, and the Wallace Vote"; Birdsall, "Preliminary Analysis of the 1968 Wallace Vote in the Southeast"; Heard, *A Two-Party South?*

24. On racially hostile white attitudes, see Giles, "Percent Black and Racial Hostility: An Old Assumption Reexamined"; Blalock, *Toward a Theory of Minority-Group Relations*. On desegregation, see Ogburn and Grigg, "Factors Related to the Virginia Vote on Segregation"; Pettigrew, "Demographic Correlates of Border-state Desegregation." On resistance to black voter registration, see Matthews and Prothro, *Negroes and the New Southern Politics*. On lynchings, see Reed, "Percent Black and Lynching: A Test of Blalock's Theory."

25. Blalock, *Toward a Theory of Minority-Group Relations*.

26. Giles and Buckner, "David Duke and Black Threat: An Old Hypothesis Revisited"; Giles and Hertz, "Racial Threat and Partisan Identification."

27. Tolbert and Grummel, "Revisiting the Racial Threat Hypothesis: White Voter Support for California's Proposition 209"; Behrens, Uggen, and Manza, "Ballot Manipulation and the 'Menace of Negro Domination': Racial Threat and Felon Disenfranchisement in the United States, 1850–2002"; Hersh and Nall, "The Primacy of Race in the Geography of Income-Based Voting: New Evidence from Public Voting Records"; Giles and Evans, "The Power Approach to Intergroup Hostility"; Bobo, "Whites' Opposition to Busing: Symbolic Racism or Realistic Group Conflict."

28. These findings are, however, contested by Voss, "Beyond Racial Threat: Failure of an Old Hypothesis in the New South."

29. Matthews and Prothro, *Negroes and the New Southern Politics*; Wright Jr., "Contextual Models of Electoral Behavior: The Southern Wallace Vote"; Giles and Evans, "The Power Approach to Intergroup Hostility"; Fossett and Kiecolt, "The Relative Size of Minority Populations and White Racial Attitudes"; Fitzpatrick and Hwang, "The Effects of Community Structure on Opportunities for Interracial Contact"; Sigelman and Welch, "The Contact Hypothesis Revisited: Black-White Interaction and Positive Racial Attitudes"; Quillian, "Group Threat and Regional Change in Attitudes Toward African-Americans"; Bobo and Hutchings, "Perceptions of Racial Group Competition: Extending Blumer's Theory of Group Position to a Multiracial Social Context"; Taylor, "How White Attitudes Vary with the Racial Composition of Local Populations: Numbers Count"; Welch et al., *Race and Place: Race Relations in an American City*.

30. There are several important exceptions and additions to this literature. For example, several studies take issue with the racial threat hypothesis (Voss, "Beyond Racial Threat: Failure of an Old Hypothesis in the New South"; Carsey, "The Contextual Effects of Race on White Voter Behavior: The 1989 New York City Mayoral Election"; Citrin, Reingold, and Green, "American Identity and the Politics of Ethnic Change") and instead argue that racial contact can in some instances improve majority-minority group relationships, in line with the classic earlier work of Allport, *The Nature of Prejudice*. This is known as the "contact theory" of racial interactions, and it has historically provided intellectual support for desegregation. Oliver and Wong, "Intergroup Prejudice in Multiethnic Settings," find similar relationships in a multiethnic setting. Kinder and Mendelberg, "Cracks in American Apartheid: The Political Impact of Prejudice Among Desegregated Whites," show that racial segregation tends to heighten the effect of prejudiced attitudes on policy choices. Other studies argue that majority group attitudes are sensitive to both geographic and socioeconomic contexts, as well as the concentrations of minorities. See also Hopkins, "Politicized Places: Explaining Where and When Immigrants Provoke Local Opposition"; Oliver and Mendelberg, "Reconsidering the Environmental Determinants of White Racial Attitudes."

31. Fields, "Ideology and Race in American History" highlights a similar idea about white supremacy in the antebellum period: "Northern free-soilism and proslavery expansionism might both be regarded as expressions of white supremacy: the one wishing to keep blacks where white farmers need not come in contact with them, the other wishing to keep blacks where white masters could have ready access to them when needed" (pp. 156–157).

32. Vansteelandt, "Estimating Direct Effects in Cohort and Case–Control Studies." This method is more technical than traditional multivariate regression analyses, but it allows us to calculate a quantity of interest called the controlled direct effect. The controlled direct effect represents the impact that slavery has on our outcomes (here, white attitudes today) if we were to fix the modern-day concentration of African Americans at a particular level. More details of this technique and additional applications in the social sciences can be found in Acharya, Blackwell, and Sen, "Explaining Causal Findings Without Bias: Detecting and Assessing Direct Effects."

33. Rosenbaum, "The Consquences of Adjustment for a Concomitant Variable That Has Been Affected by the Treatment."

34. In Acharya, Blackwell, and Sen, "The Political Legacy of American Slavery," we show that this also holds when measuring proportion black at the zip code level using the same CCES data.

35. As in chapter 3, we use data from the Cooperative Congressional Election Survey, pulling together answers (support or oppose) from the 2006, 2008, 2010, and 2011 CCES surveys.

36. We estimate this relationship via a simple bivariate ordinary least squares (OLS) regression.

37. These outcomes and models in particular are taken from Glaser, "Back to the Black Belt: Racial Environment and White Racial Attitudes in the South." See chapter 3 for the wording of the thermometer score and "generations of slavery" questions. The "gov't should help blacks" question asks respondents to place themselves on a 7-point scale according to this question: "Some people feel that the government in Washington should make every effort to improve the social and economic position of blacks. Others feel that the government should not make any special effort to help blacks because they should help themselves. Where would you place yourself on this scale, or haven't you thought much about this?" The "deserve" question asks respondents to place themselves on a 5-point agreement scale according to this statement: "Over the past few years blacks have gotten less than they deserve." The models here use OLS on both the thermometer and ordered scales; ordinal probit models for the agreement scales produce very similar results. None of these results are materially affected by including individual-level covariates.

38. The standard errors here are cluster-robust standard errors, clustered on county.

39. Changes in black proportion might matter more than absolute levels. See Hopkins, "Politicized Places: Explaining Where and When Immigrants Provoke Local Opposition"; Enos, "What the Demolition of Public Housing Teaches Us about the Impact of Racial Threat on Political Behavior."

40. Of course, some black citizens did vote during this period, perhaps especially in the Upper South. But the black voting would have been highest in magnitude in counties with high black proportions, which tended to be the areas with a legacy of slavery. If these African Americans mostly voted Republican (which we think is a reasonable assumption for this time period), then our results would understate the effect of slavery on outcomes.

41. In addition, these analyses use sequential g-estimation described in Acharya, Blackwell, and Sen, "Explaining Causal Findings Without Bias: Detecting and Assessing Direct Effects," and include additional intermediate controls to estimate the effect of proportion black on vote shares. These intermediate county-level controls include two previous Democratic president vote shares, log of the total population, and log of the average farm value.

42. These differences are standardized so that we can compare across the various characteristics. For continuous outcomes, the effects are in terms of standard deviations; for binary outcomes, they are in terms of differences in proportions. Figure 4.5 is reproduced from Acharya, Blackwell, and Sen, "The Political

Legacy of American Slavery," © 2016 by the Southern Political Science Association. All rights reserved.

43. See Dell, "The Persistent Effects of Peru's Mining *Mita*," for a similar analysis.

44. See Acharya, Blackwell, and Sen, "The Political Legacy of American Slavery," supplemental materials, section D, for more discussion of this point.

45. Farley et al., "Stereotypes and Segregation: Neighborhoods in the Detroit Area."

46. An additional advantage of this data source is that racial views are measured *before* a move takes place, which is important for evaluating sorting. The General Social Survey, for instance, asks respondents what region they lived in at age 16. One could identify those who have moved out of the South and compare their views to those who remained in the South, but this has two drawbacks. First, there exists no way to identify the proportion enslaved in their home county at age 16. Second, because attitudes are being measured as adults, it is possible that moving out of the South itself caused their opinions to change, and, if they had remained in the South, they would have maintained their views. Thus, this data cannot tell us much about whether geographic sorting is explaining our findings.

47. These comparisons were conducted on those students residing in the South in 1965. There is no correlation between the change in proportion slave of the county of residence between 1982 and 1965 and the respondent's black thermometer scores in 1965 ($\rho = 0.12$, two-sided p-value: 0.284).

Chapter 5: Antebellum Politics of Slavery and Race

1. Queener, "The Origin of the Republican Party in East Tennessee."

2. Coulter, *William G. Brownlow: Fighting Parson of the Southern Highlands*.

3. Brownlow, *Americanism Contrasted with Foreignism, Romanism, and Bogus Democracy*, p. 18, 207.

4. Brownlow, *Sketches of the Rise, Progress, and Decline of Secession*, p. 50.

5. Quoted in McKenzie, *Lincolnites and Rebels: A Divided Town in the American Civil War*, p. 193.

6. Fischer, *Albion's Seed: Four British Folkways in America*.

7. Fields, "Slavery, Race and Ideology in the United States of America," p. 143.

8. Johnson, *River of Dark Dreams: Slavery and Empire in the Cotton Kingdom*, p. 42.

9. Ransom and Sutch, *One Kind of Freedom: The Economic Consequences of Emancipation*, p. 53.

10. Wright, *The Political Economy of the Cotton South: Households, Markets, and Wealth in the Nineteenth Century*, p. 35.

11. The average slave value in the South in 1860 was around $778 (Carter et al., *Historical Statistics of the United States: Earliest Times to the Present*, Series Bb209-214), meaning that Ward had slave-wealth of around $780,000. This corresponds to approximately $22 million today. The average Black Belt farm, with its average 6.5 slaves, had a value of approximately $5,122 in 1860, approximately $140,000 today.

12. Ransom and Sutch, *One Kind of Freedom: The Economic Consequences of Emancipation*, p. 74.

13. Davis, *Inhuman Bondage: The Rise and Fall of Slavery in the New World*, p. 184.

14. Ransom, *Conflict and Compromise*, p. 69.
15. Holt, *The Rise and Fall of the American Whig Party: Jacksonian Politics and the Onset of the Civil War*.
16. Cole, *The Whig Party in the South*, p. 341.
17. Sellers, "Who Were the Southern Whigs?"
18. Carey, *Parties, Slavery, and the Union in Antebellum Georgia*, p. 111.
19. Genovese, "Yeomen Farmers in a Slaveholders' Democracy."
20. Holt, *The Rise and Fall of the American Whig Party: Jacksonian Politics and the Onset of the Civil War*, p. 179. For example, looking at North Carolina, Crofts, *Reluctant Confederates: Upper South Unionists in the Secession Crisis* points out that because "both North Carolina parties were proslavery 'without reservation,' effective mobilization of voters, especially at the initial stages of partisan development, must have required an emphasis on issues unrelated to slavery" (p. 45).
21. Holt, *The Rise and Fall of the American Whig Party: Jacksonian Politics and the Onset of the Civil War*.
22. Cooper, *The South and the Politics of Slavery, 1828–1856*.
23. Sellers, "Who Were the Southern Whigs?," writes "[i]t is often forgotten that in the ante-bellum period the South had a vigorous two-party system, an asset it has never since enjoyed. Until at least the later 1840s, the voting southerner was much more interested in the success of his own party and its policies than in banding together with southerners of the opposite party to defend the Constitution and southern rights against invitation by the North" (p. 336).
24. Holt, *The Rise and Fall of the American Whig Party: Jacksonian Politics and the Onset of the Civil War*, pp. 115–121. See also Crofts, *Reluctant Confederates: Upper South Unionists in the Secession Crisis*, chapter 2, on how these generalizations were less pronounced in the Upper South.
25. Holt, *The Rise and Fall of the American Whig Party: Jacksonian Politics and the Onset of the Civil War*, p. 58. For example, Knoxville's Brownlow, a Whig, claimed in defense of slavery that it was "established for the benefit of that class of the human family who had not the capacity to provide for their wants—and of this class are the entire African race." Brownlow and Pryne, *Ought American Slavery to be Perpetuated?*, p. 42.
26. Cole, *The Whig Party in the South*, pp. 181–189.
27. These elections also represent a shift from presidential politics. Most presidential candidates did not campaign on the issue of slavery until 1856 and, thus, a choice of different presidential candidates represented little difference to Southerners in terms of their attitudes toward the institution. We can think of these gubernatorial elections between Unionists and Southern rights supporters as, to some extent, a popular referendum on slavery in the South, as evidently some Southerners did at the time (Hahn, *The Roots of Southern Populism: Yeoman Farmers and the Transformation of the Georgia Upcountry, 1850–1890*, p. 105).
28. The election data that we use for this analysis are maintained by the Inter-university Consortium for Political and Social Research. The data file is entitled "United States Historical Election Returns, 1824–1968" (ICPSR 00001), available at https://doi.org/10.3886/ICPSR00001.v3. Because we examine voting in 1851, we use slave prevalence data from the 1850 U.S.

Census, rather than the 1860 U.S. Census. Figure 5.1 is reproduced from Acharya, Blackwell, and Sen, "The Political Legacy of American Slavery," © 2016 by the Southern Political Science Association. All rights reserved.

29. Hahn, *The Roots of Southern Populism: Yeoman Farmers and the Transformation of the Georgia Upcountry, 1850–1890*, p. 107.

30. Cole, *The Whig Party in the South*, p. 205.

31. See Farnam, *Chapters in the History of Social Legislation in the United States to 1860*, pp. 195–196, for a fuller discussion of these laws.

32. For example, according to Carter et al., *Historical Statistics of the United States: Earliest Times to the Present*, the average slave price went from $377 in 1840, to $440 in 1851, to $601 in 1854, and then to $778 in 1860—an increase of roughly 200% in twenty years.

33. Genovese, "Yeomen Farmers in a Slaveholders' Democracy," p. 338.

34. For additional discussion on these points, see Johnson, *River of Dark Dreams: Slavery and Empire in the Cotton Kingdom*, pp. 371–380, and Hahn, *The Roots of Southern Populism: Yeoman Farmers and the Transformation of the Georgia Upcountry, 1850–1890*, pp. 105–116.

35. Crofts, *Reluctant Confederates: Upper South Unionists in the Secession Crisis*, pp. 53–4.

36. The Constitutional Union Party grew in part out of the Whigs' collapse and represented the interests of Southerners against secession.

37. These men were two out of the four candidates seeking the presidency alongside Abraham Lincoln (Republican) and Stephen A. Douglas (Democrat). Both Lincoln and Douglas were uncompetitive in the South, however, with the former left off of many ballots in the South.

38. The results of this vote come from the Nashville Union and American, June 27, 1861, p. 3.

39. Over time, as is well known, the Democratic Party became the more progressive party, both more generally and also on racial issues (e.g., Franklin Roosevelt, Lyndon Johnson) and the Republicans more conservative (e.g., Barry Goldwater, Richard Nixon). One reason to use the Democratic share of the total vote (as opposed to the share of the two-party vote) is that third-party candidates have often performed well in the South. For example, Populist candidate James B. Weaver outperformed incumbent Republican Benjamin Harrison in several Southern states in 1892, but both of these choices represented a more racially liberal choice than the Democratic ticket. We highlight the two third-party candidates that could be considered more racially conservative (particularly on race issues) than the Democratic ticket: South Carolina's Strom Thurmond in 1948 and Mississippi's George Wallace in 1968.

40. This approach is discussed in further detail in chapter 3. Figure 5.4 is reproduced from Acharya, Blackwell, and Sen, "The Political Legacy of American Slavery," © 2016 by the Southern Political Science Association. All rights reserved.

41. Between the 1890s and the 1940s, we can assume that these are nearly exclusively white (and for the most part male) voters. Starting in Reconstruction larger numbers of African Americans began voting before they were disenfranchised. We discuss this more below.

42. We omit the elections after 1964 since, after the Voting Rights Act's passage in 1965, blacks started voting in large numbers. This means that we can no longer disaggregate white from black votes. For reference, however, we do show the effect of slavery on the vote for Barack Obama in the election of 2008, estimated using individual-level survey data from the Cooperative Congressional Election Survey (CCES). Specifically, we run the instrumental variables analysis on the self-reported decision to vote for Obama.

43. We omit the 1864 and 1868 presidential elections because only a handful of the states in our sample actually voted in those elections, and, in 1868, a broad class of Southern whites was temporarily disenfranchised.

44. Kousser, *The Shaping of Southern Politics: Suffrage Restriction and the Establishment of the One-Party South, 1880–1910*, pp. 11–29.

45. One issue with our analysis in figure 5.4 is that these vote shares aggregate white and black votes, making it difficult to isolate the white vote share. (This is the ecological inference problem we have discussed elsewhere.) In considering historical vote shares, African Americans were unable to vote before 1865, enfranchised during parts of Reconstruction, and then nearly fully disenfranchised again following Redemption. Thus, for nearly a 40-year stretch between roughly 1900 and 1944, when the white primary ended, we can be fairly confident that what we capture are the leanings of Southern whites. However, our results for the Reconstruction era may misestimate the effect of slavery on Democratic vote shares. The direction of the bias is unclear. For example, many newly freed blacks voted for the Republican Party. However, racial violence, ballot stuffing, and voter intimidation were common, so some scholarly accounts note that Democratic candidates earned more votes than would be expected in Black Belt areas. See, e.g., McMillan, *Constitutional Development in Alabama, 1798–1901: A Study in Politics, the Negro, and Sectionalism.*

46. There is a substantial literature exploring the possible origins of racism—and whether the transatlantic slave trade and the subsequent enslavement of African Americans reflected racism against people of African descent, or whether slavery itself was an engine that further fanned the flames of racism. Although we do not enter this complicated debate, we orient the reader to the writings of scholars such as Barbara Fields, Eric Foner, Edmund Morgan, Winthrop Jordan, Oscar and Mary Handlin, and many others on these points.

47. King and Smith, *Still a House Divided: Race and Politics in Obama's America*, chapter 2, provides a review of the overarching racial ideologies in the antebellum period. Their argument is that racial ideologies were organized into pro- and antislavery forces. Support or opposition to slavery, though, was not a perfect indicator of view on race. For example, as King and Smith argue, even much of the antislavery alliance embraced white supremacy for a variety of reasons.

48. Johnson, *River of Dark Dreams: Slavery and Empire in the Cotton Kingdom*, p. 201.

49. Hahn, *The Roots of Southern Populism: Yeoman Farmers and the Transformation of the Georgia Upcountry, 1850–1890*, p. 90.

50. Genovese, "Yeomen Farmers in a Slaveholders' Democracy," p. 338.
51. See Girard, *The Slaves Who Defeated Napoleon: Toussaint Louverture and the Haitian War of Independence, 1801–1804*, for more on the Haitian Revolution, especially pp. 319–322, on the massacre of whites.
52. Denman, *The Secession Movement in Alabama*, p. 16.
53. In our analyses in chapter 3, we included a battery of antebellum factors that could serve as proxies for social attitudes in our statistical analyses: controls for economic conditions, geographic factors such as access to water- and railways, and social factors such as the number and share of mixed race and freedmen populations.
54. Fogel and Engerman, *Time on the Cross: The Economics of American Negro Slavery*; Steckel, "A Dreadful Childhood: The Excess Mortality of American Slaves."
55. Technically, we measure the mortality rate as the ratio of slave deaths to the total number of slaves in the county. We use the log of the ratio of slave mortality rates and white mortality rates as our measure of relative slave mortality.
56. As has been noted by economic historians, nutrition was an important factor in slave mortality. Since nutritional needs vary according to age, gender, and caloric expenditures, the nutritional health of enslaved people varied as well. There is evidence that enslaved children experienced nutritional deficiencies, but that workers of peak laboring age were well-fed. See Steckel, "A Peculiar Population: The Nutrition, Health, and Mortality of American Slaves from Childhood to Maturity"; Steckel, "A Dreadful Childhood: The Excess Mortality of American Slaves."
57. The counties with slave mortality rates lower than white mortality rates tend to have small populations and are thus subject to more measurement error. Weighting by the population size leads to similar results.
58. Steckel, "A Peculiar Population: The Nutrition, Health, and Mortality of American Slaves from Childhood to Maturity."
59. The technical details of how we constructed the slave dwelling variable are as follows. We first looked to a sample of the 1860 Slave Schedule from the 1860 U.S. Census conducted by the Minnesota Population Center. Menard et al., *Public Use Microdata Samples of the Slave Population of 1850–1860*. From this data, we took, for every farm in the sample, the number of slaves in that farm divided by the number of dwellings in that farm. We repeated this for every farm in the county, and then averaged over all of the farms in the county to create a measure that captures, to the extent possible, the average number of enslaved people living per dwelling in the county.
60. In addition, and more pressing for our conclusions in part I, neither of these measures can explain the variation we see in white attitudes today. That is, including either of these variables in our main specifications from chapter 3 does not change our estimates of the effect of slavery on contemporary white attitudes in terms of partisanship, sentiments on affirmative action, and racial resentment toward African Americans. See Acharya, Blackwell, and Sen, "The Political Legacy of American Slavery," for more details.
61. Woodward, *The Strange Career of Jim Crow*, p. 23.

Chapter 6: Emancipation as a Critical Juncture

1. Arkansas Department of Education, *Local Education Agency Application for School Improvement Grant Funds*.
2. For a more detailed account of the massacre, see Rogers Jr., "The Elaine Race Riots of 1919." He reports that the Farmers and Household Union had the goal "to advance the interests of the Negro, morally and intellectually, and to make him a better citizen and a better farmer." Of the white elite, Rogers Jr. notes that "[a]ll Negro Union activities were known to the white planters who did not approve."
3. Rogers Jr., "The Elaine Race Riots of 1919," p. 148.
4. The Court vacated six of the convictions in the case in *Moore v. Dempsey*, 261 U.S. 86 (1923), a rare victory for black defendants in the early twentieth century.
5. Woodward, *The Strange Career of Jim Crow*.
6. By "emancipation," we mean Abraham Lincoln's Emancipation Proclamation, which went into effect on January 1, 1863, and freed enslaved people living in areas of the Confederacy that were not under federal control. Some enslaved people gained freedom immediately; others were subject to the control of unwilling whites and gained freedom only as the war progressed and the South's position increasingly weakened. Note that, as Foner, *Reconstruction: America's Unfinished Revolution, 1863–1877*, writes, "the Proclamation only confirmed what was already happening on farms and plantations throughout the South. War, it has been said, is the midwife of revolution, and well before 1863 the disintegration of slavery had begun" (p. 3).
7. Ransom, *Conflict and Compromise*, p. 227.
8. Ibid., p. 228.
9. Ibid., table 7.1.
10. Economic historians have written extensively about the economic costs of the Civil War. See Goldin and Lewis, "The Economic Cost of the American Civil War: Estimates and Implications"; Goldin, "The Economics of Emancipation"; Engerman, "The Economic Impact of the Civil War"; Ransom, *Conflict and Compromise*; Ransom and Sutch, *One Kind of Freedom: The Economic Consequences of Emancipation*.
11. We omit Texas from this plot due to massive changes in the distribution of farming in Texas during this time period, which makes it difficult to compare it to other states in the same analysis. The same qualitative results hold for Texas as well, however.
12. Ransom and Sutch, *One Kind of Freedom: The Economic Consequences of Emancipation*, p. 52, estimate the dollar "value" of these enslaved people in the five principal cotton states (Alabama, Louisiana, Mississippi, Georgia, South Carolina) in 1860 at $1.6 billion ($44 billion in 2015 dollars), or around half of all wealth in these states.
13. Quoted in Ransom, *Conflict and Compromise*, pp. 119–220.
14. Du Bois, *Black Reconstruction in America, 1860–1880*, p. 22. In addition to Du Bois's writings on this topic, economists have written extensively about the postwar economic labor market environment. See, for example, Ransom and Sutch, *One Kind of Freedom: The Economic Consequences of Emancipation*, chapters 4–5,

and Wright, *Old South, New South: Revolutions in the Southern Economy Since the Civil War*, chapter 4.

15. Ransom and Sutch, *One Kind of Freedom: The Economic Consequences of Emancipation*, pp. 59–60.

16. Ransom and Sutch, *One Kind of Freedom: The Economic Consequences of Emancipation*; Wright, *Old South, New South: Revolutions in the Southern Economy Since the Civil War*.

17. Du Bois, *Black Reconstruction in America, 1860–1880*, p. 184.

18. By contrast, blacks hardly had political majorities in several counties we have looked at—for example, Buncombe County, North Carolina (12% enslaved in 1860) or Knox County, Tennessee (10% enslaved).

19. Kousser, *The Shaping of Southern Politics: Suffrage Restriction and the Establishment of the One-Party South, 1880–1910*, p. 17.

20. Davidson, "The Voting Rights Act: A Brief History," p. 10.

21. Foner, *Freedom's Lawmakers: A Directory of Black Officeholders During Reconstruction*.

22. Poor whites were not so substantially well off compared to newly freed slaves. Blackmon, *Slavery by Another Name: The Re-Enslavement of Black Americans from the Civil War to World War II*, p. 85, for example, notes that "more than half of southern blacks—about 2.5 million—could not read, [but] there were 1.3 whites among their neighbors who were also illiterate."

23. Early in Reconstruction, some alliances developed between upcountry whites and freedmen in Union Leagues that apparently had some positive effect on race relations between the two groups, though it would be a stretch to say that upcountry whites were strong supporters of black political equality (Foner, *Reconstruction: America's Unfinished Revolution, 1863–1877*, p. 303). This potential alliance never fully matured. Historians have identified several reasons for the eventual failure, among the most important of which was the eventual (and highly effective) disenfranchisement of blacks. As the historian C. Vann Woodward later noted, "The determination of the Negro's 'place' took shape gradually under the influence of economic and political conflicts among divided white people—conflicts that were eventually resolved in part at the expense of the Negro." Woodward, *The Strange Career of Jim Crow*, p. 6.

24. Foner, *Reconstruction: America's Unfinished Revolution, 1863–1877*, p. 592.

25. For example, Valelly, *The Two Reconstructions: The Struggle for Black Enfranchisement*, has noted the importance of political coalitions in the Reconstruction era and gives an account of how these forces played out with respect to the Readjusters in Virginia (pp. 57–64).

26. Woodward, *The Strange Career of Jim Crow*; McMillan, *Constitutional Development in Alabama, 1798–1901: A Study in Politics, the Negro, and Sectionalism*.

27. There are many excellent discussions of the Reconstruction period. See, e.g., Foner, *Reconstruction: America's Unfinished Revolution, 1863–1877*; Du Bois, *Black Reconstruction in America, 1860–1880*. Work that specifically looks at the political reactions include Valelly, *The Two Reconstructions: The Struggle for Black Enfranchisement*; Klinkner and Smith, *The Unsteady March: The Rise and Decline of Racial Equality in America*.

28. Some refer to this as the "First" or the "First Era" Ku Klux Klan to distinguish it from Klan activities in the 1920s and 1930s.

29. Chalmers, *Hooded Americanism: The History of the Ku Klux Klan*. Specifically, some note that the Klan's early involvement arose in places where the reconfigured black political and economic power was, due to preexisting norms and social customs, the most threatening to whites. Chalmers writes that the Klan "rode where the economic distinction between Negro and white was less pronounced, where society had been less hierarchical before the war, where the Negro had been less respectful of the whites ('the pore no-count white trash') whose status was less differentiated from his own" (p. 10).

30. Horn, *Invisible Empire: The Story of the Ku Klux Klan, 1866–1871*, p. 117.

31. Chalmers, *Hooded Americanism: The History of the Ku Klux Klan*; Horn, *Invisible Empire: The Story of the Ku Klux Klan, 1866–1871*.

32. Beck and Tolnay, "The Killing Fields of the Deep South: The Market for Cotton and the Lynching of Blacks, 1882–1930."

33. Ransom and Sutch, *One Kind of Freedom: The Economic Consequences of Emancipation*, pp. 86–87.

34. Foner, *Reconstruction: America's Unfinished Revolution, 1863–1877*, p. 428.

35. Alston and Ferrie, *Southern Paternalism and the American Welfare State: Economics, Politics, and Institutions in the South, 1865–1965*. Alston and Ferrie point out that Southern whites turned to paternalistic wage contracts. These contracts were agreements between newly freed slaves and their former "owners," whereby blacks could obtain basic health care and protection from racial violence. While ostensibly beneficial to the newly freed slaves, these paternalistic wage contacts, as Alston and Ferrie argue, also had several beneficial effects for the white planter. Paternalistic contracts increased the productivity of farmers because their provision induced loyalty among workers and, perhaps more importantly, increased the cost of being caught shirking in their work. This had the dual benefits of suppressing black economic mobility (which decreased black labor power) and increasing the yields to the planters.

36. Foner, *Reconstruction: America's Unfinished Revolution, 1863–1877*, p. 429.

37. Holmes, "Whitecapping: Agrarian Violence in Mississippi, 1902–1906."

38. Beck and Tolnay, "The Killing Fields of the Deep South: The Market for Cotton and the Lynching of Blacks, 1882–1930."

39. Arnett, *The Populist Movement in Georgia*.

40. Foner, *Reconstruction: America's Unfinished Revolution, 1863–1877*, pp. 425–426.

41. Valelly, *The Two Reconstructions: The Struggle for Black Enfranchisement*.

42. As evidence of the latter, ibid. observes in post-Reconstruction Alabama (1882) that "fifty-two of one hundred black male voters actually voted, but only sixteen were counted by Democratic-controlled elections commissioners as they wished and intended to be counted, that is, as voting for the Republican candidate. The other thirty-six black voters showed up and voted but then had their votes fraudulently allocated to the Democratic total in order to guarantee a Democratic victory" (p. 54).

43. McMillan, *Constitutional Development in Alabama, 1798–1901: A Study in Politics, the Negro, and Sectionalism*.

44. Olzak, "The Political Context of Competition: Lynching and Urban Racial Violence, 1882–1914"; Inverarity, "Populism and Lynching in Louisiana, 1889–1896: A Test of Erikson's Theory of the Relationship between Boundary Crises and Repressive Justice."

45. Tolnay and Beck, *A Festival of Violence: An Analysis of Southern Lynchings, 1882–1930*, p. 19.

46. For example, Tolnay and Beck detail the appalling story of Sam Holt, from Coweta County, Georgia (49% enslaved in 1860), who, according to contemporaneous newspaper accounts, "was burned at the sake in the public road, one and a half miles from [Newman, Georgia]. Before the torch was applied to the pyre, the Negro was deprived of his ears, fingers and other portions of his body with surprising fortitude. Before the body was cool, it was cut to pieces, the bones were crushed into small bits and even the tree upon which the wretch met his fate was torn up and disposed of as souvenirs."

47. In Acharya, Blackwell, and Sen, "Explaining Attitudes from Behavior: A Cognitive Dissonance Approach," we propose a psychological mechanism by which committing an act of violence creates or reinforces preexisting negative attitudes towards the victim group, thus providing a mechanism for how violence contributed to the propagation and perpetuation of racial hostility in the South. The mechanism is based on the idea that individuals who commit acts of violence increase their hostility to the victim group to minimize the "cognitive dissonance" between their actions and their attitudes.

48. Raper, *The Tragedy of Lynching*.

49. Beck and Tolnay, "Confirmed Inventory of Southern Lynch Victims, 1882–1930." These data include all states in our analysis except Maryland, Missouri, Texas, and West Virginia and cover the period between 1877 and 1950. A lynching is defined as an illegal killing with at least 3 people involved in killing the victim, and the killing was "justified" with reference to tradition, justice, or honor. This database expanded an initial list collected from the *Chicago Tribune*, the NAACP, and the Tuskegee Institute. These data can be accessed at http://lynching.csde.washington.edu/.

50. Cook, "The Color of Lynching."

51. These results are also substantively similar if we run the basic modeling strategies of chapter 3 with the lynching rate as the outcome. The relationship between slavery in 1860 and lynchings is strong and significant: a 10-percentage-point increase in slave proportion is associated with a 1.6 increase in lynchings per 100,000 residents. These results are similar if we use an indicator for the presence of any lynching in the county as the dependent variable. Using alternative databases of lynchings produces very similar results.

52. Raper, *The Tragedy of Lynching*, p. 57.

53. Foner, *Reconstruction: America's Unfinished Revolution, 1863–1877*, pp. 199–201.

54. Section 5 of the Mississippi Black Code (1865). Quoted in DuBois, Black Reconstruction, pp. 174–175.

55. Blackmon, *Slavery by Another Name: The Re-Enslavement of Black Americans from the Civil War to World War II*.

56. Cited in Dickerson, *The Reconstruction Era: Primary Documents on Events from 1865 to 1877*, p. 52.

57. The Mississippi Code was, for example, declared invalid—and thus unenforceable—by General O. O. Howard, the director of the Freedmen's Bureau (and one of the founders of Howard University), while an army general declared the South Carolina Black Codes invalid. In addition, the Civil Rights Act of 1866 and the three Civil Rights Amendments—the Thirteenth, Fourteenth, and Fifteenth Amendments—further (albeit temporarily) undercut these attempts at restricting blacks' rights.

58. Foner, *Reconstruction: America's Unfinished Revolution, 1863–1877*, p. 421.

59. Cited in Dickerson, *The Reconstruction Era: Primary Documents on Events from 1865 to 1877*, p. 48.

60. Murray, *States' Laws on Race and Color*; Wallenstein, "Reconstruction, Segregation, and Miscegenation: Interracial Marriage and the Law in the Lower South, 1865–1900."

61. Alsobrook, "The Mobile Streetcar Boycott of 1902: African American Protest or Capitulation?"; Woodward, *The Strange Career of Jim Crow*, p. 101.

62. Birmingham Racial Segregation Ordinance Section 309 (amended in 1930).

63. Birmingham Racial Segregation Ordinance Section 597.

64. For a historical perspective, see Foner, *Reconstruction: America's Unfinished Revolution, 1863–1877*; Cohen, "Negro Involuntary Servitude in the South, 1865–1940: A Preliminary Analysis." For an economic history perspective, see Naidu, "Recruitment Restrictions and Labor Markets: Evidence from the Postbellum U.S. South"; Wright, *Old South, New South: Revolutions in the Southern Economy Since the Civil War*; Ransom and Sutch, *One Kind of Freedom: The Economic Consequences of Emancipation*. A journalistic account is proved by Blackmon, *Slavery by Another Name: The Re-Enslavement of Black Americans from the Civil War to World War II*.

65. See, e.g., Naidu, "Recruitment Restrictions and Labor Markets: Evidence from the Postbellum U.S. South," for a study of how these labor coercive criminal laws affected economic efficiency.

66. Blackmon's narratives provide extraordinary accounts of some of the lives behind this systematic increase in incarceration of African Americans. He describes, for example, how Green Cottenham, a black man living in Alabama, was convicted of vagrancy and forced into hard labor as punishment. He was sold by the court to a mine and died soon after. Blackmon, *Slavery by Another Name: The Re-Enslavement of Black Americans from the Civil War to World War II*.

67. McLennan, *The Crisis of Imprisonment: Protest, Politics, and the Making of the American Penal State, 1776–1941*, p. 109.

68. Alabama and Mississippi were states that leased convicts from county jails; other states leased convicts from state penitentiaries, which makes it by far more difficult to ascertain where these convicts came from.

69. We calculated the total population in 1886 by interpolating from the total county population reported in the 1880 U.S. Census and the total county population reported in the 1890 U.S. Census.

70. Haines, *Historical, Demographic, Economic, and Social Data: The United States, 1790–2002*.

71. Both of these trends are confirmed by both OLS and IV estimation strategies.

72. Kousser, *The Shaping of Southern Politics: Suffrage Restriction and the Establishment of the One-Party South, 1880–1910*, table 1.3, p. 27.

73. A cousin of literacy tests were "understanding" tests, for which the presumptive voter would need to provide an interpretation of text, such as a phrase or excerpt from the U.S. or state constitution. Again, such questions were difficult for even a well-educated person to answer.

74. Pildes, "Democracy, Anti-Democracy, and the Cannon"; Kousser, *The Shaping of Southern Politics: Suffrage Restriction and the Establishment of the One-Party South, 1880–1910*.

75. Ibid. p. 303.

76. Ibid.

77. For more, see Kousser, *The Shaping of Southern Politics: Suffrage Restriction and the Establishment of the One-Party South, 1880–1910*, and, for a succinct summary of the legal environment, Pildes, "Democracy, Anti-Democracy, and the Cannon," which reports that "[i]n Alabama, in 1900 there were 181,471 eligible black voters, but only 3,000 were registered after the new constitutional provisions took effect. In Virginia, there was a 100% drop—in other words, to zero—in estimated black voter turnout between the Presidential elections of 1900 and 1904. North Carolina managed the same complete elimination of black voter turnout over an eight-year period, between the Presidential elections of 1896 and 1904" (pp. 303–304).

78. Kousser, *The Shaping of Southern Politics: Suffrage Restriction and the Establishment of the One-Party South, 1880–1910*, p. 241.

79. McMillan, *Constitutional Development in Alabama, 1798–1901: A Study in Politics, the Negro, and Sectionalism*.

80. Alabama Constitutional Convention, *Journal of the Proceedings of the Constitutional Convention of the State of Alabama: Held in the City of Montgomery, Commencing May 21st, 1901*, p. 15.

81. McMillan, *Constitutional Development in Alabama, 1798–1901: A Study in Politics, the Negro, and Sectionalism*, p. 261. There is also historical evidence that Black Belt representatives were the most active in the convention and the most vocal in support of the constitution itself. Flynt, "Alabama's Shame: The Historical Origins of the 1901 Constitution." Interestingly, younger representatives from the Black Belt appear to be those with the most vehement antiblack views. McMillan, *Constitutional Development in Alabama, 1798–1901: A Study in Politics, the Negro, and Sectionalism*. For example, Gesner Williams of Marengo County (78% enslaved in 1860) declared that "[w]e of the younger generation, we have known but one slavery, and that—slaves to the negro vote."

82. One important point here is that we cannot rule out the possibility that these results are driven in part by ballot fraud and other forms of voter intimidation. Indeed, what we see here is that the higher the share of the county that was enslaved, the more the county supported a constitution that would, if enacted, suppress the votes of those people (African Americans) who pushed it through. This could be consistent with blacks either not voting or, if they were voting, extensive voter intimidation or fraud at play. Answering the question definitively is impossible; nonetheless, these findings do highlight one of the patterns endemic to the South in this period: the importance of

Black Belt politics and political actors. Indeed, one of the lasting legacies of the Alabama constitution was to turn the preferences of the Black Belt whites (e.g., preferences toward increased disenfranchisement of blacks) into state-wide policies.

83. Ritterhouse, *Growing Up Jim Crow: How Black and White Southern Children Learned Race*, p. 25.

84. DuRocher, *Raising Racists: The Socialization of White Children in the Jim Crow South*; Ritterhouse, *Growing Up Jim Crow: How Black and White Southern Children Learned Race*.

85. For more on this childhood socialization, see Ritterhouse, *Growing Up Jim Crow: How Black and White Southern Children Learned Race*, and DuRocher, *Raising Racists: The Socialization of White Children in the Jim Crow South*.

86. For example, consider Deutsch and Collins, *Interracial Housing: A Psychological Evaluation of a Social Experiment*. This is a pathbreaking study of segregated versus "interracial" housing in 1950s Newark, New Jersey, that observes that segregated housing actually had the effect of altering how whites viewed African Americans. Of their findings, the authors noted that this change hinged on the degree of forced separation between individuals of the two races: "If social custom leads one to avoid intimate contact with Negroes, then Negroes are obviously not the kind of people one would like to be intimate with." The authors further noted that "[t]here is little doubt that public laws and official policies do provide a standard of behavior; by providing a standard favorable to nonsegregated interracial tensions they help to stimulate such behavior" (p. 42). Although no similar studies have looked at the postbellum South, we can imagine similar factors nurtured and reinforced the prevalence of antiblack attitudes.

87. Woodward, *The Strange Career of Jim Crow*; Du Bois, *Black Reconstruction in America, 1860–1880*.

88. Ritterhouse, *Growing Up Jim Crow: How Black and White Southern Children Learned Race*, pp. 40–42.

89. This quote is from James Baldwin's 1965 debate with William F. Buckley at Cambridge University.

90. Woodward, *Origins of the New South, 1877–1913: A History of the South*, p. 339.

91. Foner, *Reconstruction: America's Unfinished Revolution, 1863–1877*, p. 293.

92. Key, *Southern Politics in State and Nation*, p. 9.

93. Du Bois, *Black Reconstruction in America, 1860–1880*.

94. Rather than uniting politically in their shared economic station, he wrote, calls for poorer whites to ally with newly emancipated black workers were quickly set aside by "a deep-rooted antagonism toward the Negro, slave or free." In fact, Du Bois (p. 27) observed that

> the poor whites and their leaders could not for a moment contemplate a fight of united white and black labor against the exploiters. Indeed, the natural leaders of the poor whites, the small farmer, the merchant, the professional man, white mechanic and slave overseer, were bound to the planters and repelled from the slaves and even from the mass of the white laborers in two ways: first, they constituted the police patrol who

could ride with planters and now and then exercise unlimited force upon recalcitrant or runaway slaves; and then, too, there was always a chance that they themselves might also become planters by saving money, by investment, by the power of good luck.

93. Woodward, *The Strange Career of Jim Crow*, p. 6.
94. Woodward, writes, "Before the South capitulated completely to the doctrines of the extreme racists, three alternative philosophies of race relations were put forward to compete for the region's adherence and support." Woodward, *The Strange Career of Jim Crow*, pp. 44–45. These were (1) the conservative approach, (2) the Southern radical approach, and (3) what Vann Woodward calls the liberal philosophy.
95. Ibid., p. 23.
96. Ibid., p. 24.
97. Ibid., pp. 25–26.
98. Ayers, *The Promise of the New South: Life after Reconstruction*, p. 137.
99. Woodward, *The Strange Career of Jim Crow*, p. 137.
100. Ayers, *The Promise of the New South: Life after Reconstruction*.
101. Engerman, "Slavery Without Racism, Racism Without Slavery: Mainland North America and Elsewhere."
102. A particularly revealing observation cited by Ransom and Sutch is made by one Benjamin Truman, who wrote on an 1865 visit to the South that "[i]nheriting his slaves, and finding them always brutish, stupid, and slow of understanding, [the planter] committed the logical inaccuracy of preventing them from ever becoming anything else, and proceeded to argue that they never could become so." Ransom and Sutch, *One Kind of Freedom: The Economic Consequences of Emancipation*, p. 22. More generally, other research in economics has documented that when an entrenched social institution, like slavery, is abolished as a result of external pressures, previously powerful groups (for example, the ex-slave owners) often seek to establish other local and informal institutions that serve a similar purpose to that of the previous, forcibly abolished, formal institution. See Acemoglu et al., "The Consequences of Radical Reform: The French Revolution."
103. See Woodward, *The Strange Career of Jim Crow*, for a discussion of these "forgotten alternatives."
104. Ritterhouse, *Growing Up Jim Crow: How Black and White Southern Children Learned Race*.

Chapter 7: Persistence and the Mechanisms of Reproduction

1. Thompson, *Reconstruction in Georgia, Economic, Social, Political, 1865–1872*, p. 375.
2. Lumpkin, *The Making of a Southerner*.
3. While some of this club was purely social, the children would also engage in the "planning of pretend punitive expeditions against mythical recalcitrant Negroes." Lumpkin, *The Making of a Southerner*, p. 136.

4. Ritterhouse, *Growing Up Jim Crow: How Black and White Southern Children Learned Race*.

5. Using language evoking the relationship between enslaved and "master," Lumpkin writes of this encounter, "Our little black cook, a woman small in stature though full grown, was receiving a severe thrashing. I could see her withering under the blows of a descending stick wielded by the white master of the house. I could see her face distorted with fear and agony and his with stern range." Lumpkin, *The Making of a Southerner*, p. 132.

6. Lumpkin, *The Making of a Southerner*; Ritterhouse, *Growing Up Jim Crow: How Black and White Southern Children Learned Race*; DuRocher, *Raising Racists: The Socialization of White Children in the Jim Crow South*.

7. Ritterhouse, *Growing Up Jim Crow: How Black and White Southern Children Learned Race*; DuRocher, *Raising Racists: The Socialization of White Children in the Jim Crow South*; Jennings, Stoker, and Bowers, "Politics across Generations: Family Transmission Reexamined."

8. Additional discussion of the methodology behind this figure, as well as findings predating the 20th century, can be found in chapter 5.

9. Kuziemko and Washington, "Why Did the Democrats Lose the South? Bringing New Data to an Old Debate."

10. To be more specific, Thurmond ran under the auspices of the States' Rights Democratic Party and Wallace under the auspices of the American Independent Party.

11. Tesler and Sears, *Obama's Race: The 2008 Election and the Dream of a Post-Racial America*.

12. As some scholars—e.g., Sokol—point out, informal Jim Crow segregation persisted even after it was legally banned. As late as the 1980s, for example, white and black residents of Terrell County, Georgia (46.3% enslaved in 1860), continued to use some separate facilities and some restaurants and bars continued to prohibit black patrons. Sokol, *There Goes My Everything: White Southerners in the Age of Civil Rights, 1945–1975*.

13. Rosenberg, *The Hollow Hope: Can Courts Bring About Social Change?*

14. Jennings and Niemi, "The Transmission of Political Values from Parent to Child"; Jennings and Niemi, *Generations and Politics: A Panel Study of Young Adults and Their Parents*; Jennings, Stoker, and Bowers, "Politics across Generations: Family Transmission Reexamined."

15. Smith, *Killers of the Dream*, p. 91.

16. A value of zero would indicate that parents' and children's views are unrelated.

17. For uses of this data, see Jennings and Niemi, "The Transmission of Political Values from Parent to Child"; Jennings and Niemi, *Generations and Politics: A Panel Study of Young Adults and Their Parents*; Jennings, Stoker, and Bowers, "Politics across Generations: Family Transmission Reexamined." Note that in these data there could be multiple entries per student in 1965 if they have multiple parents interviewed. Weighting to account for this sampling design does not change any of these results.

18. Unfortunately, there are too few counties in these samples (roughly 20) to conduct any analyses using county-level data, such as proportion slave.

19. The question we use for this simply asks where the respondent grew up (and in which state, if in the United States). This was asked in each wave of our ANES sample except 1998. We include those respondents who answered that they grew up in the South in a general manner or mentioned more than one state in the South.

20. Ritterhouse, *Growing Up Jim Crow: How Black and White Southern Children Learned Race*; DuRocher, *Raising Racists: The Socialization of White Children in the Jim Crow South*.

21. Musoke, "Mechanizing Cotton Production in the American South: The Tractor, 1915–1960," p. 348.

22. Musoke reports that the use of pickers "rose from 1522 in 1948 to 15,550 in 1953, an average increase of better than 2800 machines per year." Ibid., p. 348.

23. Hurst and Church, *Power and Machinery in Agriculture*.

24. Haines, *Historical, Demographic, Economic, and Social Data: The United States, 1790–2002*. Unfortunately, no county-level data on the increased use of cotton pickers exist, to our knowledge. However, using state-level data, we know that tractor growth was higher in states that adopted mechanization more quickly, as measured by the year by which the mechanized fraction of the state cotton production was greater than 10%.

25. These models include a host of area background characteristics, including terrain variability, which some have argued is an important predictor of which areas mechanized sooner or later. See, for example, Muskoe, "Mechanizing Cotton Production in the American South: The Tractor, 1915–1960," p. 355. To help identify the effects of this interaction, we additionally control for tractors in 1930.

26. For a full description of the methodology of this analysis, see Acharya, Blackwell, and Sen, "The Political Legacy of American Slavery."

27. We note two potential concerns with this test. First, the results could be consistent with a racial threat explanation—early mechanization could lead to decreases in the black population in these areas, thus diminishing racial threat later on. In our results from chapter 4, however, we found no evidence that decreases in the black population from the Great Migrations attenuated the effects of slavery, so this seems unlikely. Furthermore, tractor growth is also positively related to proportion black in 2000 and the change in the black proportion between 1930 and 2000. Given the results later in this chapter of how local black concentrations enhance the effect of slavery, it seems unlikely that the attenuating effect of tractor growth is operating through these demographic variables. Second, it could be that more racially tolerant counties chose to mechanize early to minimize racial exploitation. However, the number of tractors is itself never independently predictive of political or racial attitudes, and the change in mechanization has an insignificant effect for most values of proportion slave. Furthermore, there is no effect of proportion slave on the change in tractors, nor is there a relationship between the change in mechanization and the rate of lynchings, making it doubtful that tractors are an indicator of racial attitudes. Moreover, Hornbeck and Naidu argue that some of the counties that mechanized early were those affected by an exogenous

shock—that of the Mississippi floods of 1927—and are thus ex ante similar to counties that mechanized later. Other studies—for example, Muskoe on tractor adoption—make the argument that regional terrain (hilly versus flat) was a significant determinant of early tractor adoption; for that reason, the analysis here controls for the ruggedness of the terrain. Hornbeck and Naidu, "When the Levee Breaks: Black Migration and Economic Development in the American South"; Muskoe, "Mechanizing Cotton Production in the American South: The Tractor, 1915–1960."

28. DuRocher, *Raising Racists: The Socialization of White Children in the Jim Crow South*, pp. 102–103.

29. Ritterhouse, *Growing Up Jim Crow: How Black and White Southern Children Learned Race*, p. 75.

30. Smith, *Killers of the Dream*, p. 82.

31. DuRocher, *Raising Racists: The Socialization of White Children in the Jim Crow South*, pp. 93, 7–8.

32. Ritterhouse, *Growing Up Jim Crow: How Black and White Southern Children Learned Race*, p. 75.

33. DuRocher, *Raising Racists: The Socialization of White Children in the Jim Crow South*, p. 97.

34. Ibid., p. 100.

35. The effects in figure 7.7 come from a statistical model specified as in the baseline models in chapter 3, but with an additional interaction between slavery and whether (or not) there was a lynching measured in the county in the Beck and Tolnay database. See Beck and Tolnay,"Confirmed Inventory of Southern Lynch Victims, 1882–1930." In each of these models, the interaction between slavery and the lynching indicator is statistically significant at typical levels.

36. Another possibility is that there is post-treatment bias here and that the higher effects of slavery in counties with lynchings is due to this bias. This could be partly due to the fact that lynchings are indicators of racism in the late 19th and early 20th centuries and this could be driving the interaction. We believe this is unlikely since the higher levels of racism in the lynchings counties should lead to weaker or even negative effects of slavery since the low-slave counties that engage in lynchings obviously harbor antiblack sentiment for reasons unrelated to slavery.

37. We use the baseline model with 1860 controls from chapter 3 and add an interaction term between the proportion enslaved in 1860 and the proportion black in 2000 (from the Census). The estimated effects in the plot are predicted marginal effects and their 90% confidence intervals at the two levels of proportion black in 2000. The interaction is statistically significant across the three outcome measures.

38. DuRocher, *Raising Racists: The Socialization of White Children in the Jim Crow South*, p. 39.

39. Rosenberg, *The Hollow Hope: Can Courts Bring About Social Change?*

40. On the effects of segregation, see, e.g., Deutsch and Collins, *Interracial Housing: A Psychological Evaluation of a Social Experiment.*

41. Mickey, *Paths Out of Dixie: The Democratization of Authoritarian Enclaves in America's Deep South, 1944–1972.*
42. Matthews and Prothro, "Political Factors and Negro Voter Registration in the South."
43. Deutsch and Collins, *Interracial Housing: A Psychological Evaluation of a Social Experiment.*
44. Sokol, *There Goes My Everything: White Southerners in the Age of Civil Rights. 1945–1975*; Allport, *The Nature of Prejudice.*

Chapter 8: Interventions and Attenuation

1. Valelly, *The Two Reconstructions: The Struggle for Black Enfranchisement*, p. 193.
2. Edmund Pettus himself was a Confederate general and also an active member of the first Ku Klux Klan.
3. Schuman, Steeh, and Bobo, *Racial Trends in America: Trends and Interpretations.*
4. We use the term "attenuation" to refer to the lessening of previously detectable differences between former slaveholding and nonslaveholding areas. By contrast, we use the term "decay" to refer to the slow decrease or change in political attitudes over time. Both are interrelated concepts, which are discussed more fully in chapter 2. Decay can occur within an area; attenuation is fundamentally about comparisons across areas.
5. Key, *Southern Politics in State and Nation*, p. 670.
6. Ibid., p. 652.
7. Mickey, *Paths Out of Dixie: The Democratization of Authoritarian Enclaves in America's Deep South, 1944–1972.*
8. See Woodward, *The Strange Career of Jim Crow*, pp. 122–134, and Chappell, *A Stone of Hope: Prophetic Religion and the Death of Jim Crow*, chapter 2, for discussions of how white liberals in the North evolved in terms of their racial attitudes in this time period.
9. All eleven former Confederate states enacted a white primary at some point between 1896 and 1915.
10. See, e.g., Garrow, *Protest at Selma: Martin Luther King Jr., and the Voting Rights Act of 1965*, pp. 6–7.
11. 321 U.S. 649 (1944).
12. Key, *Southern Politics in State and Nation*, p. 626. Key also noted that *Smith* was met with comparably less resistance outside of the Black Belt. "Contrariwise, in the states around the edge of the Deep South," he wrote, "the more rapid growth of white population, and perhaps also some attrition of attitude, come gradually to produce a less-excitable social situation." (p. 626).
13. This case, *Elmore v. Rice*, 72 F. Supp. 516 (1947), involved a challenge to Richland County (60% enslaved in 1860) whites-only primaries.
14. Berg, *The Ticket to Freedom: The NAACP and the Struggle for Black Political Integration*, p. 142.
15. Ibid., chapter 6. As documented by Berg, the NAACP's efforts involved interplay between the national organization, local NAACP branches, and local black institutions, such as churches. However, despite the NAACP's efforts and a particularly well funded 1952 registration drive, "much groundwork

remained, however, especially in the Black Belt counties of the deep South. A report from Alabama in early 1953 showed that in eleven counties where the black population equaled or exceeded that of whites, only a minuscule average of 1.3 percent of all eligible African-Americans were registered. Two counties had no black voters at all" (p. 155).

16. 339 U.S. 629 (1950).
17. 339 U.S. 637 (1950).
18. The final case, *Brown v. Board*, 347 U.S. 483 (1954), was actually a set of five consolidated cases. Three of these originated in the South: (1) *Brown v. Topeka Board of Education of Topeka* (originating out of Shawnee County, Kansas); (2) *Briggs v. Elliott* (Clarendon County, South Carolina, 65% enslaved in 1860); and (3) *Davis v. County School Board of Prince Edward County* (Prince Edward County, Virginia, 62% enslaved). One, *Gebhart v. Belton* (New Castle County, Delaware), originated in the North, and another, *Bolling v. Sharpe* (District of Columbia), served as a vehicle for challenging segregation by the federal government.
19. DuRocher, *Raising Racists: The Socialization of White Children in the Jim Crow South*.
20. The focus of the opinion was in arguing about the effects of segregation on black children specifically. For example, Warren wrote that "[s]egregation of white and colored children in public schools has a detrimental effect upon the colored children. The impact is greater when it has the sanction of the law, for the policy of separating the races is usually interpreted as denoting the inferiority of the Negro group." However, *Brown* also notes, importantly, the broad importance of education for society writ large—for example, that education "is a principal instrument in awakening the child to cultural values, in preparing him for later professional training, and in helping him to adjust normally to his environment."
21. 349 U.S. 294 (1955).
22. Rosenberg, *The Hollow Hope: Can Courts Bring About Social Change?*
23. Among these were the four main groups: the NAACP, the Southern Christian Leadership Conference (SCLC), the Student Nonviolent Coordinating Committee (SNCC), and the Congress of Racial Equality (CORE).
24. Chappell, *A Stone of Hope: Prophetic Religion and the Death of Jim Crow*.
25. Mickey, *Paths Out of Dixie: The Democratization of Authoritarian Enclaves in America's Deep South, 1944–1972*, pp. 274–277.
26. On this point, we note a sizable literature documenting the possible impact of mass unrest on subsequent political attitudes (including subsequent policy outcomes). For example, looking at race relations in the U.S. specifically, Wasow, "Nonviolence, Violence and Voting: The Effects of the 1960s Black Protest Movements on White Attitudes and Voting Behavior," finds that the race riots through the 1960s served to make many Americans more conservative on law and order issues. See also Sears and McConahay, *The Politics of Violence: The New Urban Blacks and the Watts Riot*. However, other papers have found that protests or mass unrest have the effect of making the dominant group *more favorable* toward the protesting group. In a comparative context, Beber, Roessler, and Scacco, "Intergroup Violence and Political Attitudes: Evidence

from a Dividing Sudan," have found that riots in Sudan increased support for the policy positions supported by protestors. Looking more locally at Los Angeles in the 1990s, Enos, Kaufman, and Sands, "Can Violent Protest Change Local Policy Support? Evidence from the Aftermath of the 1992 Los Angeles Riot," find that protests made the local population more liberal on the issues central to the protestors' concerns.

27. Andrews, *Freedom Is a Constant Struggle: The Mississippi Civil Rights Movement and Its Legacy*.

28. Of course, several significant events did *not* take place in the Southern Black Belt, particularly as the civil rights movement progressed and grew. These later events included the March on Washington, D.C. (1963), and later race-related riots in the Watts neighborhood of Los Angeles (1965), Newark (1967), and Detroit (1967). These events highlighted the effects of Northern segregation, white flight, and the responses (or lack thereof) of Northern elites. However, the history of this period makes it clear that (1) the Black Belt played a significant role in the civil unrest that led to the seminal events of the civil rights movement and (2) white oppression and responses to the unrest furthered racial tensions.

29. One of the earliest interventions came when reluctant President Dwight Eisenhower sent federal troops to Little Rock to assist the desegregation of Little Rock Central High School, but subsequent interventions were limited. The administration of John F. Kennedy provided some support via the Attorney General's office, which was headed by Robert F. Kennedy, a strong—albeit cautious—advocate of civil rights. Robert Kennedy played a key role in the support of the Freedom Riders by the Department of Justice in the summer of 1961, including several instances where Department of Justice intervention guaranteed the riders safe passage out of dangerous situations.

30. King, *Why We Can't Wait*, pp. 73–74.

31. Rosenberg, *The Hollow Hope: Can Courts Bring About Social Change?*

32. The final Senate vote on the bill was 74–27 with only 1 vote in favor out of 22 in the former Confederate states. The House vote on the final version of the bill was 296–132 with 8 votes of approval out of 105 from Southern districts. All vote data are from the Voteview database at http://www.voteview.com.

In terms of less successful legislation, the Civil Rights Act of 1875, enacted during Reconstruction, targeted discrimination by private actors (including business), but was eventually ruled unconstitutional by the U.S. Supreme Court in the *Civil Rights Cases* (1883) on the grounds that Congress could not regulate private behavior.

33. Title I of the Civil Rights Act did require that voting laws apply equally to people of all races, but it stopped short of barring those discriminatory tests or restrictions that made it nearly impossible for millions of Southern blacks to vote.

34. As we discussed in chapter 5, Goldwater was a popular candidate in the presidential election of 1964 across the South, winning a large share of the white vote in Black Belt counties.

35. Berg, *The Ticket to Freedom: The NAACP and the Struggle for Black Political Integration*.

36. The final vote was 335–80 in the House and 81–19 in the Senate. Four Southern senators and 32 Southern representatives, only 3 of which were from the Deep South, voted for the bill.

37. In order to determine which jurisdictions would be subject to preclearance, the Voting Rights Act used a "coverage formula," which was established in Section 4 of the Act. Section 4 determined that a jurisdiction would be "covered" (and thus subject for preclearance) if (1) the jurisdiction had used a "test or device" to prevent the opportunities of people to register to vote, as of November 1, 1964, 1968, or 1972; and (2) fewer than one half of the citizens eligible to vote had actually registered as of November 1, 1964, 1968, or 1972, or fewer than one half of citizens eligible to vote had voted in the general elections of November 1964, 1968, or 1972.

38. The covered jurisdictions at the time of the Voting Rights Act's passage included Alabama, Alaska, Georgia, Louisiana, Mississippi, South Carolina, and Virginia, as well as subdivisions in Arizona, Hawaii, Idaho, and North Carolina. In the early 1970s, Texas and parts of Florida would be added to this list.

39. Rosenberg, *The Hollow Hope: Can Courts Bring About Social Change?*

40. For example, Rosenberg, *The Hollow Hope: Can Courts Bring About Social Change?*

41. Ibid.

42. Ibid.

43. Ibid.

44. On this point, O'Connell, "The Impact of Slavery on Racial Inequality in Poverty in the Contemporary U.S. South," finds that the county-level prevalence of slavery in 1860 actually predicts greater black-white income inequality. This is a similar finding to Nunn, "Slavery, Inequality, and Economic Development in the Americas." Both of these relationships are in the current period and neither can quite provide a straightforward explanation for our results, as we discuss further in Acharya, Blackwell, and Sen, "The Political Legacy of American Slavery."

45. We note that it is possible that the local economic inequality between whites and blacks could be driving the persistence of whites' attitudes that we presented in chapter 3 and that we revisit here. However, this possibility seems unlikely. The relationship between inequality and political attitudes in the South is almost nonexistent once between-state variation is removed. In fact, the difference in Democratic identification between counties with inequality above the median versus those with inequality below the median is 0.2 percentage points with a 95% confidence interval that overlaps with zero. Similar results hold for support for the other outcomes we examined, affirmative action and racial resentment. Making this explanation even less likely is the fact that we find that high-inequality counties actually have *more liberal* views than low-inequality areas after controlling for historical covariates.

46. 570 U.S. 2 (2013).

47. The Voter Education Project (VEP), for instance, organized activists and sent them across the South to increase voter registration in 1962–64. SNCC also organized the Freedom Summer (1964), in which thousands of volunteers

attempted to register Southern blacks to vote. These efforts produced major increases in the total number of African Americans in the South registered to vote, with roughly a million registered by 1962 alone. By 1964, this number had grown to almost 2 million, representing roughly 39% of the black voting-age population. See also Black and Black, *Politics and Society in the South*; Mickey, *Paths Out of Dixie: The Democratization of Authoritarian Enclaves in America's Deep South, 1944–1972.*

48. These results are robust to the inclusion of state fixed effects, as well as the various pre-1860 covariates that we have described elsewhere.

49. We note that a possible explanation here is that these patterns were part of an ongoing upward trend in voter registration specific to these regions, but this seems unlikely given the cool response of Black Belt whites to the Voting Rights Act. See, e.g., Black, "Racial Composition of Congressional Districts and Support for Federal Voting Rights in the American South," who shows that congressional support for the Voting Rights Act in 1965 was higher outside the Black Belt than within it. In tandem with low black registration, this suggests that Black Belt whites desired to maintain Jim Crow as long as possible.

50. See also Schuman, Steeh, and Bobo, *Racial Attitudes in America: Trends and Interpretations.* The literature on symbolic racism would argue that this progress on racial attitudes in the South masks how racism is now expressed in different, more subtle ways. Sears and Kinder, "Whites' Opposition to Busing: On Conceptualizing and Operationalizing Group Conflict"; Kinder and Sears, "Prejudice and Politics: Symbolic Racism Versus Racial Threats to the Good Life"; Valentino and Sears, "Old Times There are Not Forgotten: Race and Partisan Realignment in the Contemporary South."

51. We measured this by running our baseline ANES models and interacting slavery with a linear time trend. There were no significant interactions in any of the models with a p-value of 0.39 in the model with full 1860 controls.

52. The data here comes from an extension of the data from Matthews and Prothro, *Negroes and the New Southern Politics*, compiled for Alt, "Race and Voter Registration in the South Before and After the Voting Rights Act."

53. Our argument is not that this was the appropriate distribution of federal effort during this time period. Mickey, *Paths Out of Dixie: The Democratization of Authoritarian Enclaves in America's Deep South, 1944–1972*, pp. 269–270, makes the argument that the Department of Justice was not very responsive to complaints from black protest organizations and that they made allocation decisions based in part on political factors.

54. The relationship between black and white racial organizations and slavery is not as robust as other results in this book. They hold under state fixed effects, disappear with full 1860 controls, and reappear with the IV approach. Data come from Matthews and Prothro, "Political Factors and Negro Voter Registration in the South."

55. There is no evidence that the effect of slavery varies with the presence of racial organizations, with one exception. The effect of slavery on racial resentment is higher for counties with white racial organizations as compared to those without them. Across our outcome measures, controlling for state fixed effects,

presence of black racial organization in a county is correlated with more liberal whites today, while there is no systematic relationship with white racial organizations.

56. Becker, *The Economics of Discrimination*.

57. What differences we do see in the South across high- and low-slave areas are in the white populations. Whites in former high-slave counties have lower arrest rates, have higher educational attainment, and have higher incomes.

Chapter 9: Conclusion & Lessons

1. Key, *Southern Politics in State and Nation*, p. 11.

2. Ibid. p. 5.

3. Ibid., p. 5.

4. Woodward, *The Strange Career of Jim Crow*; Ritterhouse, *Growing Up Jim Crow: How Black and White Southern Children Learned Race*.

5. Ritterhouse, *Growing Up Jim Crow: How Black and White Southern Children Learned Race*; DuRocher, *Raising Racists: The Socialization of White Children in the Jim Crow South*.

6. Woodward, *The Strange Career of Jim Crow*.

7. Voigtländer and Voth, "Persecution Perpetuated: The Medieval Origins of Anti-Semitic Violence in Nazi Germany"; Nunn and Wantchekon, "The Slave Trade and the Origins of Mistrust in Africa"; Jha, "Trade, Institutions, and Ethnic Tolerance: Evidence from South Asia"; Alesina and Fuchs-Schündeln, "Goodbye Lenin (or Not?): The Effect of Communism on People's Preferences"; Rozenas, Schutte, and Zhukov, "The Political Legacy of Violence: The Long-Term Impact of Stalin's Repression in Ukraine."

8. Du Bois, *Black Reconstruction in America, 1860–1880*, pp. 185, 30.

9. Woodward, *The Strange Career of Jim Crow*.

10. Key, *Southern Politics in State and Nation*.

11. Ibid., pp. 5–6.

12. A prominent example is Senator Ellison D. "Cotton Ed" Smith, from Lynchburg, South Carolina. Smith, a virulent racist, was chair of the powerful Agricultural Committee and himself a cotton planter. He famously walked out of the 1936 Democratic Convention after witnessing a prayer being led by a black pastor, recounting that he wouldn't be ministered to by a "slew-footed, blue-gummed, kinky-headed Senegambian." Quoted in Hayes, *South Carolina and the New Deal*, p. 153.

13. Katznelson, *Fear Itself: The New Deal and the Origins of Our Time*, p. 128.

14. Ibid., pp. 161–66.

15. Some of these views are themselves intimately tied up with race. See Alexander, *The New Jim Crow: Mass Incarceration in the Age of Colorblindness*.

16. Gilens, *Why Americans Hate Welfare: Race, Media, and the Politics of Antipoverty Policy*.

17. Gilens, *Why Americans Hate Welfare: Race, Media, and the Politics of Antipoverty Policy*; Alexander, *The New Jim Crow: Mass Incarceration in the Age of Colorblindness*; Kinder and Sanders, *Divided by Color: Racial Politics and Democratic Ideals*.

18. Glaze, *Correctional Populations in the United States, 2010*.

19. See, e.g., Schuman, Steeh, and Bobo, *Racial Attitudes in America: Trends and Interpretations*.
20. Highton, "Voter Identification Laws and Turnout in the United States."
21. Key, *Southern Political in State and Nation*, p. 6.

Appendix A: Data Notes

1. It's not entirely clear from the CCES questions who was asked the following question—Independents, "Others," or both.
2. Saporito et al., "From Here to There: Methods of Allocating Data Between Census Geography and Socially Meaningful Areas."
3. O'Connell, "The Impact of Slavery on Racial Inequality in Poverty in the Contemporary U.S. South"; Reece and O'Connell, "How the Legacy of Slavery and Racial Composition Shape Public School Enrollment in the American South."
4. Siczewicz, *U.S. Historical Counties*.

BIBLIOGRAPHY

Acemoglu, Daron, and James Robinson. *Why Nations Fail: Origins of Power, Poverty and Prosperity*. New York: Crown Publishers, 2012.

Acemoglu, Daron, Davide Cantoni, Simon Johnson, and James Robinson. "The Consequences of Radical Reform: The French Revolution." *American Economic Review* 101, no. 7 (2011): 3286–3307.

Acharya, Avidit, Matthew Blackwell, and Maya Sen. "Explaining Attitudes from Behavior: A Cognitive Dissonance Approach." *The Journal of Politics*, Forthcoming.

———. "Explaining Causal Findings Without Bias: Detecting and Assessing Direct Effects." *American Political Science Review* 110, no. 3 (2016): 512–529.

———. "The Political Legacy of American Slavery." *The Journal of Politics* 78, no. 3 (2016): 621–641.

Alabama Constitutional Convention. *Journal of the Proceedings of the Constitutional Convention of the State of Alabama: Held in the City of Montgomery, Commencing May 21st, 1901*. Brown Printing Company, 1901.

Alesina, Alberto, and Nicola Fuchs-Schündeln. "Goodbye Lenin (or Not?): The Effect of Communism on People's Preferences." *American Economic Review* 97, no. 4 (2007): 1507–1528.

Alesina, Alberto, Paola Giuliano, and Nathan Nunn. "On the Origins of Gender Roles: Women and the Plough." *Quarterly Journal of Economics* 128, no. 2 (2013): 469–530.

Alexander, Michelle. *The New Jim Crow: Mass Incarceration in the Age of Colorblindness*. New York: The New Press, 2012.

Allport, Gordon Willard. *The Nature of Prejudice*. Cambridge, MA: Addison-Wesley, 1954.

Alsobrook, David E. "The Mobile Streetcar Boycott of 1902: African American Protest or Capitulation?" *Alabama Review* 56, no. 2 (2003): 83–103.

Alsobrook, David E. "William D. Jelks, December 1900, June 1901–1907." In *Alabama Governors: A Political History of the State*, edited by Samuel L. Webb, and Margaret E. Armbrester, 163–169. Tuscaloosa: University of Alabama Press, 2014.

Alston, Lee J., and Joseph P. Ferrie. *Southern Paternalism and the American Welfare State: Economics, Politics, and Institutions in the South, 1865–1965*. New York: Cambridge University Press, 2007.

Alt, James E. "Race and Voter Registration in the South Before and After the Voting Rights Act." In *Quiet Revolution in the South: The Impact of the Voting Rights Act, 1965–1990*, edited by Chandler Davidson, and Bernard Grofman, 351–377. Princeton: Princeton University Press, 1994.

"America's Oldest Citizen Dies in Mississippi at 130," *Jet*, November 4, 1971.

Andrews, Kenneth T. *Freedom Is a Constant Struggle: The Mississippi Civil Rights Movement and Its Legacy*. Chicago: University of Chicago Press, 2005.

Angrist, Joshua D., and Jörn-Steffen Pischke. *Mostly Harmless Econometrics: An Empiricist's Companion*. Princeton: Princeton University Press, 2008.

Ansolabehere, Stephen, and Brian F. Schaffner. "Does Survey Mode Still Matter? Findings from a 2010 Multi-Mode Comparison." *Political Analysis* 22, no. 3 (2014): 285–303.

Arkansas Department of Education. *Local Education Agency Application for School Improvement Grant Funds*. Division of Learning Services, 2010.

Arnett, Alex Mathews. *The Populist Movement in Georgia*. New York: Columbia University Press, 1922.

Ayers, Edward L. *The Promise of the New South: Life after Reconstruction*. Oxford: Oxford University Press, 1992.

Banerjee, Abhijit, and Lakshmi Iyer. "History, Institutions, and Economic Performance: The Legacy of Colonial Land Tenure Systems in India." *American Economic Review* 95, no. 4 (2005): 1190–1213.

Beam, Adam. "Racist Graffiti Causes Furor," *The State*. (Columbia, SC) December 31, 2009. Accessed October 27, 2017. http://www.thestate.com/news/politics-government/election/article14369321.html.

Beber, Bernd, Philip Roessler, and Alexandra Scacco. "Intergroup Violence and Political Attitudes: Evidence from a Dividing Sudan." *The Journal of Politics* 76, no. 3 (2014): 649–665.

Beck, Ellwood M., and Stewart E. Tolnay. *Confirmed Inventory of Southern Lynch Victims, 1882–1930*. Center for Studies in Demography and Ecology, University of Washington. 2004. http://lynching.csde.washington.edu/.

———. "The Killing Fields of the Deep South: The Market for Cotton and the Lynching of Blacks, 1882–1930." *American Sociological Review* 55, no. 4 (1990): 526–539.

Becker, Gary S. *The Economics of Discrimination*. Chicago: University of Chicago Press, 1957.

Bednar, Jenna, and Scott E. Page. "When Order Affects Performance: Institutional Sequencing, Cultural Sway, and Behavioral Path Dependence." Working Paper, 2015.

Behrens, Angela, Christopher Uggen, and Jeff Manza. "Ballot Manipulation and the 'Menace of Negro Domination': Racial Threat and Felon Disenfranchisement in the United States, 1850–2002." *American Journal of Sociology* 109, no. 3 (2003): 559–605.

Bendix, Reinhard. *Nation-building and Citizenship: Studies of Our Changing Social Order*. New York: John Wiley & Sons, 1964.

Berg, Manfred. *The Ticket to Freedom: The NAACP and the Struggle for Black Political Integration*. Gainesville: University Press of Florida, 2007.

Berinsky, Adam J. "The Two Faces of Public Opinion." *American Journal of Political Science* 43, no. 4 (1999): 1209–1230.

Berlin, Ira. *Many Thousands Gone: The First Two Centuries of Slavery in North America*. Cambridge, MA: Harvard University Press, 1998.

Birdsall, Stephen S. "Preliminary Analysis of the 1968 Wallace Vote in the Southeast." *Southeastern Geographer* 9, no. 2 (1969): 55–66.

Bisin, Alberto, and Thierry Verdier. "The Economics of Cultural Transmission and the Dynamics of Preferences." *Journal of Economic Theory* 97, no. 2 (2001): 298–319.

Black, Earl, and Merle Black. *Politics and Society in the South*. Cambridge, MA: Harvard University Press, 1987.

———. "The Wallace Vote in Alabama: A Multiple Regression Analysis." *Journal of Politics* 35, no. 3 (1973): 730–736.

Black, Merle. "Racial Composition of Congressional Districts and Support for Federal Voting Rights in the American South." *Social Science Quarterly* 59, no. 3 (1978): 435–450.

Blackmon, Douglas A. *Slavery by Another Name: The Re-Enslavement of Black Americans from the Civil War to World War II*. New York: Anchor Books, 2008.

Blalock, Hubert M. *Toward a Theory of Minority-Group Relations*. New York: John Wiley & Sons, 1967.

Bobo, Lawrence. "Whites' Opposition to Busing: Symbolic Racism or Realistic Group Conflict." *Journal of Personality and Social Psychology* 45, no. 6 (1983): 1196–1210.

Bobo, Lawrence, and Vincent L. Hutchings. "Perceptions of Racial Group Competition: Extending Blumer's Theory of Group Position to a Multiracial Social Context." *American Sociological Review* 61, no. 6 (1996): 951–972.

Booker's Place: A Mississippi Story. Directed by Raymond De Felitta. Hangover Lounge, 2012. Film.

Borden, Jeremy. "KKK Met with Skirmishes at Rally to Protest Confederate Flag Removal." *Washington Post*, July 18, 2015. Accessed January 19, 2016.

Bowles, Samuel. *Microeconomics: Behavior, Institutions, and Evolution*. Princeton: Princeton University Press, 2004.

Bowles, Samuel, and Herbert Gintis. "The Evolutionary Origins of Collective Action." In *Oxford Handbook of Political Economy*, edited by Barry R. Weingast and Donald A. Wittman, 952–967. Oxford: Oxford University Press, 2006.

Boyd, Robert, and Peter J. Richerson. *Culture and the Evolutionary Process*. Chicago: University of Chicago Press, 1985.

Broockman, David, and Joshua Kalla. "Durably Reducing Transphobia: A Field Experiment on Door-to-Door Canvassing." *Science* 352, no. 6282 (2016): 220–224.

Broom, W. B. *So. Ca. College to W. B. Broom*. Servant Hire, Box 1, Vice President of Finance and Office of the Treasurer, 1805–1977, University Archives, South Caroliniana Library, University of South Carolina, 2011.

Brownlow, William Gannaway. *Americanism Contrasted with Foreignism, Romanism, and Bogus Democracy*. Nashville: Published by the Author, 1856.

Brownlow, William Gannaway. *Sketches of the Rise, Progress, and Decline of Secession*. Philadelphia: George W. Childs, 1862.

Brownlow, William Gannaway, and Abraham Pryne. *Ought American Slavery to be Perpetuated?* Philadelphia: J. B. Lippincott & Co., 1858.

Bullock III, Charles S., Donna R. Hoffman, and Ronald Keith Gaddie. "The Consolidation of the White Southern Congressional Vote." *Political Research Quarterly* 58, no. 2 (2005): 231–243.

Byrd, William N., Jr. "Wiregrass: The Transformation of Southeast Alabama, 1880–1930." PhD diss., Auburn University, 2009.

Campante, Filipe, and David Yanagizawa-Drott. "The Intergenerational Transmission of War." Working Paper, 2016.

Carey, Anthony Gene. *Parties, Slavery, and the Union in Antebellum Georgia*. Athens, GA: University of Georgia Press, 1997.

Carney, Judith Ann. *Black Rice: The African Origins of Rice Cultivation in the Americas*. Cambridge, MA: Harvard University Press, 2001.

Carsey, Thomas M. "The Contextual Effects of Race on White Voter Behavior: The 1989 New York City Mayoral Election." *The Journal of Politics* 57, no. 1 (1995): 221–228.

Carter, Dan T. *The Politics of Rage: George Wallace, the Origins of the New Conservatism, and the Transformation of American Politics*. Baton Rouge: Louisiana State University Press, 2000.

Carter, Susan B., Scott Sigmund Gartner, Michael R. Haines, Alan L. Olmstead, Richard Sutch, and Gavin Wright. *Historical Statistics of the United States: Earliest Times to the Present*. New York: Cambridge University Press, 2006.

Chalmers, David M. *Hooded Americanism: The History of the Ku Klux Klan*. Durham: Duke University Press, 1981.

Chappell, David L. *A Stone of Hope: Prophetic Religion and the Death of Jim Crow*. Chapel Hill: University of North Carolina Press, 2004.

Charnysh, Volha. "Historical Legacies of Interethnic Competition: Anti-Semitism and the EU Referendum in Poland." *Comparative Political Studies* 48, no. 13 (2015): 1711–1745.

Citrin, Jack, Beth Reingold, and Donald P. Green. "American Identity and the Politics of Ethnic Change." *The Journal of Politics* 52, no. 4 (1990): 1124–1154.

Clubb, Jerome M., William H. Flanigan, and Nancy H. Zingale. *Electoral Data for Counties in the United States: Presidential and Congressional Races, 1840–1972*. Inter-university Consortium for Political and Social Research (ICPSR) [distributor], 2006.

Cohen, William. "Negro Involuntary Servitude in the South, 1865–1940: A Preliminary Analysis." *Journal of Southern History* 42, no. 1 (1976): 31–60.

Cole, Arthur Charles. *The Whig Party in the South*. London: Oxford University Press, 1914.

Collier, Ruth Berins and David Collier. *Shaping the Political Arena: Critical Junctures, the Labor Movement, and Regime Dynamics in Latin America*. Princeton: Princeton University Press, 1991.

Cook, Lisa D. "The Color of Lynching." Working Paper, 2011.

Cooper, William J. *The South and the Politics of Slavery, 1828–1856*. Baton Rouge: Louisiana State University Press, 1978.

Coulter, E. Merton. *William G. Brownlow: Fighting Parson of the Southern Highlands*. Knoxville: University of Tennessee Press, 1999.

Crofts, Daniel W. *Reluctant Confederates: Upper South Unionists in the Secession Crisis*. Chapel Hill: University of North Carolina Press, 1989.

Davidson, Chandler. "The Voting Rights Act: A Brief History." In *Controversies in Minority Voting: The Voting Rights Act in Perspective*, edited by Bernard Grofman, and Chandler Davidson, 7–34. Washington, DC: Brookings, 1992.

Davis, David Brion. *Inhuman Bondage: The Rise and Fall of Slavery in the New World*. Oxford: Oxford University Press, 2006.

Degler, Carl N. *Neither Black nor White: Slavery and Race Relations in Brazil and the United States*. New York: Macmillan, 1971.

Dell, Melissa. "The Persistent Effects of Peru's Mining *Mita*." *Econometrica* 78, no. 6 (2010): 1863–1903.

Denman, Clarence Phillips. *The Secession Movement in Alabama*. Montgomery: Alabama State Department of Archives and History, 1933.

Deutsch, Morton, and Mary Evans Collins. *Interracial Housing: A Psychological Evaluation of a Social Experiment*. Minneapolis: University of Minnesota Press, 1951.

Dhar, Diva, Tarun Jain, and Seema Jayachandran. *The Intergenerational Transmission of Gender Attitudes: Evidence from India*. Working Paper, 2016.

Dickerson, Donna Lee. *The Reconstruction Era: Primary Documents on Events from 1865 to 1877*. Westport, CT: Greenwood Publishing, 2003.

Dogan, Mattei. "Political Cleavage and Social Stratification in France and Italy." In *Party Systems and Voter Alignements: A Cross-National Perspective*, edited by Seymour M. Lipset, and Stein Rokkan, 129–196. New York: Free Press, 1967.

Du Bois, W.E.B. *Black Reconstruction in America, 1860–1880*. New York: Free Press, 1998. First published 1935 by Harcourt, Brace, and Company.

DuRocher, Kristina. *Raising Racists: The Socialization of White Children in the Jim Crow South*. Lexington: The University Press of Kentucky, 2011.

Engerman, Stanley L. "Slavery Without Racism, Racism Without Slavery: Mainland North America and Elsewhere." *Proceedings of the Fifth Annual Gilder Lehrman Center International Conference*, 2003, 1–41.

———. "The Economic Impact of the Civil War." *Explorations in Economic History* 3, no. 2 (1966): 176–199.

Enos, Ryan D., Aaron Russell Kaufman, and Melissa L. Sands. "Can Violent Protest Change Local Policy Support? Evidence from the Aftermath of the 1992 Los Angeles Riot." Working Paper, 2017.

Enos, Ryan D. "What the Demolition of Public Housing Teaches Us about the Impact of Racial Threat on Political Behavior." *American Journal of Political Science* 60, no. 1 (2016): 123–142.

Ertman, Thomas. *Birth of the Leviathan: Building States and Regimes in Medieval and Early Modern Europe*. Cambridge: Cambridge University Press, 1997.

Farley, Reynolds, Charlotte Steeh, Maria Krysan, Tara Jackson, and Keith Reeves. "Stereotypes and Segregation: Neighborhoods in the Detroit Area." *American Journal of Sociology* 100, no. 3 (1994): 750–780.

Farnam, Henry W. *Chapters in the History of Social Legislation in the United States to 1860*. Edited by Clive Day. Washington, DC: Carnegie Institution of Washington, 1938.

Fausset, Richard, and Ashley Southall. "Video Shows Officer Flipping Student in South Carolina, Prompting Inquiry." *The New York Times*, October 26, 2015. Accessed January 19, 2016.

Feldman, Stanley, and Leonie Huddy. "Racial Resentment and White Opposition to Race-Conscious Programs: Principles or Prejudice?" *American Journal of Political Science* 49, no. 1 (2005): 168–183.

Ferris, William R. *Blues from the Delta*. Garden City, NY: Anchor Press/Doubleday, 1978.

Fields, Barbara Jeanne. "Ideology and Race in American History." In *Region, Race, and Reconstruction: Essays in Honor of C. Vann Woodward*, edited by J. Morgan Kousser, and James M. McPherson, 143–177. New York: Oxford University Press, 1982.

———. "Slavery, Race and Ideology in the United States of America." *New Left Review* 181, no. 1 (1990): 95–118.

Fischer, David Hackett. *Albion's Seed: Four British Folkways in America*. Oxford: Oxford University Press, 1989.

Fitzpatrick, Kevin M., and Sean-Shong Hwang. "The Effects of Community Structure on Opportunities for Interracial Contact: Extending Blau's Macrostructural Theory." *The Sociological Quarterly* 33, no. 1 (1992): 51–61.

Flynt, Wayne. "Alabama's Shame: The Historical Origins of the 1901 Constitution." *Alabama Law Review* 53, no. 1 (2001): 67–76.

Fogel, Robert William, and Stanley L. Engerman. *Time on the Cross: The Economics of American Negro Slavery*. New York: W.W. Norton & Company, 1995. First published 1974 by Little, Brown, and Company.

Folsom, James E. *Speeches of Governor James E. Folsom, 1947–1950*. Wetumpka, AL: Wetumpka Printing Company, n.d.

Foner, Eric. *Freedom's Lawmakers: A Directory of Black Officeholders During Reconstruction*. New York: Oxford University Press, 1993.

———. *Nothing But Freedom: Emancipation and Its Legacy*. Baton Rouge: Louisiana State University Press, 1983.

———. *Reconstruction: America's Unfinished Revolution, 1863–1877*. New York: Harper Perennial, 2011.

Fontana, Nicola, Tommaso Nannicini, and Guido Tabellini. "Historical Roots of Political Extremism: The Effects of Nazi Occupation of Italy." IZA Discussion Paper No. 10551, 2017.

Fossett, Mark A., and K Jill Kiecolt. "The Relative Size of Minority Populations and White Racial Attitudes." *Social Science Quarterly* 70, no. 4 (1989): 820–835.

Garrow, David J. *Protest at Selma: Martin Luther King Jr., and the Voting Rights Act of 1965*. New Haven: Yale University Press, 1978.

Genovese, Eugene D. "Yeomen Farmers in a Slaveholders' Democracy." *Agricultural History* 49, no. 2 (1975): 331–342.

Gerber, Alan S., and Donald P. Green. "The Effects of Canvassing, Telephone Calls, and Direct Mail on Voter Turnout: A Field Experiment." *American Political Science Review* 94, no. 3 (2000): 653–663.

Gerber, Alan S., Donald P. Green, and Christopher W. Larimer. "Social Pressure and Voter Turnout: Evidence from a Large-Scale Field Experiment." *American Political Science Review* 102, no. 1 (2008): 33–48.

Gilens, Martin. *Why Americans Hate Welfare: Race, Media, and the Politics of Antipoverty Policy*. Chicago: University of Chicago Press, 1999.

Giles, Micheal W. "Percent Black and Racial Hostility: An Old Assumption Reexamined." *Social Science Quarterly* 58, no. 3 (1977): 412–417.

Giles, Micheal W., and Melanie A. Buckner. "Comment on 'Beyond Racial Threat: Failure of an Old Hypothesis in the New South'." *The Journal of Politics* 58, no. 4 (1996): 1171–1180.

———. "David Duke and Black Threat: An Old Hypothesis Revisited." *The Journal of Politics* 55, no. 3 (1993): 702–713.

Giles, Micheal W., and Arthur Evans. "The Power Approach to Intergroup Hostility." *Journal of Conflict Resolution* 30, no. 3 (1986): 469–486.

Giles, Micheal W., and Kaenan Hertz. "Racial Threat and Partisan Identification." *American Political Science Review* 88, no. 2 (1994): 317–326.

Gintis, Herbert. "The Hitchhiker's Guide to Altruism: Gene-Culture Coevolution and the Internalization of Norms." *Journal of Theoretical Biology* 220, no. 4 (2003): 407–418.

Girard, Philippe R. *The Slaves Who Defeated Napoleon: Toussaint Louverture and the Haitian War of Independence, 1801–1804*. Tuscaloosa: The University of Alabama Press, 2011.

Glaser, James M. "Back to the Black Belt: Racial Environment and White Racial Attitudes in the South." *The Journal of Politics* 56, no. 1 (1994): 21–41.

Glass, Jennifer, Vern L. Bengtson, and Charlotte Chorn Dunham. "Attitude Similarity in Three-Generation Families: Socialization, Status Inheritance, or Reciprocal Influence?" *American Sociological Review* 51, no. 5 (1986): 685–698.

Glaze, Lauren E. *Correctional Populations in the United States, 2010*. Bulletin. Washington, DC: Bureau of Justice Statistics, Department of Justice, 2011.

Goldin, Claudia D. "The Economics of Emancipation." *The Journal of Economic History* 33, no. 1 (1973): 66–85.

Goldin, Claudia D., and Frank D. Lewis. "The Economic Cost of the American Civil War: Estimates and Implications." *The Journal of Economic History* 35, no. 2 (1975): 299–326.

Green, Donald P., Bradley Palmquist, and Eric Schickler. *Partisan Hearts and Minds: Political Parties and the Social Identities of Voters*. New Haven: Yale University Press, 2002.

Gregory, James N. *The Southern Diaspora: How the Great Migration of Black and White Southerners Transformed America*. Chapel Hill: University of North Carolina Press, 2005.

Guiso, Luigi, Paola Sapienza, and Luigi Zingales. "Long-Term Persistence." *Journal of the European Economic Association* 14, no. 6 (2016): 1401–1436.

Hacker, Jacob S. *The Divided Welfare State: The Battle over Public and Private Social Benefits in the United States*. Cambridge: Cambridge University Press, 2002.

Hahn, Steven. *The Roots of Southern Populism: Yeoman Farmers and the Transformation of the Georgia Upcountry, 1850–1890*. New York: Oxford University Press, 1983.

Haines, Michael R. *Historical, Demographic, Economic, and Social Data: The United States, 1790-2002.* Inter-university Consortium for Political and Social Research (ICPSR) [distributor], 2010.

Hayes, Jack I. *South Carolina and the New Deal.* Columbia, SC: University of South Carolina Press, 2001.

Heard, Alexander. *A Two-Party South?* Chapel Hill: University of North Carolina Press, 1952.

Hammerstein, Oscar. "You've Got to Be Carefully Taught." *South Pacific,* 1949.

Hersh, Eitan. *Hacking the Electorate: How Campaigns Perceive Voters.* Cambridge: Cambridge University Press, 2015.

Hersh, Eitan D., and Clayton Nall. "The Primacy of Race in the Geography of Income-Based Voting: New Evidence from Public Voting Records." *American Journal of Political Science* 60, no. 2 (2016): 289–303.

Highton, Benjamin. "Voter Identification Laws and Turnout in the United States." *Annual Review of Political Science* 20 (2017): 149–167.

Holloway, Vanessa A. *Getting Away with Murder: The Twentieth-Century Struggle for Civil Rights in the U.S. Senate.* Lanham, MD: University Press of America, 2014.

Holmes, William F. "Whitecapping: Agrarian Violence in Mississippi, 1902-1906." *The Journal of Southern History* 35, no. 2 (1969): 165–185.

Holt, Michael F. *The Rise and Fall of the American Whig Party: Jacksonian Politics and the Onset of the Civil War.* Oxford: Oxford University Press, 1999.

Hopkins, Daniel J. "Politicized Places: Explaining Where and When Immigrants Provoke Local Opposition." *American Political Science Review* 104, no. 1 (2010): 40–60.

Horn, Stanley F. *Invisible Empire: The Story of the Ku Klux Klan, 1866–1871.* Boston: Houghton Mifflin, 1939.

Hornbeck, Richard, and Suresh Naidu. "When the Levee Breaks: Black Migration and Economic Development in the American South." *American Economic Review* 104, no. 3 (2014): 963–990.

Huckfeldt, Robert, and John Sprague. *Citizens, Politics, and Social Communication: Information and Influence in an Election Campaign.* New York: Cambridge University Press, 1995.

———. "Networks in Context: The Social Flow of Political Information." *American Political Science Review* 81, no. 4 (1987): 1197–1216.

Hurst, Wilbur M., and Lillian M. Church. *Power and Machinery in Agriculture.* Washington, DC: United States Department of Agriculture, 1933.

Inverarity, James M. "Populism and Lynching in Louisiana, 1889-1896: A Test of Erikson's Theory of the Relationship between Boundary Crises and Repressive Justice." *American Sociological Review* 41, no. 2 (1976): pp. 262–280.

Jelks, William D. "The Acuteness of the Negro Question: A Suggested Remedy." *North American Review* 184 (1907): pp. 389–395.

Jennings, M. Kent, and Richard G. Niemi. *The Political Character of Adolescents: The Influence of Families and Schools.* Princeton: Princeton University Press, 1974.

———. *Generations and Politics: A Panel Study of Young Adults and Their Parents*. Princeton: Princeton University Press, 1981.

———. "The Transmission of Political Values from Parent to Child." *American Political Science Review* 62, no. 1 (1968): 169–184.

Jennings, M. Kent, Laura Stoker, and Jake Bowers. "Politics across Generations: Family Transmission Reexamined." *The Journal of Politics* 71, no. 3 (2009): 782–799.

Jha, Saumitra. "Trade, Institutions, and Ethnic Tolerance: Evidence from South Asia." *American Political Science Review* 107, no. 4 (2013): 806–832.

Johnson, Walter. *River of Dark Dreams: Slavery and Empire in the Cotton Kingdom*. Cambridge, MA: Harvard University Press, 2013.

Jones, Jeffrey M. "In U.S., Most Reject Considering Race in College Admissions." *Gallup*, July 24, 2013.

Jordan, Winthrop D. *White Over Black: American Attitudes Toward the Negro, 1550–1812*. Chapel Hill: University of North Carolina Press, 1968.

Katznelson, Ira. *Fear Itself: The New Deal and the Origins of Our Time*. New York: W. W. Norton & Company, 2013.

Kennedy, Helen. "GOP Activist DePass Apologizes after Joking on Facebook that Gorilla is Related to Michelle Obama." *The New York Daily News*, June 15, 2009. Accessed January 19, 2016.

Key, V.O. *Southern Politics in State and Nation*. Knoxville: University of Tennessee Press, 1984. First published 1949 by Knopf Books.

Key, V. O., and Frank Munger. "Social Determinism and Electoral Decision: the Case of Indiana." In *American Voting Behavior*, edited by Eugene Burdick, and Arthur J. Brodbeck, 281–299. Glencoe, IL: Free Press, 1959.

Kinder, Donald R., and Tali Mendelberg. "Cracks in American Apartheid: The Political Impact of Prejudice Among Desegregated Whites." *The Journal of Politics* 57, no. 2 (1995): 402–424.

Kinder, Donald R., and Lynn M. Sanders. *Divided by Color: Racial Politics and Democratic Ideals*. Chicago: University of Chicago Press, 1996.

Kinder, Donald R., and David O. Sears. "Prejudice and Politics: Symbolic Racism Versus Racial Threats to the Good Life." *Journal of Personality and Social Psychology* 40, no. 3 (1981): 414–431.

King, Desmond S., and Rogers M. Smith. *Still a House Divided: Race and Politics in Obama's America*. Princeton: Princeton University Press, 2011.

King, Gary. *A Solution to the Ecological Inference Problem: Reconstructing Individual Behavior from Aggregate Data*. Princeton: Princeton University Press, 1997.

King, Martin Luther, Jr. *Why We Can't Wait*. New York: New American Library, 2000. First published 1964 by Harper & Row.

Klinkner, Philip A., and Rogers M. Smith. *The Unsteady March: The Rise and Decline of Racial Equality in America*. Chicago: University of Chicago Press, 2002.

Knoke, David, and Natalie Kyriazis. "The Persistence of the Black-Belt Vote: A Test of Key's Hypothesis." *Social Science Quarterly* 57, no. 4 (1977): 889–906.

Kolchin, Peter. *American Slavery: 1619–1877*. New York: Hill & Wang, 2003.

Kousser, J. Morgan. "The Immutability of Categories and the Reshaping of Southern Politics." *Annual Review of Political Science* 13 (2010): 365–383.

———. *The Shaping of Southern Politics: Suffrage Restriction and the Establishment of the One-Party South, 1880–1910*. New Haven: Yale University Press, 1974.

Krasner, Stephen D. "Sovereignty: An Institutional Perspective." *Comparative Political Studies* 21, no. 1 (1988): 66–94.

Kuziemko, Ilyana, and Ebonya Washington. "Why did the Democrats Lose the South? Bringing New Data to an Old Debate." Working Paper, 2016.

Lawson, Steven F. *Black Ballots: Voting Rights in the South, 1944–1969*. Lexington: Lexington Books, 1999.

Lee, Alexander, and Kenneth A. Schultz. "Comparing British and French Colonial Legacies: A Discontinuity Analysis of Cameroon." *Quarterly Journal of Political Science* 7, no. 4 (2012): 365–410.

Leip, David. *Atlas of U.S. Presidential Elections*, 2008. http://www.uselectionatlas.org.

Levi, Margaret. *Consent, Dissent, and Patriotism*. New York: Cambridge University Press, 1997.

Lipset, Seymour M., and Stein Rokkan. "Cleavage Structures, Party Systems, and Voter Alignments: An Introduction." In *Party Systems and Voter Alignements: A Cross-National Perspective*, edited by Seymour M. Lipset, and Stein Rokkan, 1–64. New York: Free Press, 1967.

Lumpkin, Katharine Du Pre. *The Making of a Southerner*. New York: Alfred A. Knopf, 1946.

Matthews, Donald R. and James W. Prothro. *Negroes and the New Southern Politics*. Harcourt, Brace, and World, 1966.

———. "Political Factors and Negro Voter Registration in the South." *American Political Science Review* 57, no. 2 (1963): 355–367.

McKenzie, Robert. *Lincolnites and Rebels: A Divided Town in the American Civil War*. New York: Oxford University Press, 2006.

McLennan, Rebecca M. *The Crisis of Imprisonment: Protest, Politics, and the Making of the American Penal State, 1776–1941*. New York: Cambridge University Press, 2008.

McMillan, Malcolm Cook. *Constitutional Development in Alabama, 1798–1901: A Study in Politics, the Negro, and Sectionalism*. Chapel Hill: University of North Carolina Press, 1955.

McMillen, Neil R. *Dark Journey: Black Mississippians in the Age of Jim Crow*. Champaign, IL: University of Illinois Press, 1989.

Menard, Russell, Trent Alexander, Jason Digman, and J. David Hacker. *Public Use Microdata Samples of the Slave Population of 1850–1860*. University of Minnesota Press, Minnesota Population Center, Minneapolis, MN, 2004.

Mendelberg, Tali. *The Race Card: Campaign Strategy, Implicit Messages, and the Norm of Equality*. Princeton: Princeton University Press, 2001.

Mickey, Robert. *Paths Out of Dixie: The Democratization of Authoritarian Enclaves in America's Deep South, 1944–1972*. Princeton: Princeton University Press, 2015.

Mitchener, Kris James, and Ian W. McLean. "The Productivity of U.S. States Since 1880." *Journal of Economic Growth* 8, no. 1 (2003): 73–114.

Morgan, Edmund S. *American Slavery, American Freedom: The Ordeal of Colonial Virginia*. New York: W.W. Norton & Company, 1975.

Murray, Pauli, ed. *States' Laws on Race and Color*. Athens, GA: University of Georgia Press, 1997.

Musoke, Moses S. "Mechanizing Cotton Production in the American South: The Tractor, 1915–1960." *Explorations in Economic History* 18, no. 4 (1981): 347–375.

Naidu, Suresh. "Recruitment Restrictions and Labor Markets: Evidence from the Postbellum U.S. South." *Journal of Labor Economics* 28, no. 2 (2010): 413–445.

North, Douglass C. *Institutions, Institutional Change and Economic Performance*. Cambridge: Cambridge University Press, 1990.

North, Douglass C., and Barry R. Weingast. "Constitutions and Commitment: The Evolution of Institutions Governing Public Choice in Seventeenth-Century England." *The Journal of Economic History* 49, no. 4 (1989): 803–832.

Nunn, Nathan. "Slavery, Inequality, and Economic Development in the Americas." In *Institutions and Economic Performance*, edited by Elhanan Helpman. Cambridge, MA: Harvard University Press, 2008.

Nunn, Nathan, and Leonard Wantchekon. "The Slave Trade and the Origins of Mistrust in Africa." *American Economic Review* 101, no. 7 (2011): 3221–3252.

O'Connell, Heather A. "The Impact of Slavery on Racial Inequality in Poverty in the Contemporary U.S. South." *Social Forces* 90, no. 3 (2012): 713–734.

Ogburn, William F., and Charles M. Grigg. "Factors Related to the Virginia Vote on Segregation." *Social Forces* 34, no. 4 (1956): 301–308.

Oliver, J. Eric, and Tali Mendelberg. "Reconsidering the Environmental Determinants of White Racial Attitudes." *American Journal of Political Science* 44, no. 3 (2000) 574–589.

Oliver, J. Eric, and Janelle Wong. "Intergroup Prejudice in Multiethnic Settings." *American Journal of Political Science* 47, no. 4 (2003): 567–582.

Olzak, Susan. "The Political Context of Competition: Lynching and Urban Racial Violence, 1882–1914." *Social Forces* 69, no. 2 (1990): 395–421.

Orren, Karen. *Belated Feudalism: Labor, the Law, and Liberal Development in the United States*. Cambridge: Cambridge University Press, 1992.

Page, Scott E. "Path Dependence." *Quarterly Journal of Political Science* 1, no. 1 (2006): 87–115.

Peisakhin, Leonid V. "Living Historical Legacies: The 'Why' and 'How' of Institutional Persistence–The Case of Ukraine." Working Paper, 2010.

Pettigrew, Thomas F. "Demographic Correlates of Border-State Desegregation." *American Sociological Review* 22, no. 6 (1957): 683–689.

Pierson, Paul. "Increasing Returns, Path Dependence, and the Study of Politics." *American Political Science Review* 94, no. 2 (2000): 251–267.

———. *Politics in Time: History, Institutions, and Social Analysis*. Princeton: Princeton University Press, 2004.

Pierson, Paul, and Theda Skocpol. "Historical Institutionalism in Contemporary Political Science." In *Political Science: The State of the Discipline*, edited by Ira Katznelson, and Helen V. Milner, 693–721. New York: W. W. Norton, 2002.

Pildes, Richard H. "Democracy, Anti-Democracy, and the Cannon." *Constitutional Commentary* 17, no. 2 (2000): 295–319.

Polanyi, Karl. *The Great Transformation: The Political and Economic Origins of Our Time*. Boston: Beacon Press, 1944.

Putnam, Robert D., Robert Leonardi, and Raffaella Y. Nanetti. *Making Democracy Work: Civic Traditions in Modern Italy*. Princeton: Princeton University Press, 1993.

Queener, Verton M. "The Origin of the Republican Party in East Tennessee." *The East Tennessee Historical Society's Publications* 13 (1941): 66–90.

Quillian, Lincoln. "Group Threat and Regional Change in Attitudes Toward African-Americans." *American Journal of Sociology* 102, no. 3 (1996): 816–860.

Ransom, Roger L. *Conflict and Compromise: The Political Economy of Slavery, Emancipation, and the American Civil War*. New York: Cambridge University Press, 1989.

Ransom, Roger L., and Richard Sutch. *One Kind of Freedom: The Economic Consequences of Emancipation*. New York: Cambridge University Press, 2001. First published 1977 by Cambridge University Press.

Raper, Arthur Franklin. *The Tragedy of Lynching*. Courier Corporation, 1969. First published 1933 by The University of North Carolina Press.

Reece, Robert L, and Heather A. O'Connell. "How the Legacy of Slavery and Racial Composition Shape Public School Enrollment in the American South." *Sociology of Race and Ethnicity* 2, no. 1 (2015): 42–57.

Reed, John Shelton. "Percent Black and Lynching: A Test of Blalock's Theory." *Social Forces* 50, no. 3 (1972): 356–360.

Ritterhouse, Jennifer. *Growing Up Jim Crow: How Black and White Southern Children Learned Race*. Chapel Hill: University of North Carolina Press, 2006.

Rogers Jr., O. A. "The Elaine Race Riots of 1919." *The Arkansas Historical Quarterly* 19, no. 2 (1960): 142–150.

Rogin, Michael. "Politics, Emotion, and the Wallace Vote." *The British Journal of Sociology* 20, no. 1 (1969): 27–49.

Rosenbaum, Paul R. "The Consquences of Adjustment for a Concomitant Variable That Has Been Affected by the Treatment." *Journal of the Royal Statistical Society. Series A (General)* 147, no. 5 (1984): 656–666.

Rosenberg, Gerald N. *The Hollow Hope: Can Courts Bring About Social Change?* Chicago: University of Chicago Press, 2008.

Rozenas, Arturas, Sebastian Schutte, and Yuri Zhukov. "The Political Legacy of Violence: The Long-Term Impact of Stalin's Repression in Ukraine." *The Journal of Politics*, 79, no. 5 (2017): 1147–1161.

Saporito, Salvatore, Jana M. Chavers, Laura C. Nixon, and Megan R. McQuiddy. "From Here to There: Methods of Allocating Data Between Census Geography and Socially Meaningful Areas." *Social Science Research* 36, no. 3 (2007): 897–920.

Schoenberger, Robert A., and David R. Segal. "The Ecology of Dissent: The Southern Wallace Vote in 1968." *Midwest Journal of Political Science* 15, no. 3 (1971): 583–586.

Schuman, Howard, Charlotte Steeh, and Lawrence Bobo. *Racial Attitudes in America: Trends and Interpretations*. Cambridge, MA: Harvard University Press, 1985.

Sears, David O., and Patrick J. Henry. "The Origins of Symbolic Racism." *Journal of Personality and Social Psychology* 85, no. 2 (2003): 259–275.

Sears, David O., and Donald R. Kinder. *Racial Tension and Voting in Los Angeles.* Los Angeles: Institute of Government and Public Affairs, University of California, 1971.

———. "Whites' Opposition to Busing: On Conceptualizing and Operationalizing Group Conflict." *Journal of Personality and Social Psychology* 48, no. 5 (1985): 1141–1147.

Sears, David O., and John B. McConahay. *The Politics of Violence: The New Urban Blacks and the Watts Riot.* Boston: Houghton Mifflin, 1973.

Sellers, Charles Grier, Jr. "Who Were the Southern Whigs?" *The American Historical Review* 59, no. 2 (1954): 335–346.

Sewell, William H. "Three Temporalities: Toward an Eventful Sociology." In *The Historic Turn in the Human Sciences*, edited by Terrence J. McDonald, 245–280. Ann Arbor: University of Michigan Press, 1996.

Siczewicz, Peter. *U.S. Historical Counties.* Dataset. Emily Kelley, digital comp., ed. by John H. Long, 2011. http://publications.newberry.org/ahcbp.

Sigelman, Lee, and Susan Welch. "The Contact Hypothesis Revisited: Black-White Interaction and Positive Racial Attitudes." *Social Forces* 71, no. 3 (1993): 781–795.

Skocpol, Theda. *States and Social Revolutions: A Comparative Analysis of France, Russia, and China.* New York: Cambridge University Press, 1979.

Skowronek, Stephen. *The Politics Presidents Make: Leadership from John Adams to George Bush.* Cambridge, MA: Harvard University Press, 1993.

Smith, Lillian Eugenia. *Killers of the Dream.* W. W. Norton & Company, 1994. First published 1949 by W.W. Norton.

Smith, Rogers M. *Civic Ideals: Conflicting Visions of Citizenship in U.S. History.* New Haven: Yale University Press, 1997.

Sniderman, Paul M., and Edward G. Carmines. *Reaching Beyond Race.* Cambridge, MA: Harvard University Press, 1997.

Sokol, Jason. *There Goes My Everything: White Southerners in the Age of Civil Rights, 1945–1975.* New York: Alfred E. Knopf, 2006.

Steckel, Richard H. "A Dreadful Childhood: The Excess Mortality of American Slaves." *Social Science History* 10, no. 4 (1986): 427–465.

Steckel, Richard H. "A Peculiar Population: The Nutrition, Health, and Mortality of American Slaves from Childhood to Maturity." *The Journal of Economic History* 46, no. 3 (1986): 721–741.

Tabellini, Guido. "Culture and Institutions: Economic Development in the Regions of Europe." *Journal of the European Economic Association* 8, no. 4 (2010): 677–716.

Taylor, Marylee C. "How White Attitudes Vary with the Racial Composition of Local Populations: Numbers Count." *American Sociological Review* 63, no. 4 (1998): 512–535.

Tesler, Michael, and David O. Sears. *Obama's Race: The 2008 Election and the Dream of a Post-Racial America.* Chicago: University of Chicago Press, 2010.

Thelen, Kathleen. *How Institutions Evolve: The Political Economy of Skills in Germany, Britain, the United States, and Japan*. Cambridge, UK: Cambridge University Press, 2004.

Thompson, Calara Mildred. *Reconstruction in Georgia, Economic, Social, Political, 1865–1872*. New York: Columbia University Press, 1915.

Tocqueville, Alexis de. *Democracy in America*. Chicago: University of Chicago Press, 2002. First published 1840.

Tolbert, Caroline J., and John A. Grummel. "Revisiting the Racial Threat Hypothesis: White Voter Support for California's Proposition 209." *State Politics and Policy Quarterly* 3, no. 2 (2003): 183–202.

Tolnay, Stewart E., and Ellwood M. Beck. *A Festival of Violence: An Analysis of Southern Lynchings, 1882–1930*. Champaign, IL: University of Illinois Press, 1995.

Valelly, Richard M. *The Two Reconstructions: The Struggle for Black Enfranchisement*. Chicago: University of Chicago Press, 2004.

Valentino, Nicholas A., and David O. Sears. "Old Times There are Not Forgotten: Race and Partisan Realignment in the Contemporary South." *American Journal of Political Science* 49, no. 3 (2005): 672–688.

Vansteelandt, Sijn. "Estimating Direct Effects in Cohort and Case–Control Studies." *Epidemiology* 20, no. 6 (2009): 851–860.

Voigtländer, Nico, and Hans-Joachim Voth. "Persecution Perpetuated: The Medieval Origins of Anti-Semitic Violence in Nazi Germany." *Quarterly Journal of Economics* 127, no. 3 (2012): 1339–1392.

Voss, D. Stephen. "Beyond Racial Threat: Failure of an Old Hypothesis in the New South." *The Journal of Politics* 58, no. 4 (1996): 1156–1170.

Wallenstein, Peter. "Reconstruction, Segregation, and Miscegenation: Interracial Marriage and the Law in the Lower South, 1865–1900." *American Nineteenth Century History* 6, no. 1 (2005): 57–76.

Wantchekon, Leonard, and Omar García-Ponce. "Critical Junctures: Independence Movements and Democracy in Africa." Working Paper, 2017.

Wasow, Omar. "Do Protests Matter? Evidence from the 1960s Black Insurgency." Working Paper, 2017.

Welch, Susan, Lee Sigelman, Timothy Bledsoe, and Michael Combs. *Race and Place: Race Relations in an American City*. New York: Cambridge University Press, 2001.

Wittenberg, Jason. *Crucibles of Political Loyalty: Church Institutions and Electoral Continuity in Hungary*. Cambridge, UK: Cambridge University Press, 2006.

Woodward, C. Vann. *Origins of the New South, 1877–1913: A History of the South*. Baton Rouge: Louisiana State University Press, 1981. First published 1951.

———. *The Strange Career of Jim Crow*. New York: Oxford University Press, 2002. First published 1955.

Wright, Carroll D. *Second Annual Report of the Commisioner of Labor, 1886: Convict Labor*. Technical report. Washington, DC: Bureau of Labor, 1887.

Wright, Gavin. *Old South, New South: Revolutions in the Southern Economy Since the Civil War*. New York: Basic Books, 1986.

———. *Sharing the Prize: The Economics of the Civil Rights Revolution in the American South*. Cambridge, MA: Harvard University Press, 2013.

————. *The Political Economy of the Cotton South: Households, Markets, and Wealth in the Nineteenth Century*. New York: W. W. Norton, 1978.

Wright Jr., Gerald C. "Contextual Models of Electoral Behavior: The Southern Wallace Vote." *American Political Science Review* 71, no. 2 (1977): 497–508.

Wrinkle, Robert D., and Jerry L. Polinard. "Populism and Dissent: The Wallace Vote in Texas." *Social Science Quarterly* 54, no. 2 (1973): 306–320.

Yglesias, Matthew. "Charles Shooting Suspect Dylann Roof's Apparent Manifesto Surfaces." *Vox*, June 20, 2015. Accessed June 27, 2017. https://www.vox.com/2015/6/20/8818389/dylann-roof-manifesto.

INDEX

Note: Page numbers in italics indicate illustrations; those with a *t* indicate tables.